Library of
Davidson College

Garden Cities for America

Garden Cities for America

The Radburn Experience

Daniel Schaffer

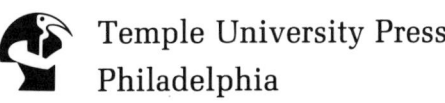
Temple University Press
Philadelphia

Temple University Press, Philadelphia 19122
© 1982 by Temple University. All rights reserved
Published 1982
Printed in the United States of America

Library of Congress Cataloging in Publication Data

Schaffer, Daniel, 1950–
  Garden cities for America.

  Includes bibliographical references and index.
  1. Garden cities—United States. 2. Radburn (N.J.)—City planning. 3. City planning—New Jersey. 4. Regional planning—United States.
I. Title.
HT164.U6S3   307.7'68'0974921   82-736
ISBN 0-8722-258-4   AACR2

To Denise

Contents

Illustrations   ix
Preface   xi
Acknowledgments   xiii
Introduction   3
1. The Garden City Invention   15
2. The Path to an American Garden City   29
3. The Regional Planning Association of America   49
   Theory and Practice
4. Toward a Regional Plan   79
5. The Six Percent Solution   101
6. Sunnyside Up   119
7. A Town for the Motor Age   145
8. Pioneering in Suburbia   167
   Radburn's Early Years
9. A Bankrupt Vision   189
   Radburn, Sunnyside, and the Depression
10. Public Policy, Private Wealth   217
    The Lost Vision of the Regional Planning
    Association of America

Notes   233
Index   265

Illustrations

The English Garden City   23
    The Three Magnets
    The Garden City and Rural Belt
    Ward and Center of a Garden City
    The Social City
    Letchworth (1908, two photos)
    Welwyn Garden City (c. 1925)

Toward a Regional Plan   95
    The Appalachian Trail (two photos)
    Wright's Regional Plan for New York, Epoch I (1840–1880)
    Wright's Regional Plan for New York, Epoch II (1880–1920)
    Wright's Regional Plan for New York, Epoch III
    A Vision of Regional Growth for New York

The Evolution of the Radburn Idea   135
    General Plan for Sunnyside Gardens (1924)
    Interior Courtyard at Sunnyside (c. 1935)
    The Birth of the Radburn Plan (1928)
    The Radburn Superblock (1929, two illustrations)
    The Cul-de-sac (c. 1932)
    Turned-around Houses
    A View of the Family Entrance (c. 1932, two photos)
    Radburn Architecture (c. 1932)

Howard Avenue Underpass (c. 1949)
Eye-level View of the Interior Parkland (c. 1932)
The Neighborhood Unit (1929)

The Radburn Legacy   211

General Plan for Radburn (c. 1929)
The Radburn Motif (two photos)
Aerial View of Radburn (c. 1940)
Aerial View of Radburn (c. 1975)

Preface

When this book began in the winter of 1977, the American dream of a suburban home on a spacious lot was in serious trouble. Since that time the prospects for home ownership have grown worse, victimized by escalating interest rates, land prices, and construction costs. But though the types of shelters we live in have changed somewhat, the nation's profligate use of land has not. Preliminary results of the 1980 census indicate that Americans are now moving to non-metropolitan districts in once remote areas in the same way that they migrated from cities to suburbs in the post–World War II period. If the present trend persists then the American landscape will assume a splattered, amorphous pattern that is neither rural, urban, nor suburban—a pattern that will defy conventional descriptions.

While forces have been altering internal land use patterns in cities, suburbs, and villages throughout the nation, profound regional shifts in population have been reshaping the historic relationships between North and South, East and West. The dramatic growth of the "sunbelt" has been matched by the economic decline of the "frostbelt," tipping the scale of regional imbalance as if the nation's sections had a reciprocal relationship which allowed one region to advance only at the expense of the others.

These two demographic developments have helped to crystallize my analysis of the American garden city movement and the Radburn idea. When the garden city gained currency in the 1920's, it was viewed as an alternative to unchecked metropolitan growth; after World War II, it was presented as a counterpoint to suburban sprawl; now, in the post-suburban era, the garden city and Radburn may emerge as a way to save our farmland from the spread of non-metropolitan villages.

With these ideas taking shape during the course of my thinking, the garden city movement emerged as not only presenting an alternative to the existing physical landscape, but more importantly as a challenge to the prevailing method of financing real estate development—as a reform movement which asked basic questions about America's economic and social system (though without directly confronting the sources of power). These questions, which address the economics of land use, allow us to see the demographic trend from city to suburb to semi-rural townhouse and condominium as part of the same process, and enable the garden city movement and the Radburn idea to emerge as concepts as relevant today as they were in the 1920's. Issues of adequate housing for all citizens, the preservation of "undeveloped" land, and balanced regional growth all were addressed by garden city advocates with criticisms leveled against speculative capitalist real estate development; a process which takes many forms but always heads in one direction—toward the intensification of land use as a means of maximizing its profitability for private, not social, gain. How to build stable communities and stable regions within a system that breeds instability was the central question faced by garden city and Radburn advocates. Over the past half century, and especially over the past five years as our available land and resources have diminished, such questions have grown even more critical.

Acknowledgments

This book would not have been possible without the assistance of many able and talented people. Robert Fishman, a friend and teacher, offered insightful organizational and thematic suggestions that substantially improved the work. Stimulating discussions with Warren Sussman gave me a larger social and cultural context in which to place my ideas. Gerald Grob, James Hughes, and Seth Scheiner commented on an early draft of the manuscript. Although I have met Roy Lubove but once and Park Dixon Goist, Carl Sussman, and Mark Lapping not at all, their previous work on the American garden city movement provided a sound foundation on which to build my analysis.

As a staff member of the Radburn Association in 1978 and 1979, I had the good fortune of working with Ronald Gatti, the town manager. He not only opened the Radburn Archives to me, but also gave me a first-hand look at contemporary issues in the community. At Radburn, I also received valuable assistance from Nancy Moreland and Karen Oppici. The first generation of Radburn residents and administrators, among them William Elbow, George Sporn, Robert Hudson, and John Walker, gave generously of their time to reminisce about Radburn's first years. The late Charles Ascher spoke with me at length about Radburn's history; and Lewis Mumford's short series of keenly perceptive letters helped to shape my early analysis. While working with Philip Dolce and Mary Darragh on two CBS-TV Sunrise Semester series focusing on contemporary land use and planning, I received a superb background for writing a history of Radburn and the garden city movement, a background that helped me relate issues of historical significance to today's problems. They also created an energized environment of commitment that spilled over to my research and writing. I also am grateful to Kenneth Arnold and his staff at Temple University Press, especially to Zachary Simpson, who guided the manuscript from its first draft to its completion, and to Cynthia Davis Buffington, who supplied able editorial assistance. Time for research and writing, a scholar's most valuable commodity, was made possible through fellowships from the New Jersey Historical Commission and Rutgers University.

Portions of Chapter 3 first appeared in "A Garden City for the Motor Age," in *Town & Country Planning* 48, no. 2 (May 1979): 57–59, and parts of Chapter 7 were originally published in "Lessons in Land Use: Radburn and the Regional Planning Association of America," in *Planned & Utopian Experiments: Four New Jersey Towns* (Trenton, N.J.: New Jersey Historical Commission, 1980), pp. 52–71.

Finally, I would like to thank Megan and Hilary, my two-year-old twins, for providing ample diversions and for keeping priorities in order; and Denise who unselfishly contributed her intelligence, understanding and patience, making this book as much a product of her wisdom and concern as it is of my persistence.

To all who have helped . . . thanks. I, of course, assume full responsibility for any shortcomings or errors.

Garden Cities for America

Introduction

With the aid of ideals, a community may select, among a multitude of possibilities, those which are consonant with its own nature or that promise to further human development.—Lewis Mumford[1]

TO travel through Bergen County in northern New Jersey is to travel through the archetypal affluent American suburb: the values and lifestyles of most of its families are basically the same as those of suburbanites throughout the country. Its ideal is the pursuit of private wealth and of satisfaction defined by material success; its meaning and structure are provided by the privately owned home and automobile. It has detached single-family houses centered on spacious, well-kept lawns; busy state roads lined with a variety of malls and light industrial plants; an eight-lane interstate highway, turnpike, and parkway to facilitate access to other areas; and a sprinkling of colleges, parks, golf courses, and country clubs.

With a median family income exceeding $21,000 a year, with 22 percent of its adult population college educated, and with every conceivable type of store and service available in its three large shopping centers or along its two state highways, Bergen County represents the prevailing perception of a suburban paradise.[2] Though pockets of poverty exist, and the construction of high-rise apartments on the Palisades in Fort Lee has changed the complexion of the southeastern section of the county, the private houses, highways, and bustling shopping centers have left an indelible mark on the landscape and the residents.

Picture, if you will, an alternative environment. Instead of an endless stream of individual lots, houses, and commercial establishments strung along the length of each major highway, imagine a constellation of relatively self-contained communities separated by green, open space. Each community would contain between 25,000 and 50,000 people. Housing, commerce, and industry would all be integrated in the original site plan so that most of the residents' daily needs could be met within the confines of the community. Yet the towns would not be entirely isolated entities. A sophisticated transportation network would bind them together to permit diverse cultural activities that only a large population of several hundred thousand people could support; and a system of mass transit facilities and "townless highways" or parkways would lace through open space permanently devoted to agriculture and recreation. This "undeveloped" area would not only provide food for nearby communities, but also give each of them a physical definition absent from other American suburbs. Unplanned growth—or what one student of urban planning has called "land pollution"—would be replaced by orderly, systematic land use. Indeed the word "undeveloped" in its conventional sense would no longer apply, for each parcel of land would be developed to fill a specific need in a balanced urban-and-rural environment.[3]

In the center of Bergen County, almost inconspicuous among the extensive suburbs, lies Radburn, a small manifestation of such a vision. When Radburn was planned in 1929, it was conceived as a town for 25,000 to 30,000 people to be built on one square mile of land. Today it consists of 149 acres, less than a quarter of a square mile, and houses 677 families, or fewer than 3,000 people. Of these, only 100 acres and about 500 families are to be found in the historic area, built before 1940, the rest of its residents living in conventional suburban homes constructed after World War II.[4] Radburn's diminished size, however, has not diminished its importance in the history of urban planning. With its pattern of cul-de-sacs, interior parkland, and cluster housing, the physical environment of Radburn's older sections remains an unique alternative to conventional suburban development. From Thomas Adams' description of Radburn in the early 1930's as an "ideally planned place to live" to Lewis Mumford's assertion in the early 1960's that Radburn "was the most forward step in town planning since Venice," professional planners have held Radburn in high regard.[5] In 1974, Radburn was declared a state and national historic site for "its special place in the realm of community planning and architecture" and for serving as "a world-wide example of the harmonious blending of private space and open area."[6]

This special sort of esteem, which Radburn has enjoyed among both American and European planners, however, is not shared by the vast majority of people living in or near the community. The community is not—nor has it ever been—an historic artifact for the people who live there, and if it ever did become a museum, instead of a vibrant community, it would probably lose its real significance. With the influence Radburn has exerted on post–World War II European development, it is undoubtedly a special place in the minds of planning professionals. But the residents usually view its special qualities in a different light than do students and scholars who study the community. For most Radburnites, the community is simply a good place to live. The physical environment, with its absence of through streets, creates a safe place for their children; the commuter trains and buses to Manhattan, plus the major highways leading to suburban offices and shopping centers, make Radburn convenient for work and play; and the well-organized recreational programs keep both youngsters and adults active and healthy. In short, the pools, parkland, and social programs fit perfectly into the family-centered lifestyles preferred by most residents.

In fact, despite some inevitable differences probably attributable more to the social composition of Bergen County than to the uniqueness of Radburn, the portrait of a Radburn family looks like the one most observers would draw of a conventional suburban household. Indeed Radburn's demographic composition resembles that of Bergen County as a whole and is similar to that of any affluent, mature suburb in the United States: the community is white, professional, and middle to upper middle class. The price of a house ranges from $65,000 to $130,000, with the typical house selling for $75,000; over 75 percent of the work force are professionals or businesspeople who commute to New York City or to the mushrooming commercial and industrial parks in suburban northern New Jersey. Like so many new communities, Radburn had a youthful population in 1929 when it first opened, one consisting primarily of recently married couples with young children; but the population has aged with the community. In a recent survey, the mean age of the residents was forty-nine, a figure slightly high due to the disproportionate number of senior citizens who responded, but one nevertheless indicative of Radburn's maturity—and also a reflection of the significant number of residents who have decided to remain in Radburn throughout their adult lives. As a young community, Radburn consisted predominantly of Protestant families. Today the religious composition is mixed, a recent survey indicating that 42 percent of the population are Protestant, 23 percent Catholic, and 23 percent Jewish. This demographic change parallels the transformation that has taken place in many of the nation's suburbs, especially those in the northeast since World War II.[7]

Lifestyles are conventional, the family remaining the focal point of community concern. In 1929, Radburn was hailed as "a town for children," and to a large extent the community still concentrates its efforts on their needs—or, more precisely, on their needs as perceived by middle class suburban parents. Throughout the entire year, the Radburn [homeowners'] Association conducts a comprehensive program for those between the ages of two and seventeen. The summer is particularly busy, as the community puts together a well-staffed recreational program that amounts to a day camp for its children, and the most important event on the annual calendar is "Family Day" held each July.

In Family Day's festive environment, the entire community participates in a continuous series of games and recreational activities ranging from softball for adults to a watermelon-eating contest for children. The day is consciously designed to celebrate the family, as adults and children play together in a well-organized atmosphere of friendly competition. Planning for the day begins in the winter; families alter or postpone vacations to attend; resident photographers often capture the event on film and present a slide show during the winter so that the community can relive the excitement.

The family-exalting attitude expressed in Family Day, like so many others in Radburn, resembles those found throughout suburban America. But the town's physical environment, with its swatches of interior parkland and continuous thread of pedestrian walkways, facilitates rather than impedes family and community interaction. And in its melding of the family and community spirits in a degree rarely experienced in conventional suburbs, Family Day more than any other social program makes Radburn an unusual place to live for the residents. Thus the day is more meaningful to the residents than any rendition of the community's unique site plan or statement of its historical significance.

When Radburn first opened, the social amenities and country club atmosphere were unique. Even by today's standards, the facilities and programs at Radburn are better than average. But many affluent suburban towns, such as neighboring Paramus, Ridgewood, and Saddle River, have developed elaborate recreational programs of their own. The ballfields, swimming pools, tennis courts, and playgrounds that made Radburn an outstanding example of community planning fifty years ago have since been adopted by most post–World War II suburban American towns. The direct relationship between physical and social planning, so carefully drawn in Radburn, is usually absent in those other, more modern, communities. The amenities available elsewhere are often developed as part of the public school curriculum—they are tied to each house, as they emphatically are not in Radburn, by the omnipresent automobile.[8]

Though on the average each Radburn family owns nearly two cars, a figure comparable to the national average for households enjoying similar incomes,[9] residents can—if they choose—be car-free within the community. There are more than eight miles of walkways in Radburn. These paths connect those houses built according to the original site plan—about half of the total number—to both the elementary school and the shopping center, enabling residents to utilize basic community facilities without confronting vehicular traffic. Radburn is safe, then, especially for children. On the north side of the community, youngsters may walk to school or to the store or to a play area without crossing a street.[10] Over the past fifty years, only two fatalities have occurred on Radburn's cul-de-sacs, the system of dead-end streets specifically designed to thwart traffic in the residential areas. And Radburn is convenient for both children and adults who walk or ride bicycles. In a survey taken in 1970, almost 50 percent of the respondents stated that they had walked to the grocery store at least once during the previous week and the same number claimed they had used the community paths to stroll to a friend's house. Indeed about 20 percent of the adult population asserted that they did a good deal of walking along the community paths both for relaxation and convenience. The privatized landscape of America's conventional suburbs, with its devotion to the automobile and individual yards, virtually destroys this type of activity; and even the new planned communities of Columbia, Maryland, and Reston, Virginia, cannot match Radburn's pedestrian system. When it comes to wrestling with the problems created by the automobile, planners are well advised to return to the fifty year old Radburn site plan.

Fifty years of history have not minimized its ingenious qualities.[11] Along with the recreational activities, the residents find such convenience and safety the community's most appealing qualities. Radburn's planners undoubtedly had these considerations in mind when they drafted the original plan. But their vision extended beyond the desire to improve the physical environment. Indeed Radburn was as much an exercise in social planning as it was in physical planning. Those who built Radburn were part of a generation who believed site planning could both express and promote certain social values. Safety from the dangers posed by the automobile was certainly an important feature of the community, and, as we shall see later, it was the one element of the plan that received the most publicity. But structuring the physical landscape in a way that would promote face-to-face interaction and participatory democracy was a more significant goal. By removing the automobile from the fabric of the residential neighborhood, increased safety would be enhanced by a new social and political environment characterized by more active citizen involvement.

To some extent, planners in the post–World War II period have grown skeptical about the role the physical environment plays in the formation of social values. Although contemporary planners believe site planning might determine patterns of neighborliness, few argue that it will exert a dramatic influence on basic values and principles. Closely placed houses compel neighbors to pass each other more often and relationships may evolve from these informal exchanges, but their depth is determined by elements that have little to do with the physical environment. Income levels, occupations, common interests, family responsibilities, and the distinctive personalities of residents all—for example—play vital roles in patterns of neighborliness.

Radburn's layout has had some effect on the quality of life in the community, convenience and safety quite aside. Its small size, which the planners believed to be a fundamental prerequisite for local democracy, has made its political structure more informal and more accessible to the residents. First, Radburnites have direct access to the manager of the community. Responsible to only 3,000 people, the manager can afford to discuss problems as they arise with each family. And the town meetings, held as often as once a month, provide an excellent forum for debating community issues. Second, there is a clear and direct relationship between the assessment fee each family pays to the Radburn Association and the quality of services the community enjoys. No tax revolt exists in Radburn. Except for the Depression years, the residents have rarely protested *en masse* against their additional tax burden. They appear genuinely satisfied with the services they receive for their money.

But the communal atmosphere the designers hoped to generate in Radburn was subject to forces far more powerful than the physical environment, and Radburn is far from a communal village. The community's unique physical environment has not made its families substantially different from other contemporary suburban families. Indeed, a sociologist would be hard-pressed to distinguish the values, behavior patterns, and lifestyles of Radburnites from those of residents living in the conventional suburban landscape. Their personal expectations and goals are the same as other suburbanites'. Most families share the private vision so characteristic of middle class America. One's house is a refuge from the outside world, as well as an investment that hopefully will increase in value. Education is important because it will help children compete for wealth and status in adulthood. Recreation is emphasized not only because it improves the health of adults and children, but also because it sharpens their competitive tools. The focal point of concern throughout Radburn is the family, with special attention paid to children, the community structure being perceived as an agent which promotes that sacred institution. For the residents, Radburn works well because it creates an excellent environment nurturing and expressing their traditional values. If Radburn had generated the communal principles and participatory democratic framework the designers envisaged, it is doubtful the residents would find it as appealing as they do. Sociologists Thomas Ktsanes and Leonard Reissman once described the mass produced suburbs of the post–World War II period as "new homes for old values."[12] The persistently traditional attitudes expressed by Radburnites make this an apt phrase to describe America's most noteworthy planned community as well.

Thus Radburn can be considered from a variety of perspectives. For the designers it was not only a physical and social plan for community development but also the "first step" in a new pattern of regional growth. Haphazard linear development would be replaced by a polynucleated land use design. A network of relatively small communities, girdled by swatches of green open space, would focus on the natural landscape rather than the man-made street, embodying on a regional scale the same values the planners hoped to introduce in the Radburn experiment. On both the community and regional levels, then, the Radburn idea was an offshoot of the English garden city movement: it was an attempt to transplant those turn-of-the-century European concepts onto the post–World War I American landscape. The first chapter will examine those European roots.

Radburn might also be viewed as the most visible product of one of the most innovative planning groups in American history—the Regional Planning Association of America. The RPAA, formed in 1923, remained in existence only a decade and was nothing more than a group of close friends who shared similar ideas on land use and planning. But the association contained some of the brightest minds in the profession—Lewis Mumford, Henry Wright, Sr., Benton MacKaye, Clarence Stein, and Stuart Chase. Despite the group's lack of financial resources and its reluctance to engage in political activity, the force of the RPAA's ideas placed it on center stage for a fleeting moment in the late 1920's. A history of the organization and an analysis of how it compared to conventional planning associations in the early twentieth century will be the topics of Chapters 2 and 3. The regional vision of Radburn's planners is outlined in Chapter 4.

As a multi-million dollar project, Radburn was a real estate venture of the first magnitude. The City Housing Corporation (CHC), which financed Radburn's construction, found its difficult task complicated by a commitment to curtail the cost of money (and thus the price of homes) by placing a lid on the dividend rate for stocks and bonds. The limited dividend concept has a long but frustrating history among progressive housing reformers. That history, and why Radburn's developers thought they could reintroduce the idea in the late 1920's without suffering the same fate, will be the topic of Chapters 5 and 9.

Radburn was also one in a series of carefully planned experiments. While visionary ideas remained central to their arguments, Radburn's designers never strayed far from the practical realities of land development in this country. The first experiment to bear the imprint of these planners was Sunnyside Gardens, in Queens, New York, built between 1924 and 1928. The 1,200 housing units were modest in scope. Yet it marks an important stage in the development of the garden city movement. Chapter 6, then, will focus on Sunnyside. Sunnyside's success ignited wide-spread enthusiasm for the development of Radburn. When plans for the construction of Radburn were announced in January 1928, support for the CHC was never greater. The site plan, with its cul-de-sacs, pedestrian walkways, interior parkland, and cluster housing, captured the imagination of the planning profession. And the emphasis placed on the sanctity of the family and community appealed to experts and the public alike. The "Radburn idea," which remains the enduring legacy of the RPAA, will be described in Chapter 7.

Ultimately, the principles behind the Radburn plan were tempered by both the town's administrators and the people who moved into the community. This raises the key question of how the "Radburn idea" compares with the Radburn experience, or how the community was and is "lived in."[13] This question will be pursued throughout the book and especially in the eighth chapter.

When the first residents arrived in May 1929, Radburn's future appeared bright. Public response was unanimous in its approval of the idea and the CHC's ability to solicit investment capital was never stronger. However, within five months after the first residents moved in, the stock market crashed; and within three years, the Radburn project was abandoned. Many of the people in both Radburn and Sunnyside faced financial ruin and they petitioned the CHC for relief. But expressions of protest in each community were remarkably different, and CHC executives, who unexpectedly found themselves in the midst of a complete economic collapse, were unable to respond adequately to the scope of the problem. By 1933, the Raburn project was all but defunct; one year later, the CHC went into bankruptcy. The story of the unraveling of the "Radburn idea" and the collapse of the CHC will be the subject of Chapter 9.

The Great Depression ended private attempts at a garden cities program in America, but at the same time it opened up opportunities for public investment. Many of those who were involved in the creation of the "Radburn idea" subsequently moved on to government service in the Roosevelt administration during the 1930's. For several years, conflicting visions of land use and community development were debated by policy makers. But the "Radburn idea" and the larger vision of regional growth that it embodied were overshadowed by more conventional planning methods. Radburn has been referred to as a child of the roaring twenties and a victim of the Great Depression. As far as the physical development of the community is concerned, this statement is true. But in terms of the fulfillment of the idea as the basis of a regional plan, forces even larger than the particular events following the economic collapse were operating against it. These were forces of tradition and ideology and they will be the topics of the concluding chapter.

THE history I have chosen to write about Radburn is, then, on the one hand, the story of a small, and in most ways a rather commonplace, suburban community; and, on the other hand, it is the history of one of the most innovative planning schemes in twentieth-century America, a scheme that has been honored and emulated throughout the world. The full meaning of the Radburn experiment cannot be understood unless we explore both of these closely related histories. For ultimately, it is the intriguing dialectic between the "Radburn idea" and the Radburn community that not only tells us a great deal about political and social reform in the late 1920's but also provides us with insights into the process of twentieth-century land use and development. Thus both the success and the failure of Radburn and the garden cities movement in America cast a great deal of light on the contours of community development in the United States.

The Garden City Invention   1

The time for the complete reconstruction of London—which will eventually take place on a far more comprehensive scale than that now exhibited in Paris, Berlin, Glasgow, Birmingham, or Vienna—has, however, not yet come. A simpler problem must be first solved. One small Garden City must be built as a working model, and then a group of cities.... These tasks done, and done well, the reconstruction of London must inevitably follow, and the power of vested interests to block the way will have been almost, if not entirely, removed.—Ebenezer Howard[1]

It was by unselfconscious common sense and humane understanding, rather than by systematic fact-finding and analysis, that Howard got to the heart of the urban problem.—Frederic J. Osborn[2]

The very building of Letchworth and Welwyn, while it immensely helped the idea, by bringing it down to earth, also limited it; for admirable though each of them is, they each have weaknesses in plan and execution which people too easily identify with the original idea, instead of realizing that both the improvements and lapses from key proposals are the inevitable price one pays for transportation into actual life.—Lewis Mumford[3]

THE garden city was not an American invention; nor was it a product of the twentieth century. Rather, the movement originated from the writings of an obscure English court stenographer, Ebenezer Howard, who in 1898 published a manuscript entitled *To-morrow: A Peaceful Path to Real Reform* (now known under the title of the 1902 edition, *Garden Cities of To-morrow*).[4] Howard was responding to the urban and industrial squalor of nineteenth-century England. He was particularly disturbed by his nation's inability to deal with the problems of human misery despite unprecedented growth and prosperity. To overcome this socio-political paralysis, Howard prescribed preplanning, a limited population for each town, open space, unified land ownership, and a process of "internal colonization" to create a matrix of clearly defined, self-contained cities. These concepts would form the intellectual core of the garden city movement.

None of Howard's ideas was entirely new. Neither was his approach dictated by violent revolutionary ideals: Howard was a "gentleman reformer" who believed that his moderate, gradualist measures would lead to dramatic political and social change. The disturbing conditions found among England's dispossessed population called for a comprehensive reform program, but marvelous technological advances combined with the inherent practicality and social concern of England's leaders meant that these reforms could be instituted without a great deal of disruption or conflict—once the proper course had been charted. Howard's "prime contribution," according to Lewis

Mumford, one of his most articulate disciples, "was to outline the nature of a balanced community and to show what steps were necessary in an ill-organized and disoriented society to bring it into existence."[5]

Howard's "peaceful path to real reform" was physically embodied in the garden city. His plan called for relatively self-contained towns approximately 5,000 acres or eight square miles in size. An area of concentrated settlement would be located in the center of each tract, covering 1,000 acres; the remainder of the land—amounting to 80 percent of the total—would be reserved for agriculture, forestry, and recreation. Each garden city would support a maximum population of 32,000 people. About 30,000 would live in the densely populated section at its center, and 2,000 persons engaged in agriculture would cultivate the fields on a large part of the remaining land surrounding it. Factories would be situated between the area developed for residential settlement and the farms and forests, thus close enough to where the laborers lived, yet sufficiently removed from the residential sections so as not to interfere with leisurely, family activities.

Howard chose a circular design for the garden city, with a maximum distance of three-quarters of a mile from the center to the circumference. But he did not rule out other configurations. Indeed, it was the process of growth rather than the precise shape of the garden city that remained paramount in his mind. To emphasize this point, he warned his readers that his description of the town was "merely suggestive and will probably be much departed from." In bold type he cautioned that each diagram was "a diagram only," not a definitive portrait of a garden city. He emphasized that each plan "must depend upon the site selected." Even the maximum population of 32,000 was not to be immutable. Thus what remained sancrosanct to him were the principles embodied by the garden city concept and the orderly, peaceful method by which his goals were to be achieved.[6]

Each city would enjoy a large, but by no means a complete, degree of self-sufficiency. The environment would provide a proper mixture and balance of residential, agricultural, commercial, and industrial activities. With its precise geometrical pattern, the physical layout of Howard's prototypical landscape retained many of the features of a Victorian city. But his call to limit the population growth of each city, his emphasis upon open space and social amenities, and his attention to the housing needs of all citizens—not just the wealthy—made his proposal a unique contribution to town planning. Howard was not simply offering a plan to ameliorate the worse aspects of the urban environment. He was proposing a new vision of land use. "Town and country must be married," he proclaimed, "and out of this joyous union will spring a new hope, a new life, a new civilization."[7]

In 1892 Howard was prepared to take his ideas to the public, but the initial response to his garden city principles was far from enthusiastic. Howard could not find a receptive forum to publicize his proposals; indeed he could not even find a publisher for his manuscript. Finally, in 1898, he personally financed the publication of his book with money borrowed from an American friend. Reaction to it was limited to a number of unflattering reviews that disappointingly characterized him as an impractical utopian dreamer. Throughout the late nineteenth century, such indifference and ridicule stalled the movement he hoped to create.

Despite that limited public support, Howard, with the assistance of radical land reformers, organized the Garden City Association in 1899. But it was not until he garnered the support of a prominent London lawyer, Ralph Neville, that the garden city movement became a visible political force. Neville introduced Howard to George Cadbury, whose family had gained a fortune in the chocolate industry, and to W. H. Lever, the millionaire soap manufacturer. Both these philanthropic capitalists were interested in housing reform and had constructed highly praised nineteenth-century working class model villages: Cadbury had financed the building of Bourneville, in 1895, and Lever provided the capital for Port Sunlight, erected in 1898. Through the support of these men Howard was able to obtain the capital and recognition he could have never acquired on his own or through his affiliation with English radicals. With their backing, a conference was held in Bourneville in 1901 to promote garden city principles. Attracting 1,500 individuals interested in the plight of English housing, it launched the movement into national prominence. At the age of fifty-one, "the inventor of the garden city" saw his ideas achieve a degree of fame that had eluded him for almost a decade.

In 1904 the Garden City Association had accumulated enough capital to purchase land for the construction of the first garden city. The site chosen was Letchworth, in Hertfordshire, about forty miles north of London. Howard's principles were applied there to a remarkable degree, though Letchworth's architects and site planners, Raymond Unwin and Barry Parker, softened the sharp edges of Howard's geometric design by forgoing his strict circular pattern. They preferred instead to respect and to utilize the contour of the land in formulating their site plan. But Letchworth suffered from two problems that were continually to plague the garden city movement in both Europe and the United States—undercapitalization and the inability to provide decent low cost housing for the poor. Despite the support of several wealthy entrepreneurs, the community suffered from a shortage of "front-end" capital. The amount of investment money necessary to construct a new town was (and is) enormous, and a substantial return could only be secured as the town matured over time. Since the annual return on bonds issued for the construction of Letchworth was limited to 5 percent, capitalists could find more lucrative investments elsewhere. Moreover, the untested plan did not offer them the security provided by more traditional and profitable methods of land development. "There is no doubt that the shortage of capital, due to public disbelief in the schemes, retarded development at times when it could have been profitably accelerated," Frederic Osborn, the most important spokesperson for the garden city in post–World War II England, asserted almost a half-century after the construction of Letchworth commenced. "This delayed the overtaking of interest on capital expenditure by revenue, and in turn intensified the disbelief of investors—the usual vicious circle of undercapitalization."[8]

Failing to dispose of its bonds on the private market, the Letchworth development company was forced to borrow money on mortgaged property. The high rate of interest charged for that capital raised construction costs and thus slowed the community's growth; it also, in turn, intensified the problem of financing adequately constructed housing for low income families, a goal that Howard had so earnestly hoped the garden city movement could achieve. The experience at Letchworth thus proved that the pull of conditions in the larger economic sphere could (and probably would) restrain the orbit of the garden city's social reform measures. Howard later disclosed that many workers in Letchworth's own factories could not afford housing there: they bicycled each day to the factories from substandard cottages located in the old English villages beyond the greenbelt.[9]

But despite these difficulties and limitations, Letchworth achieved a moderate degree of success. There was a good deal of truth to Howard's contention that, "whether viewed from the ethical or the economic standpoint," the garden city was a sound method of community development.[10] Although the town grew slowly and investors had to wait years for a profitable return on their money, the company was able to pay its debts, as well as to assume all of its municipal responsibilities. Since Letchworth was an experiment designed to prove the practicality of large scale reform, those who directed construction were understandably preoccupied with thus proving its economic feasibility. The approach conformed to Howard's notion that a single garden city must be built and be a proven success before demands for more garden cities would emerge. "One small Garden City must be built as a working model, and then a group" of the planned communities could be constructed. With "these tasks done, and done well," Howard had predicted, "the power of vested interest to block the way will have been almost, if not entirely, removed."[11]

However it would be 1920—sixteen years—before the second garden city was built, on a tract of land twenty-one miles east of London, at Welwyn. The Parliament's Housing Act of 1919 had provided a subsidy for the construction of working class homes, thus permitting Welwyn to meet the housing needs of a larger spectrum of English society than had Letchworth. But once again the management of the new town suffered from a shortage of capital which forced the community to grow slowly. Thus the limited success of each garden city, which required so much attention and capital—ultimately stymied Howard's plan for broad social reform. The actual experience of constructing a garden city, a process Howard had perceived as a stepping stone to more significant social change on a national level, had ironically narrowed the focus of the movement. As Letchworth and Welwyn matured and the financial investments in those experiments were made secure, Howard's vision of a constellation of garden cities, or what he called "social cities," was obscured. By the time Welwyn was built there would be little pretense about its significance. It would be a well-kept town providing an environment superior to either the rural or urban traditional landscapes in England, but not part of a larger social movement that would lead to a radical transformation of society. Before he died in 1928, Howard had lived long enough to see his principles leave their mark; but instead of transforming English society, the garden city had been neatly worked into the existing contours of Britain's social and political terrain. This paradox would remain at the heart of the garden city experience in both England and America: the potentially revolutionary aspects of Howard's principles would be lost in the translation of his ideals into reality.

The English Garden City

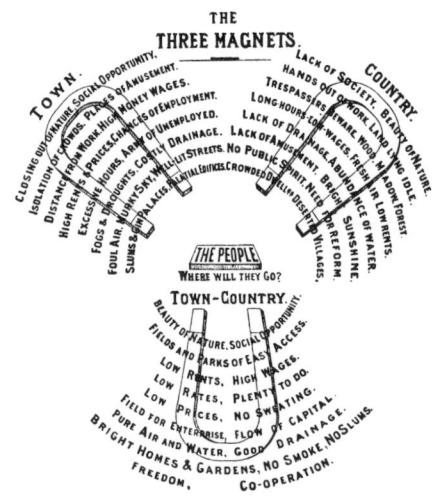

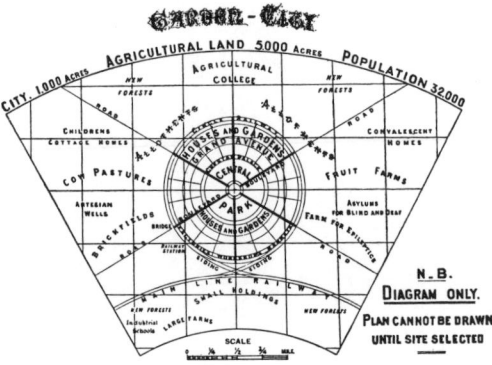

Top: The Three Magnets: melding the best qualities of town and country. The philosophical basis of the garden city movement that Howard envisioned as a path to a "new civilization." From Ebenezer Howard, *Garden Cities of To-morrow* (London: Swan Sonnenschien and Co., 1902).

Bottom: The Garden City and Rural Belt: translating abstract principles into a discernible form. Howard's geometric design. From Ebenezer Howard, *Garden Cities of To-morrow* (London: Swan Sonnenschien and Co., 1902).

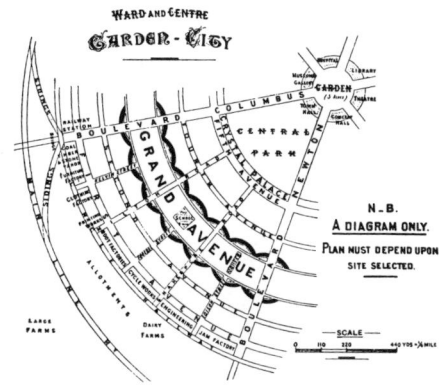

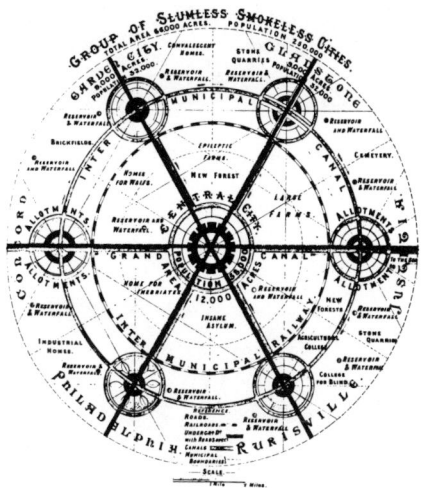

Top: Ward and Center of a Garden City: illustrating the concept of cellular growth within a garden city. Each ward represented a microcosm of the whole. From Ebenezer Howard, *Garden Cities of Tomorrow* (London: Swan Sonnenschien and Co., 1902).

Bottom: The Social City: demonstrating the concept of cellular growth on a regional scale. Six garden cities anchored by a central city. All towns are separated by green open space, but connected by a rapid transit system. From *To-morrow: A Peaceful Path to Real Reform* (London: Swan Sonnenschien and Co., 1898).

Opposite: Letchworth (1908): translating Howard's theory into practice at a site 40 miles north of London. Planners Raymond Unwin and Barry Parker, while they incorporated most of Howard's basic principles, softened the harsh edges of the original diagrams. Limited capital stymied the pace of development, and the high cost of housing closed Letchworth's doors to England's working class. Courtesy of the Central Office of Information, London.

Above: Welwyn Garden City (c. 1925): the second example of Howard's ideas, established 1920, 21 miles east of London. Public subsidies enabled Welwyn to accommodate a broader cross section of England's population than Letchworth. But the 16-year lag between the construction of the first and second garden cities underlined the movement's inability to raise adequate funds. Howard's ideas were partially realized, but in the process, elements of social reform and balanced regional growth were compromised. Courtesy of the Central Office of Information, London.

The Path to an American Garden City 2

What is a house? . . . it is the backbone of the nation. By the quality of its appearance, its convenience, its durability, one may infallibly determine the real degree of a nation's prosperity and civilization.—Charles H. Whitaker[1]

The public now, for the first time in this century, is seeing housing undertaken on a large scale for the good of those to be housed and not for the profit of the real-estate speculator or builder. The memory of the American public is short, and it is while we are carrying on war-housing that we must prepare for similar peace-problems.—Clarence S. Stein[2]

Let us quit thinking of town-planning in terms of quarter sections and prepare to plan counties, states and the nation. Is there any logical reason why we should not? We may not know how, but we can learn.—Frederick L. Ackerman[3]

THE writings of Howard and the construction of Letchworth did not go unnoticed in the United States. Indeed, as historian Roy Lubove has noted, "all progressive housing reformers endorsed the garden city program or its modifications."[4] But during the first decade of the twentieth century, the dominant motifs of American city planning were dictated by the City Beautiful movement that emerged from the enormous popularity of the Chicago World's Fair (1893–1894). Throughout the period, urban planners concentrated on civic centers, landscaped parks, boulevards, and parkways, all of which fit well into traditional patterns of growth. Business districts and posh residential areas became the physical expressions of a city's status, and the large metropolitan center which dominated the hinterland emerged as the central vision of urban America. But even while these themes shaped the nascent urban planning profession, such other ideas as Howard's garden city were not entirely dismissed.

One of the most articulate spokespersons for the garden city movement prior to World War I was the progressive reformer Frederick C. Howe. Although he reserved his most lavish praise for the advances in urban planning made in Germany, Howe spoke favorably of Howard's ideas as offering a method of decentralizing the urban population.[5] Moreover, articles praising the garden city appeared in literary and professional journals ranging from Gustav Stickley's "arts and crafts magazine," *The Craftsman*, to the *American City*, a journal for professional planners. Despite the praise, American observers often misrepresented the principles of the garden city or extracted certain elements from Howard's program without accepting the totality of his social or regional vision. For example, the well-known and influential housing reformer Lawrence Veiller concurred with Howard's argument on the need to reduce population density in urban centers, but rejected Howard's call for municipal land ownership and, for the most part, ignored the comprehensive portrait of land use found in *Garden Cities of To-morrow*. He chose instead to emphasize the need to decentralize population within the prevailing contours of urban growth. Thus Howard's concerns with open space, improved housing, and orderly growth were addressed differently by most American social reformers of the same period—even if they adopted his terminology and expressed their support for his general principles.[6]

As an outgrowth of such American interest in Howard's ideas, the Garden Cities Association of America was formed in 1906, the year Letchworth opened its doors in England. Louis Childs, a former New York senator, served as the first president. Other members of the organization included Bishop Henry C. Potter of the Episcopal Church; Ralph Peters, head of the Long Island Railroad; William D. P. Bliss and Josiah Strong, well-known Christian Socialist ministers; Elgin R. L. Gould, president of the City and Suburban Homes Company; Felix Adler of Columbia University and founder of the Society for Ethical Culture; and banker August Belmont, who had been a prominent figure in New York City politics for the previous forty years. Thus those individuals belonging to America's first garden cities association were the same kinds of civic and political leaders who had supported Howard's ideas in England at the turn of the century. As we will see later, their experience also paralleled that of the individuals who during the 1920's became members of the City Housing Corporation's board of directors. Felix Adler, for example, whose involvement in the American garden city movement was to span its history from its inception through the CHC's construction of Radburn, was urbane, well-educated, and middle class. Like Howard himself, he was a gentleman reformer who abhorred the degradation found in the city, but saw in fighting it great opportunity for fundamental social change.[7]

The Garden Cities Association immediately drew tentative plans for the construction of a series of garden communities to house 375,000 families in Long Island, Connecticut, New Jersey, Pennsylvania, and Virginia; but its aspirations outreached its resources. The recession of 1907 quickly undermined any hopes for a concrete demonstration of Howard's principles in the United States and deflated the initial enthusiasm expressed by the organization's supporters. The Association never recovered from this setback. It continued to advocate garden city principles through its journal, *The Village*, but not a single house was ever constructed under its direction, and persistent, debilitating financial problems made it an insignificant force in early twentieth-century social reform. After languishing for over a decade, the first Garden Cities Association in America was dissolved in 1921.[8]

Despite the failure of organized support, garden city principles were partially expressed in several planned communities built during the early years of the twentieth century—most notably in Forest Hills, New York, designed by Grosvenor Atterbury and Frederick Law Olmsted, Jr., in 1912. Indeed the site plan at Forest Hills later inspired Clarence Perry to devise the "neighborhood unit" concept, which became a key component of the American garden city idea in the late 1920's. Other communities to display some debt to Howard included Mariemont, Ohio, near Cincinnati, and the Palos Verdes Estates in California, twenty miles from Los Angeles. As historian Mel Scott has pointed out, unlike Howard's ideal garden city these towns lacked "any relation to broad public policy for the distribution of population and the development of regions"; moreover, by identifying improved street patterns and house groupings with garden city principles, such planned communities blurred the broad vision of reform proposed by Howard. Nevertheless, combined with the extensive literature on the subject, they indicate that American planners found garden city principles appealing and incorporated some of Howard's concepts into their work even though they failed to accept or appreciate the full dimensions of his proposals.[9]

It would be the effects of World War I on housing conditions in the United States, not the construction of the pre-war "garden suburbs," which led to the founding, in 1923, of the nation's second garden cities association—the Regional Planning Association of America. The government's temporary involvement in housing construction, followed by a critical housing shortage after the Armistice, had convinced many members of the planning profession of the need to continue government participation in low cost housing. Even reformers who previously had expressed their faith in the private market realized that the acute housing shortage could not be resolved by speculative builders, each of whom erected an average of only twenty houses per year. Noted housing reformers and planners Lawrence Veiller, Robert W. De Forest, James Ford, and John Nolen urged the government to continue a federal housing program beyond the war emergency—at least until the housing crisis subsided. Although they were unsuccessful in that appeal to Congress, more conventional economic remedies in the form of tax subsidies, moratoria, and rent control emerged from the housing debate, a debate which was particularly vigorous in the nation's urban centers, where the low cost housing crisis was most severe. It was thus in a turbulent atmosphere—though things soon quieted with the "return to normalcy"—that the RPAA emerged.[10]

The forum for RPAA principles was provided by Charles Whitaker, who, as the editor of the *Journal of the American Institute of Architects (JAIA)* between 1913 and 1928, "made that periodical one of the liveliest technical publications in the period."[11] Under his leadership, the *JAIA* emerged as a vehicle for some of the nation's most perceptive and innovative housing reformers, architects, and planners. At the same time, he opened some very important doors to intellectual exchange and friendship that would have an enduring impact on the American garden city movement. Whitaker's abiding commitment to Henry George's single-tax principles, as well as personal problems, would subsequently curtail his involvement in the RPAA during the organization's most productive period. But between 1917 and 1923, he and his journal were prime catalysts of what would become RPAA thinking.

For example it was Whitaker, personally interested in English war housing, who in 1917 commissioned architect Frederick L. Ackerman to investigate it—and to report on his findings in the *JAIA*. While the U.S. was debating the feasibility of government-financed housing, hesitantly accepting a federal program as a temporary measure "necessary for the prosecution of the war,"[12] England was pursuing a vigorous policy of building permanent working class communities with ample space and ventilation. As a disciple of the radical economist Thorstein Veblen, Ackerman was fascinated by the degree of technical knowledge and rational planning that went into these English experiments. For Ackerman, the British housing program illustrated "what the State can do when it acts with the full power of its rightful authority and with a broad enlightened conception of its aim and purpose."[13] He chided the U.S. government for being the only industrial nation that did not recognize housing as a municipal or federal responsibility, and he urged the labor unions to extend their demands beyond wages and hours to improved housing conditions.

During his tour of England, Ackerman came in contact with advocates of the garden city movement, many of whom had been employed by the government in war housing projects. Accepting their contentions, Ackerman argued that implementation of Howard's principles would be a logical extension of the current British housing program. He did not reduce Howard's concepts to a vision merely of orderly, arranged cities with lower densities, open space, and handsome residential quarters, but instead presented Howard's ideas fully, as a comprehensive scheme for balanced regional and perhaps even national growth. In his quest for rational, systematic development, he boldly called for a comprehensive housing program based upon "a national plan" designed according to Howard's polynucleated ideal of self-contained garden cities.[14]

Whitaker's commitment to alternative land use patterns led him to sponsor the writings of Lewis Mumford, a young American who was beginning to earn a reputation as a perceptive social critic. In 1919, at the age of twenty-four, Mumford published one of his first articles, "The Heritage of the Cities Movement in America: An Historical Survey," in Whitaker's *JAIA*. Although his analysis was to deepen with time, many of the ideas that remained central to his philosophy were outlined at this early date. In particular, Mumford's debt to the Scottish academician Patrick Geddes—whom he later called "his master"—is as clear in this early article as in material produced subsequently in his lengthy and fruitful career. It was in the Geddes tradition, for example, that Mumford emphasized the relationship between man and his environment. He drew upon Geddes' "valley section" to show how one's environment shapes one's personality and, more importantly, the social psychology and institutions of a region. But neither Mumford nor Geddes was presenting an argument for geographic determinism. Rather, each was illustrating how the natural environment nurtured a diversity of personalities and provided the fertile ground for a varied and productive society.[15]

From those premises, a number of important conclusions emerged: fundamental principles which were not only to remain at the core of Mumford's writings but also to be at the heart of the RPAA's program. First, since the social psychology of a region is largely determined by the interaction between the environment and people, any plan must be based upon a survey of the existing natural and human resources. Geddes' succinct instructions for a "survey–analysis–plan" became the cornerstone of the most advanced planning proposals of the first half of the twentieth century. Second, planning not only must entail the survey of an entire region but also the study of the interrelationships among "place, work, and folk—environment, function, and organism." Geddes had been inspired by the analysis of the nineteenth-century French sociologist, Le Play, who had argued that "the kind of place, and the kind of work done in it, deeply determine the ways and institutions of history." To understand the origins of these institutions required "a synoptic vision," one that incorporated a combined knowledge of sociology, biology, geography, geology, history, and technology—a monumental prerequisite that only someone who shared Geddes' relentless energy and keen intelligence could hope to duplicate. Third, the city had emerged as a container which absorbed and then expressed the diverse values of a "valley section" or region. Therefore, the urban environment and the hinterland enjoyed an essential historical relationship upon which they both depended. Mumford went so far as to describe the city as an environment which "combined the predatory habits characteristic of the folk traditions of the uplands with the peaceful ways of the lowlands." In short, the city embodied the collective heritage and personality of a region.[16]

This delicate balance between the city and the region seemed to Geddes, and in his turn to Mumford, to have been disrupted by the misuse of nineteenth-century technology—by coalburning which blackened the skies, by coalmining which scarred the landscape, and by the railroad which cut apart the natural environment and funneled people into increasingly unsightly and unhealthy metropolitan centers. The "paleotechnic era," as Geddes named it, "had used technology for the benefit of individual profit and power, not for social improvement." As paleotechs, he maintained, "we make it our private endeavor to dig up coals, to run machinery, to produce cheap cotton, to clothe cheap people, to get more coals, to run more machinery, and so on, and all this essentially toward 'extending markets.'" The result was the destruction of habitable cities and regions and the cancerous growth of "conurbations," the tentacle-like expansion of factories, mills, coalfields, slums, and suburbs characteristic of the nineteenth-century landscape. "What is the concrete goal and final generalization of paleotechnic industry and its economics alike, the synthetic achievement and concept of its main doing and thinking?" Geddes asked rhetorically. "In a single word, it is—slum."[17]

For neither Geddes nor Mumford was the source of the problem technology itself. Indeed new sources of energy—most notably, electricity—provided the seeds for "a new industrial age" which Geddes labeled the "neotechnic order." If nineteenth-century paleotechs had destroyed natural resources, twentieth-century neotechs would conserve them; if the environment had been blighted in the past, it would be beautified in the future; if drudgery and poverty had characterized the previous order, wealth and leisure would be the cornerstone of the new one. "The neotechnic order," Geddes proclaimed, "with its better use of resources and population towards the bettering of man and his environment together, means . . . the creation, city by city, region by region, of its Eutopia, each a place of effective health and well-being, even of glorious and in its way, unprecedented beauty, renewing and rivaling the best achievements of the past, and all this beginning here, there, and everywhere—even where our paleotechnic order/disorder seems to have done its very worst."[18]

Whitaker's journal not only provided a forum for the Geddesonian ideas that Mumford articulated and amplified but also publicized the innovative site planning techniques of group housing introduced by another figure of importance to the RPAA, Henry Wright, Sr. At the age of twenty-three, in 1901, Wright graduated from the University of Pennsylvania with a degree in architecture, and found employment in the firm of the well-respected landscape architect George Kessler. While working on the Louisiana Purchase Exposition of 1903, he was hired to plot a number of wealthy suburban subdivisions in his hometown of St. Louis. Notably, even at that early date, he struggled to free his designs from the restraining influence of the grid pattern and individual, private lots, so as to create a pleasing and functional relationship between each house and the larger community. In 1918, Wright moved eastward to become a town planning assistant for the wartime U.S. Shipping Board where he served as an advisor on housing projects at Newburg, New York, Bridgeport, Connecticut, and Camden, New Jersey. He began to elaborate on his theories for group housing and to formulate detailed technical studies proving that economy and aesthetic appeal could be designed into a high density community for moderate income families. Equally important to the development of the RPAA and its program, Robert D. Kohn, the director of the Shipping Board's production division, introduced Wright to Clarence Stein, an architect and planner who shared Wright's interest in large scale development. These two men, who possessed complementary talents, would soon form the key partnership—a fruitful relationship that lasted for over a decade—which would result in the town planning experiments at Sunnyside and Radburn. With Ackerman also serving on the Shipping Board as the chief of design of the Housing and Town Planning Division, the web of contacts that would result in the formation of the RPAA was being spun.[19]

After the war, Wright returned briefly to St. Louis as an architectural advisor to the City Planning Commission, which he had previously helped to organize. In reports to the Commission, Wright continued to espouse the virtues of comprehensive planning, emphasizing the need for broad street-frontage and shallow construction (two rooms deep) to avoid the dark rooms, poor ventilation, and wasteful alleyways symptomatic of urban America's housing problems. To put his theories into practice, he invested his own capital in a demonstration project of two four-family houses. Wright's "broadside flats" provided twice the frontage of the neighboring buildings and an amount of light and ventilation which was in sharp contrast to that common in the densely packed houses and deep alleyways characteristic of the area. These flats represent an important phase of Wright's evolving design concepts—though it had been his practical experience with the government's war housing agency that had actually provided him with the technical data necessary to confirm his innovative planning theories. If Mumford articulated the regional vision held by the RPAA more powerfully than any other member, then Wright provided the technical genius and expertise that could translate that lofty vision into a visible urban form.[20]

Another future member of the RPAA, Benton MacKaye, presented a distinctly romantic conception of regional development in Whitaker's *JAIA* when, in 1921, he described his Appalachian Trail project. Whereas Mumford's principles were largely graftings from European cuttings, MacKaye developed his notion of "regional ecology" from his native, American roots. As a student at Harvard, graduating in 1901 and receiving his M.A. in forestry in 1905, MacKaye had come in contact with the writings of geographers and geologists such as William Morris Davis and Nathan Southgate Shaler. Under their tutelage, he became convinced of the need to preserve the natural environment, and made it the centerpiece of his own philosophy. As a teacher at Harvard, and then more significantly as a member of the newly formed U.S. Forest Service, he began to develop unique ideas of conservation and regional planning which he expressed in a number of different agencies—the Forest Service, the Department of Labor, the Tennessee Valley Authority, the ill-fated Missouri Valley Authority—over a forty year period of government service.[21]

But MacKaye, one of the organizing members and subsequently president of the Wilderness Society, was no born-again pioneer yearning for a return to the primeval past. In his report on *Employment and Natural Resources*, issued by the Department of Labor at the conclusion of World War I, he condemned the "back to the land movement" as an unrealistic, utopian solution. "Real access to land is through industry and there is no short cut," he proclaimed. "The only way to improve this access is to improve industry. Mere living in the country will not make a living." As MacKaye understood the problem, America consisted of three elemental environments—the primeval (forest and lakes untouched by man), the rural (cultivated for food production), and the urban (oriented to industry and trade). The solution was to strike a balance among these three environments to prevent the city from becoming a metropolitan monster that not only destroyed the hinterland, and overburdened the city's own ability to function, but also sapped the rural environment of its vitality. In an argument that paralleled Geddes', MacKaye argued for a regional plan based on the maintenance of distinct, but mutually dependent, environments. Indeed he adoped Geddes' term geotechnics, literally "earth use," to describe his unique brand of environmentalism. "Geotechnics," he later wrote, "may be defined as man's ecology. For it applies to human habitation; it is our emulation of nature in her successful effort to make the earth more habitable."[22]

Finally, Whitaker provided an opportunity for the young architect and planner Clarence S. Stein to present his arguments against conventional housing reform programs. Stein, who was to become the chief American advocate for the garden city movement, was born in 1883 into a "comfortable middle class family." After a brief stay at Columbia University, he left to study architecture at the Ecole des Beaux Arts in Paris, but, "like H. H. Richardson, he emerged from its discipline without being tied to classical or renaissance clichés." As an employee in the Bertram G. Goodhue architectural firm, his first encounter with town planning came at the small mining community of Tyrone, New Mexico. As was the case with most of his eventual RPAA colleagues, however, it was his experience in the government housing agencies during World War I and his reaction to the subsequent postwar housing crisis that turned his attention to the need for social reform and his energies to public service. In 1919, Stein was made secretary of the New York Housing Committee, part of the Reconstruction Commission formed by Governor Alfred E. Smith to deal with postwar problems. On that advisory committee were future RPAA members Robert D. Kohn, Frederick L. Ackerman, and Alexander Bing.

Thus the network of contacts that would become RPAA was widening—and Stein was at its hub just as he would be at the hub of the RPAA, synthesizing the ideas of the group and formulating a coherent and forceful campaign to publicize its ideas. Mumford would later capture the unique talents of his life-long friend when he wrote that Stein's "special facility was to evaluate important ideas, to choose congenial associates, seize imaginatively on their special talents, and put them to work on tasks of research, design or construction, that drew forth their best qualities." At no time would these talents be more productive than in the decade of the 1920's. Indeed, it had been by displaying those abilities that Stein had convinced his friend Bing to devote his reformist impulses to New York City's housing crisis, rather than to the labor problems that had previously engaged him.[23]

At Stein's instigation, Governor Smith's Housing Committee uncovered the seriousness of New York's housing crisis; it also sought to disclose the root causes of that social problem and to offer solutions to it. The Committee did not deny that a housing emergency had been precipitated by World War I. Increased costs, difficulty in obtaining loans, and the shortage of labor and materials, all war-related, had led to a moratorium in housing construction. But the Committee concluded that the war was not the only reason for the problem. Indeed it suggested that in the present emergency the housing shortage was only more intense than, not radically different from, that existing previous to the war. "A shortage of homes fit for Americans," the Committee argued, "has always existed in this state." The reason was quite simple, but the Committee's solution could potentially lead to a fundamental alteration in the politics of land development in the United States. Since private builders, and speculative developers, expected at least a 10 percent return on their capital investment, a rate that pushed the cost of housing beyond the means of most citizens, the committee concluded that solving the problem required the curtailment of speculative development—the cornerstone of American land use policy. Simply put, then, "decent homes and wholesome environments in which to bring up children cost more than workers can afford," and the source of the problem was inherent in the way Americans had chosen since the nation's birth to capitalize development.[24]

The Committee recommended a number of solutions that, based as they were on such assumptions, marked a significant departure from conventional programs for housing reform. It called for the creation of local housing boards in communities of over 10,000 people to maintain an up-to-date survey of housing conditions; for the organization of a state land-bank to issue tax-exempt bonds for low cost housing construction; for the enactment of a constitutional amendment permitting the extension of state credit on a large scale (and at low rates) to construct publicly financed, moderately priced homes; and for the passage of an enabling act to allow cities to acquire land and, if necessary, to construct publicly financed housing.

These suggestions, which were for the most part ignored by the state legislature, bore the indelible mark of Stein's (and the future RPAA's) ideas. The Committee viewed the housing crisis not only as a present emergency but also as a persistent historical problem rooted in speculative patterns of investment. Its

Its interest was not solely in increasing the quantity of housing, but also in improving the quality of housing within a broad community setting. "The solution to the housing problem," the Committee reasoned, "means community planning in a large sense." In a subtle way, the Committee furthermore endorsed the general principles of the garden city when it called for "decentralized industry" and for limitations on "the size of our cities." To enact such programs would have required that large amounts in low interest loans be made available through state agencies—a solution which, although rarely ventured in the United States, had been implemented with a good deal of success (as Stein knew and the RPAA would argue) in Europe. Indeed Holland's national housing legislation of 1901 had provided loans to municipalities and housing societies for the entire cost of constructing housing, while, in the postwar period, additional legislation protected public and private low cost housing contractors from the debilitating effects of inflation. Between 1918 and 1922, the city of Amsterdam constructed (or was in the process of completing) 3,000 houses, and its building societies accounted for another 7,000 units. Thus when the New York state legislature balked at the Committee's suggestions, Stein would lament that "a program too revolutionary for New York . . . would have seemed . . . feeble in Holland."[25]

The Housing Committee was dissolved in 1921; but in 1923, a new Commission on Housing and Regional Planning was organized by Governor Smith to deal with the continuing housing crisis, and Stein was appointed to head it. He added the term "regional planning" to its title as a condition of employment, later reminiscing that "the legislators probably did not notice or did not understand its meaning, which probably accounted for why [the] suggestion was so readily accepted."[26] The first report of the Commission painted a bleak picture. "Rents have risen continuously, and congestion has increased. Families are being forced into poorer and smaller quarters. They are obliged to double up, two families living in rooms which under normal conditions, would be occupied by one family; they are increasingly forced to take in lodgers. The dilapidated, unsanitary old houses, which were considered uninhabitable in 1920, are now fully occupied and overcrowded. The conditions of upkeep and repair have grown steadily worse." The images conveyed in this portrait were given sharper detail by the statistical evidence tabulated by the Commission. Newly constructed housing rented at a minimum of $15 to $20 a room. If one applied the standard rule of the time that no more than 20 percent of a family's income should be used for rent, then only one-third of the population—those who earned over $2,500 a year—could afford a new two-room apartment. Four-room apartments would be beyond the reach of all but 10 percent of the population. In fact, only 3 percent of the new construction in New York City was within the means of 70 percent of the population. The scramble for it was intense, and the losers were then left to scramble for the inadequate old housing stock, most of which had been built before the turn of the century under outdated sanitary codes.[27]

The Commission's recommendations were similar to those presented by the Reconstruction Committee immediately following the war. The Commission asserted that "there can be no freedom of contract between tenant and landlord when"—with the vacancy rate well below 1 percent—"the tenant has neither recourse nor alternative but must yield to conditions imposed by the landlord." Although the Commission agreed that the tax-exemption law which took effect in 1921 stimulated housing construction, it argued that this legislation was a subsidy benefiting the rich, since it forced other, less able segments of society to pay more taxes to make up for the lost municipal revenues. Moreover, since the tax exemptions were not tied exclusively to low cost housing, the law often benefited developers who built high rent apartments and expensive homes. Thus the Commission contended that the spurt of housing construction in the early 1920's benefited the majority of New York residents "only indirectly," as it "relieved pressure on the housing stock from above." It went on to conclude that the law was "no longer warranted unless means can be provided to insure that the benefit of tax exemption shall be enjoyed primarily by those families of limited income who are to live in the homes which this subsidy is designed to create."[28]

The Commission argued, as the RPAA was to argue, that the key to the solution of the housing problem lay in injecting large quantities of low interest capital into the coffers of nonspeculative, limited dividend companies. "Housing must be provided by some agency operating without speculative profits, under public control, with money at a low rate of interest, aided by the exercise of the power of condemnation, producing on a large scale, with efficient organization and management." It was the only way, the Commission believed, that exorbitant rates of interest (especially for second and third mortgages) and thus the cost of construction could be contained.[29]

To understand this recurring conclusion, one must have some knowledge of the way in which housing construction was capitalized in the 1920's. The first mortgage, covering 40 to 60 percent of the cost, usually ran from three to ten years and was loaned at an interest rate ranging from 5.5 to 10 percent. For tenement construction, the cost of borrowing money began at 8.5 percent, since the financial risks were much greater. The second mortgage, taken out to cover any remaining costs, usually bore an interest rate of between 10 and 15 percent and perhaps one running as high as 20 percent. Since it was amortized in one to five years, a payback requirement few contractors or prospective homeowners could meet, borrowers had to add another .5 to 5 percent per year for brokerage fees to negotiate mortgage extensions. These were the factors that led the Commission to conclude that financing constituted the most significant factor in construction costs. Only 1 to 2 percent savings in interest could translate into a 10 percent reduction in rent or mortgage fees. Therefore, the Commission called for a maximum 6 percent return on investment for moderate and low cost housing. That standard posed no difficulty in obtaining first mortgages, most of which were issued by large financial institutions such as savings banks, life insurance companies, and trust companies. But it did conflict with the standard rate set by the private individuals or groups of small lenders who sold second mortgages at a rate at least twice that high. Of course in an industry dominated by such small entrepreneurs the economic changes sought by the Commission would not be easily accepted or implemented, unless dramatic transformations took place in traditional methods of capitalization.[30]

Still, Stein was able to keep the disclosures and urgings of the Commission before both the planning profession and the public at large. The New York Times carried stories on its findings, and Whitaker provided Stein with a regular column in the JAIA. As chairman of the American Institute of Architects' newly formed Committee on Community Planning, a post in which Wright would follow him, Stein at yet another point bridged the gap between theoretical planning and public policy-making. His ability to work within established political channels, while proposing dramatic, new programs, enabled him to bring his blueprints from the drawing board to the construction site—and with his personal qualities and his extraordinary organizational skills, he would put (and hold) the RPAA together.

WHITAKER provided the forum where future members of the RPAA first published their ideas; and the New York Housing Committee and the Commission on Housing and Regional Planning gave them much data and valuable experience in the public arena. But above all it was the experiments in group housing, neighborhood development, and functional street systems "based upon service" conducted by the World War I federal housing agencies which would be expanded on in discussions and experiments undertaken by the RPAA in the 1920's. Henry Wright spoke later about the influence that the wartime experience exerted on members of the organization and in turn on the site plan for Radburn. "I visited the other day in Chicago, a gentleman who worked in the planning of those wartime towns for munition and ship owners," he wrote in 1929 soon after construction began in Radburn. "He took me out to his home in the evening. When he went in the door with me, he said, Mary, I have brought Henry Wright home with me. He has been telling me a great fairy tale about a town they are building in the East, and they are doing all the things we used to talk about during the war."[31]

Thus many of the theoretical and practical ideas subsequently analyzed collectively by the RPAA were first explored in quite different settings by individual members. Although the RPAA was in existence for a decade after its formal organization in 1923, its position remained remarkably consistent. By exploring the ideas presented during the formative stages of the association's development, it is possible to grasp the central thrust of its program. For in the final analysis, the RPAA—like Howard—was not interested in building a city with a specific, rigid physical form, however functional and aesthetically pleasing the design might be. Rather, it was concerned with formulating a set of principles that could be used in a city (or, more precisely, a regional) building process, a process which would be more concerned with introducing a particular set of values into the urban container than in drafting a precise design for the container itself. As Stein maintained, there is no definite answer even to the question "what is the most efficient size of a town." The vital factor in planning was arrangement and grouping within and outside the boundaries of the city.[32] This was the principle of environmental design which, inspired by Howard's writings on the garden city, provided the theoretical underpinnings for the specific plans drawn by members of the RPAA over the next ten years.

The Regional Planning Association of America 3
Theory and Practice

A community with a stable population is now referred to as a "dead one.". . . If the community is growing, if concentration, congestion and traffic are increasing, the prospect is good. If not, it is poor. This point of view constitutes the core of the problem of the great city.—Frederick L. Ackerman[1]

The cutting edge of the city planning movement is now in such experimental units as Mariemont and Sunnyside and Radburn; they perform a work parallel to that achieved in education by the experimental schools; and an appraisal of tomorrow's tendencies will be incomplete without a reckoning of their failures and successes.—Lewis Mumford[2]

Other cities can avoid New York's breakdown only by making an effort to avoid New York's "greatness."—Clarence S. Stein[3]

IN the summer of 1923, while the RPPA was being organized, Bing, Stein, and Wright—in their first unified effort—prepared a "Preliminary Study of a Proposed Garden Community in the New York Region." The report contained a blueprint of a garden suburb for 25,000 residents to be built on one square mile of land. A site in Brooklyn "at the undeveloped edges of New York City," the Harkness tract, had been tentatively chosen for the experiment. But before Bing could secure the land, a speculative builder bought it: it was subdivided and auctioned in a piecemeal fashion and then developed in the conventional grid pattern. Although the "Preliminary Study" was never utilized, it is important because it constituted a feasibility report that served as the foundation of the building program later financed by Bing's City Housing Corporation—which, as we shall see, was the chief financial agent in the construction of Sunnyside and Radburn—and, moreover, because it encapsulated the land use policy to be advocated by the RPAA.[4]

The study began with a statement of what its authors intended not to do and what they intended to prove. They rejected slum clearance programs because such measures were too costly to make a significant contribution to housing and community development. Since urban land was expensive, such programs would have to devote too much of their capital to land purchase and thus too little to construction. In a statement that was to remain basic to the RPAA's program, they argued that better housing for low income groups would best be achieved where land is cheap and undeveloped because capital could then be spent on the quality of design and construction. Only under those conditions would the full savings to be derived from comprehensive financing, planning, and administration be realized. And even if that large scale approach was followed, the authors conceded, housing could not be built immediately for the lowest paid workers. The cost of construction would result in rents beyond what they could afford given their wages. But the three hoped that with the application of the limited dividend concept their experimental program would begin to reveal the soundness of semi-philanthropic investment. This would ultimately result in a revolving capital fund that could provide a firm financial foundation for the construction of a network of garden communities. Finally, the authors looked upon their experiments as educational models that other public and private institutions—most notably, well-capitalized insurance companies, workmen's pension funds, and savings associations—would study and emulate. With the types of financial resources commanded by these institutions, the authors believed, their support could eventually lead to the extensive use of innovative community planning techniques.

It was in the interests of reducing the awesome complexity of the problem before them that Bing, Wright, and Stein started a plan for a garden suburb within an urban orbit, rather than the construction of a self-contained garden city. Although that approach would severely limit the scope of the site planning techniques that could be employed, it would nevertheless ease financing and provide a training ground for more ambitious projects in the future.[5] It also would enable the developer to take advantage of municipal services, such as fire, police, and sanitation protection, thus substantially reducing administrative costs. Finally, a garden community built within a five-cent subway ride of the nation's largest metropolitan center would enjoy employment, cultural, and recreational opportunities that a new garden city constructed in the hinterland could not supply.

One problem, however, could not be denied: the authors acknowledged in the "Preliminary Study" the appeal to the consumer of the private, detached home. They admitted that the detached home enhanced privacy, reinforced a sense of ownership, allowed contact with nature, and provided fresh air. But they argued that these valuable amenities could only be secured on a very spacious lot and at an enormous expense for public utilities. Such prerequisites were becoming increasingly difficult to attain as the cost of capital, land, and construction increased. Wright, the most ardent critic of the private detached home, argued that the American "ideal" of a "house standing free and independent on its own plot, a whole country estate if we have luck, but at any rate, an independent and isolated plot," is "impossible, and . . . is precisely what stands in the way of any improvement in our housing prospects." Only by curbing "the wasteful and extravagant" cost resulting from the "individualized process of home building" could the nation begin to meet the housing needs of its citizens.[6]

Finally, the authors reminded their readers that conventional real estate methods had always failed to provide adequate housing for the "workingman." As a matter of practice, subdivision in the United States usually took place before the land was ready for development. Thus, in many cases, the realtor had to assume costly carrying charges on the subdivided land, as well as on the streets and utility lines constructed to encourage (but by no means to assure) development. Not only were these unnecessary costs passed on to the eventual homeowner, but the first families who moved into the area also inherited the expense of refurbishing the infrastructure that had deteriorated while the land lay idle. On the other hand, plotting a major subdivision and then allowing small contractors to develop it in a piecemeal fashion, which was the normal practice, could mean that housing appeared before the infrastructure was complete. The unsuspecting homeowner would then be burdened with additional taxes to build the sewers, schools, and roads that would all become necessary as the area grew.

Part of the problem, the authors pointed out, was that small contractors worked with a limited amount of capital and therefore could not take advantage of the economies of large scale production. Unbridled competition among small builders had not only resulted in wasteful, piecemeal development but had also led to shoddy, jerry-built housing design and construction—all that without providing a consistently secure profit for investors. Even industrial (or company) towns built by a single capitalist, and thus enjoying the potential benefits of unified ownership, had usually followed traditional real estate techniques and practices. The dismal failure at Pullman, Illinois, at the turn of the century (and the adverse publicity the company received as a result) put a stop to such modest attempts to reform American patterns of community development. It "led industrial corporations," the authors of the "Preliminary Study" complained, "to disassociate themselves as far as possible from the responsibilities of housing."[7]

In effect, Bing and the others wanted to devise a plan that would enable the real estate industry to enter the era of twentieth-century mass production without incorporating that system's speculative edge. Only well-capitalized, limited dividend corporations such as those advocated by the New York Housing Committee and the Commission on Housing and Regional Planning could meet the housing problem in the way proposed by Bing, Stein, and Wright. The key to financial success for the Harkness tract was to be a formula similar to that used by successful private, speculative developers, except that the investment return would be limited and the bulk of the profits would be poured back into the community (or into the creation of new communities), rather than kept as private wealth. Rapid construction, to reduce carrying costs and maintain a fluid capital base, would be critical. "It is highly desirable that the funds invested in the first garden city be realized upon as quickly as possible, so that these funds can be used to build a large number of successive communities, utilizing for each new development the experience gained in the previous ones. The success of this enterprise would also lead, in all probability, to the formation of similar companies and in a comparatively short time, the country might be dotted with these greatly improved communities."[8] This sense of experimentation and optimism characterized the collective work of these individuals and became, at the same time, a motivating force behind the RPAA.

IN 1923, Stein asserted that "American cities have been developed without any systematic planning. They are almost wholly the result, as expressed in terms of streets and buildings, of individual enterprise seeking personal ends and not of a community which has exercised its forethought for the common good."[9] The Regional Planning Association of America, formed in that year largely through Stein's own tireless efforts, hoped to transform the perceptions upon which such communities were constructed, and, in so doing, to change the shape and size of the communities themselves. The RPAA charged itself with the responsibility "to improve living and working conditions through comprehensive planning of regions including urban and rural communities and particularly through the decentralization of vast urban populations."[10] Or, as Mumford later put it, the goal of the RPAA was "the building of balanced communities, cut to human scale, in balanced regions, which would be part of an ever widening national, continental, and global whole, also in balance."[11] The organization concurred with each of Howard's basic principles: the ultimate solution resided in the garden city, placed within a regional fabric tailored by Geddes. It advocated comprehensive planning; a predetermined population limit for each garden city; a pattern of land use that would centralize dispersion so as to create a physical landscape characterized by polynucleated development; and non-speculative investment and unified ownership, preferably in the hands of the municipal government. Clearly each of these principles could be traced to the writings of Ebenezer Howard. Indeed to illustrate its affiliation with Howard's ideas, the organization was initially named the Garden City and Regional Planning Association of America, and it served as this nation's chapter of Howard's International Garden Cities and Town Planning Federation.[12]

But it was the association's approach to town planning, as much as its declared principles, that revealed the RPAA's allegiance to the English garden city. A great deal has been written about Ebenezer Howard as "the inventor of the garden city," one who responded to planning in much the same way a skilled craftsman would respond to the problem of constructing a cabinet or house. For Howard, the garden city was not an idealistic concept. Rather, it represented a set of principles or more precisely a set of tools, that could be used to forge a new landscape for England.[13] Members of the RPAA responded to town planning for America in much the same way. With sensibilities akin to Howard's, the association appreciated both the potential and the limitations placed on its theories and experiments—whether those were economic, social, or technical. Neither academically nor professionally overspecialized, the RPAA was organized as a study group or educational forum designed to broaden the expertise of its membership. In place of a strong institutional framework, it relied upon a shared commitment to solving the problems of housing through urban reform and regional development. Throughout its ten-year existence between 1923 and 1933, it rarely had more than a dozen active members, and never operated on a budget exceeding $2,500 annually. Architects and planners Clarence Stein, Henry Wright, Frederick Ackerman, and Robert Kohn; conservationist and regionalist Benton MacKaye; urban critic and author Lewis Mumford; economist Stuart Chase, editor Charles Whitaker; realtor Alexander Bing; and housing expert Catherine Bauer formed the nucleus of the group. At various times the association was able to attract progressive reformers and planners such as Edith Elmer Wood, Tracy Auger, Russel Van Nest Black, Charles Ascher, Robert Bruère, and Harold Bittenheim into its informal ranks. "Never a formal organization with an office, a staff, a regular publication, and a schedule of meetings, the association," as historian Mel Scott has observed, "was really no more than a circle of friends held together by a broad conception of planning."[14] Trained as architects, conservationists, economists, and site planners, then, each person viewed his or her discipline as one partial factor pertaining to the overall issue of land use and development. Indeed the association was convinced that a regional plan based on garden city principles would not unfold unless such a comprehensive, interdisciplinary approach was taken. Mumford captured the attitude of the group when he asserted that "unlike city planning, regional planning is not merely the concern of a profession; it is a mode of thinking and method of procedure."[15] The sense of process conveyed by this statement forms a major link between the publication of Howard's manuscript in 1898 and the construction of Radburn beginning in 1928.

To accomplish the goal of building garden cities for America, the RPAA drafted a number of basic principles. In a radical departure from existing political policy, the organization proclaimed that housing the population, especially workers, "is a community problem." Therefore, that social issue must be approached collectively, rather than through the pocketbooks of private speculators and prospective residents. The RPAA went on to say that business had been unable to resolve the housing problem and, consequently, "the provision of homes for working people must be liberated from the demand of profit-making." In a statement that articulated the moral foundation upon which the RPAA's principles were built, the organization declared that capitalists had an obligation "to invest in enterprise for the creation of better communities and better homes without demanding a profit, but merely receiving a fair rate of interest for the use of capital employed."[16]

Land sales, the RPAA concluded, must be divorced from "speculative profits," the key word being "speculative." Thus a distinction was made between an extravagant return and a more limited and "legitimate" profit. The RPAA's conviction that capitalists should accept "a minimum rate of interest for money invested in housing" reflects the organization's position that land should be treated as a public utility "important to health, efficiency and happiness," rather than as a commodity trapped by the forces of the private market. If capitalists could not finance housing for all citizens, then, the association contended, government must assume that responsibility. Thus the RPAA wanted to extract housing from the dangerous whirlpool of capitalist investment without necessarily restructuring the economy.[17] It was a difficult, often contradictory, position to be in, and the members of the RPAA rarely overestimated the influence which their organization would exert. "To produce a garden city under our present conditions," Mumford complained, "is to produce something which, if not dead, can remain alive only through artificial respiration."[18] Frederick Ackerman, the bitterest critic of capitalism within the group, continually worked under a cloud of pessimism, believing that the benefits derived from technology would not improve housing conditions until traditional patterns of profit were eliminated. But the RPAA's emphasis upon experimentation and technology, as well as its access to established political channels, enabled it to take a humanistic approach to issues of community development without assuming a dogmatic, principled position. As with Howard and the English garden city, this constituted the source both of its strength and its weakness.

For most planners, and for most citizens in the post–World War I era, the clearest manifestation of the housing problem was congestion. As Stein often pointed out, "the symptom of the disease in our cities is apparent.... Human beings crammed into subways, blocked in by streets, crowded in sidewalks, congested in inadequate living quarters, everywhere insufficient room to work or to live freely, finely, or even efficiently." The RPAA argued that congestion was caused by the lack of comprehensive planning, the centralization of industry, and the limited number of parks "within [a] walking distance of homes." All of these conditions were a consequence of speculation, since contractors, builders, and realtors were determined to intensify land use so as to maximize land values and profits.[19]

The congestion resulting from this policy was forcing families who could afford to do so to seek refuge in less crowded suburbs. But continuous unplanned growth meant that the suburban solution was only temporary, since, as Mumford noted, in the United States "it pays to keep the land undeveloped until it can be overdeveloped."[20] Stein spoke about "dinosaur cities" that could no longer support their population, and Mumford referred to "the wilderness of suburbia" where the commuter is more than "a man without a country: he is a man without a city, in short, a barbarian." "Suburbia," he concluded, "is a common refuge from life" where "the remedy is an aggravation of the disease." In the minds these men, as well as at the heart of the RPAA's program, the degradation existing within both environments was viewed as part of the same intricate process. It was

Garden Cities for America   58

not an urban or suburban problem. Rather, it was a problem of land use that could only be resolved through a comprehensive, regional approach.[21]

Thus the RPAA attacked both urban concentration and suburban diffusion. Decentralization was inevitable. The high price of land, increasing congestion, and poor housing conditions were making the city an unattractive place to live. Therefore, the question was not one of centralization versus decentralization. That issue had already been settled. What remained to be seen was whether twentieth-century technology and social conditions would lead to the development of an unstable, one-dimensional suburban environment that would eventually fall victim to the same problems plaguing the city; or whether technology and social policy would result in an efficiently planned, aesthetically pleasing, stable and harmonious environment. This was the compelling question—and choice—as perceived by the RPAA.

In recent years, the RPAA has been criticized for its "anti-urban" principles. Jane Jacobs, a well-known planner who has been the most outspoken critic, forcefully outlined that argument in her enormously influential book *The Death and Life of Great American Cities*. She began with a broadside against Howard, claiming that "his prescription for saving the people was to do-in the city." His American disciples, who were most clearly connected with the RPAA, adopted Howard's misguided principles, devising a regional plan that would "decentralize great cities, thin them out, and disperse their enterprises and populations into smaller, separated cities or, better yet, towns." The end product, Jacobs sarcastically concluded, would be "the creation of self-sufficient small towns, really very nice towns if you were docile and had no plans of your own and did not mind spending your life among others with no plans of their own."[22]

But Jacobs missed the mark when she accused the RPAA (and more generally the garden city movement) of being anti-urban. Through its various members, the RPAA spoke out against uncontrolled metropolitan growth, not the urban environment. These individuals proposed the garden city as a way to save urban America from the destructive forces of congestion and dispersion, which they saw as part of the same process rather than as separate elements. It is interesting to note that the majority of RPAA members were born and raised in urban environments and spent a good portion of their professional lives in Manhattan. Stein opened the first chapter of an unpublished manuscript written early in his career with a hymn to the diversity, excitement, and opportunity available in New York City. But he went on to say that the city's invigorating vitality had been sapped by congestion. Mumford, who spent the first forty years of his life in New York City before moving to rural upstate New York, has described himself as a "true metropolitan," a "bred-in-the-bone New Yorker." Both men have consistently displayed in their writings a life-long commitment to the city. What they detested was the impending breakdown in the metropolitan system due to the city's inability to support its teeming population. Nowhere was this failure more evident than in New York City during the 1920's, where the municipal government no longer appeared capable of dealing with the burden placed on housing; the street, water, and sewage systems; and other basic services.[23]

To overcome these problems of overdevelopment, the RPAA called for a "regional plan," characterized by "new population centers, where natural resources will be preserved for the community, where industry may be conducted efficiently, and where adequate equipment of houses, gardens, and recreational grounds will insure a healthy and stimulating environment." In the comprehensive, often romantic, portrait of regional development drawn by the RPAA, the complex relationships among climate, soil, vegetation, industry, and culture would all be a part of the plan. Rural as well as urban areas would be studied and a balanced pattern of growth established, based on Howard's principle of limiting the size of each city and preserving greenbelts of open space between them.[24]

The task was enormous. But the RPAA held that the twentieth century contained the seeds for a glorious revolution in land use patterns because technology had obviated the need for the centralization of industry and population which were characteristic of nineteenth-century growth. Drawing upon Geddes' comparison of the paleotechnic and neotechnic eras, the RPAA reasserted his belief in the possibility of new regional forms based on a polynucleated pattern that would replace nineteenth-century "conurbations," a process of incessant metropolitan growth that often left the hinterland desolate and overburdened the city with unbearable responsibilities.

As Geddes' most consistent and eloquent disciple, Mumford reiterated his argument that new sources of energy and new modes of transportation made the "new industrial age" plausible.[25] "Under modern industry," he argued, "a balanced economic life for every region has become a possibility." Whereas coal (the paleotechnic energy source) was dirty and a pollutant, electricity (the neotechnic energy source) was clean; whereas coal was heavy and difficult (not to mention expensive) to transport, electricity could travel great distances at a moderate cost through a power grid. Thus coal had encouraged the concentration of population near the mining fields. Electricity, on the other hand, would facilitate population dispersion because industry would no longer have to be near the natural resource that propelled the machines. "The electrical regime," as Mumford referred to it, "is technically and hygienically superior to the age which preceded it. Electric power is smokeless, it has no waste products, it permits the distribution of power with almost equal efficiency in a single center or in a score of centers." With these qualities, it could serve as the foundation of a new social order.[26]

The decentralization of population and industry was also reinforced by the invention of the automobile. Whereas the railroad (the paleotechnic mode of transportation) encouraged linear growth and dense pockets of settlement around major stations, the automobile (the neotechnic mode of transportation) provided the means for dispersed development. Finally, the new forms of communication made possible by twentieth-century technology would enable the spread of urbane ideas without the physical growth of the metropolitan environment. Since the radio, telephone, and movies meant that rural isolation and provincialism could be avoided, it was no longer necessary to concentrate cultural and educational activities in urban centers. Thus instead of describing members of the RPAA as nostalgic romantics yearning for a return to a serene and pastoral preindustrial environment, it would be more accurate to describe them as "reverse romantics," individuals who believed fervently that a better future could emerge from the present not by destroying or ignoring technology but rather by harnessing its enormous potential to humane ends.

Professional planners outside of the RPAA also recognized the enormous potential for change inherent in new modes of transportation and new kinds of energy. As the well-respected John Nolen commented, "the twentieth century has provided facilities in the electric power station, the motor car, telephone and wireless communication, that tend to make life in new and relatively small communities almost as satisfactory from a commercial or cultural point of view as in a large city."[27] But the RPAA maintained that an irreconcilable difference existed between their philosophy and those principles advocated by professional planners who accepted existing financial practices and the premise of unlimited metropolitan growth based upon rising land values, and then tried to work within the boundaries set by those preconditions. The solution to the housing problem, as members of the RPAA often stated, was not in applying bandages to a diseased patient but rather in rooting out the source of the malaise itself. "We can no longer patch," Stein wrote. "We must plan. We must find a new and fundamentally different basis for our plan."[28] Mumford saw the distinction as one based on different perceptions of the urban environment. "Does a city exist to promote the life of its citizens? Or do the citizens exist in order to increase the size, the importance, and the commercial turnover of the city? That is the real question that lies in back of every city plan: there is no compromise between these points of view."[29]

Thus the RPAA argued that the city planning movement had been shackled by a "tangle of private property interests."[30] Since the city had been defined as a marketplace, it was designed to attract the greatest number of consumers and industries possible. In this way, a municipality could maximize its tax revenues while private developers would enjoy ever-expanding profits. If congestion increased, an inevitable consequence of this policy, then the problem was not that there were too many people but rather that the infrastructure needed to be altered in such a way as temporarily to alleviate the overcrowdedness; and therefore create once again an environment that would encourage more people to live and work in the area. The mania for street widening and visions of multi-level roadways during the 1920's revealed those central principles of the planning profession, and, for members of the RPAA, indicated their self-defeating quality. Improving and extending roadways without a community plan not only opened the hinterland to speculative growth but also placed excessive fiscal demands on the city. Road construction required enormous sums of money that could only be obtained through the public purse: consequently, taxes would have to be increased. To recoup the losses incurred through higher taxes, realtors would engage in a more intensive use of the land, thus recreating the problem of congestion. Stein captured the cyclical essence of this problem when he argued that improvements to facilitate traffic "can only be done at vast expense which falls back on the land in the shape of assessments and taxes... and in time [will] make it necessary to build still higher buildings and more levels of streets." With specific reference to New York City's mass transit system, Stein warned that "more subways will not decrease congestion. They spread it. At one end they carry the city of tall crowded tenements and apartments on hard paved streets further and further out toward the life giving green of the country, which they never reach. At the other end they power more workers into the already crowded centers."[31] But most professional planners, who "worked under the stimulus of day-to-day interests and necessities without the aid of a comprehensive, enlightened plan to promote the common welfare," were preoccupied with such short-term technical solutions—avoiding the larger and more essential economic and social issues.[32]

According to the RPAA, the limited tools used by planners to deal with urban problems were, then, an outgrowth of their basic, self-defeating assumptions. The most common tool was zoning, a device that has remained the essential element in

American planning for the past six decades. Functional zoning had been introduced in Germany at the turn of the century; in the United States a rudimentary form of zoning (or districting) dated back to the creation, for public safety, of fire districts regulating the construction of wooden buildings. But not until 1916, in New York City, was the nation's first comprehensive zoning ordinance passed—and the motivating factors for the approval of the ordinance typify zoning's history.[33]

In 1911, New York's Commission on Congestion of Population had expressed urgent concern about the problems of congestion and inadequate light and ventilation caused by the city's increasing number of skyscrapers, and recommended a city-wide restriction on building heights. Despite widespread support, the Commission's suggestions moved slowly through the political process. Five years after the initial report, no ordinance had been passed. Then, in 1916, midtown Manhattan merchants purchased full-page ads in the daily newspapers beseeching all New Yorkers to save their city from impending doom. The northward migration of industry threatened their posh retail and residential district. If the trend were permitted to continue, the factories and warehouses would destroy profits and land values, forcing residents and merchants serving a wealthy clientele to leave. The city, in turn, would be deprived of taxes from a wealthy, revenue-producing area. The ads galvanized support for a zoning measure. With the banking and business communities allied, New York City passed the nation's first comprehensive zoning ordinance, one regulating building height, area, and use.[34]

Thus the ordinance, as would be the case in subsequent zoning ordinances passed in cities throughout America, was a document written by and for business interests. Lawrence Veiller refused to sign the final report which was used as its basis, believing that the regulations to be promulgated would compromise health and safety in favor of commercial growth. The facts confirmed his suspicions. New York's zoning ordinance permitted enough housing construction for the entire population of the United States in 1900, and it allowed enough industrial and commercial development for 300 million workers. As

Mel Scott concluded, "the wonder is that no one ever tried to overturn the resolution on the simple grounds that it was absurd." But far from being condemned or overturned, the New York City ordinance became a model for zoning legislation throughout the nation.[35]

The RPAA did not deny that zoning could play an important role in a comprehensive planning program. The need to segregate various functions from one another, such as heavy industry from residential areas, was undeniable. But too often zoning was employed as the only planning mechanism. Although it regulated usage, it could not control the physical layout or timing of development. Consequently, zoning often impeded comprehensive planning. As Henry Wright quipped, "the designer [was left] in the position of a musical composer confined to the use of a single note for each movement of his composition."[36] Zoning often had other negative impacts on housing and community development. By establishing uniform lot sizes, for example, it discouraged innovative site planning. This was one of the reasons for the RPAA's complaint that the American architect had become enslaved to the engineer. The emphasis on street systems and individual lots created a straitjacket that restrained an architect's imagination. "It is all but hopeless," Mumford argued, "for the architect to design sanely and beautifully unless he can relate his individual works to a sanely and beautifully designed city, to a sane and beautiful community."[37] And with zoning's emphasis on the individual lot, a broad regional approach to community design was impossible.

Finally, zoning laws, as was the case with the New York ordinance in 1916, were often passed to freeze or to insure high land values. Since zoning usually reflected potential, rather than actual use, municipalities planned for disproportionate percentages of commercial and industrial development to insure that maximum revenues would be derived from the land. Conforming to the nation's long tradition of city boosterism, "overzoning" for business use created plans based on extraordinarily optimistic forecasts for urban growth. For example, Burbank, California, with a population of 20,000 in the mid-1920's, zoned enough business frontage to serve a population of 1.5

million, even though the residential areas were planned to provide housing for a maximum of 125,000. In Pasadena, with a population of 75,000, the business areas designated by law could have accommodated over a million customers and employees. If conventional zoning policy had been followed in Los Angeles for all of the proposed highways of the 1920's, then Los Angeles County would have had enough business frontage to cater to the needs of the entire American population. In Duluth, Minnesota, if office space had been built to its maximum zoned allowance, then the town's business districts could have employed 20 million people. But in characteristic fashion, New York City led the way: the nation's greatest metropolis—with a population of fewer than 6 million people in 1920—zoned enough commercial and industrial space to accommodate no fewer than 300 million employees.[38] This use of zoning, repeated in town after town across the country, not only encouraged leap-frogging commercial and industrial growth disconnected from community development but also resulted in escalated land values. Thus it violated the core of the RPAA's program which called for a curtailment of speculative profits as the means of providing a comprehensive community plan.[39]

Rejecting zoning, then, as the final solution to housing and community development problems, the RPAA also rejected solutions proposed by such early twentieth century progressive housing reformers as Lawrence Veiller. These reformers had waged a staunch political campaign to upgrade the quality of housing stock by establishing minimum standards for construction and maintenance, fighting for improvements in building coverage, ventilation, fire-proofing, and room size. When rigorously enforced, such "restrictive legislation" curbed the worst abuses found in tenement housing. But the RPAA argued, with a good deal of justification, that this approach did not insure an adequate supply of housing stock; nor did it encourage innovative site planning. Restrictive legislation could never have stimulated construction to overcome, for example, the post–World War I housing shortage discussed in Chapter 2—a shortage that Edith Elmer Wood had estimated at the time of the Armistice as one of 400,000 units, one soon to grow into a shortage of a million units. Indeed such laws would compound the economic difficulties faced by contractors and discourage construction for middle and low income groups by pushing up costs, especially during inflationary periods.[40] Prior to the post–World War I period, this problem never had to be confronted directly. With the serious housing shortage of the early 1920's, however, restrictive legislation no longer seemed adequate. Robert W. De Forest, chairman of the New York Tenement House Commission of 1900 and one of its most ardent supporters, asserted that "tenement house reform would not be practical which went so far as to put a stop to building new tenement houses. Nor would it be practical if it compelled such extensive change in the old tenements that owners would turn to other uses. . . . Reform of such a kind would harm most the very persons it sought to aid."[41] And Edith Elmer Wood's forthright warning echoed with a truthfulness that could no longer be ignored. "Housing reform," she asserted, "must not be allowed to create house famines."[42] It was partially in the context of the post–World War I housing crisis, then, that the RPAA criticized previous programs for housing reform.

Just as the organization proposed that zoning must be supplemented by other, more innovative policies, RPAA members maintained that "restrictive legislation" must be joined by "constructive legislation" in any comprehensive land use program. Wright often contended that "restrictive legislation" meant the "minimum became the maximum," as builders used basic municipal standards as the criteria for all tenement construction. Ackerman put it another, more sharply critical, way. "Minimum standards," he argued, "represent, with a fair degree of accuracy, the slum at its best." For these social critics, the dismal state of housing in the nation's urban centers was proof that earlier progressive reformers had failed. And they had failed for the same reasons that city planners were not significantly improving the urban environment. As Stein noted, their reform proposals had "always been a compromise of the right to better living with the right to profit of the land owner, the speculative builder and the landlord of the existing bad housing." By trying to make housing profitable for the realtor and comfortable for all residents, they had been unable to do either. Traditional housing reform had been a false solution, Wright concluded, because "with a minimum of decent equipment the tenement house was unprofitable to build at old rentals, and at a readjusted rental, it was no longer cheap enough for a large body of workers."[43]

The RPAA agreed with the indisputable evidence that housing costs had increased substantially over time. But it found, contrary to the dominant view among urban planners, that the cause of this was not in the short-term inflationary spiral of the post–World War I period. Escalating material and labor costs, up 100 percent between 1917 and 1920, were not primarily responsible for the problem of high housing costs. Indeed, lists of figures drawn up by members of the RPAA indicated that these factors constituted only a small percentage of the total increase in cost. For the association, a key to long-term trends in the price structure of housing was found in the interrelationship between housing costs and community development costs. This relationship, a factor often neglected by conventional planners, was changing as the ratio of the cost of the external shell to the total cost of a house's construction had decreased. First of all, this was because of an increase in home appliances. Since the Revolutionary period, at least one significant invention in each century emerged as a vital component in the American house: in the eighteenth century, the Franklin Stove; in the nineteenth century, running water; and in the twentieth century, bathrooms, central heating, and complicated systems of waste removal.[44]

There had also been a dramatic rise in the demand for municipal facilities, facilities often needed to service those household appliances. Between 1850 and 1870, street grading, paving, and gas and water systems had all been introduced. By the last decade of the nineteenth century, municipal sewage disposal systems, plumbing, and electrical appliances had increased the burden on municipal equipment and thus the cost of community development. Whereas the physical shell of a house was estimated to be 90 percent of its total cost in 1800, by 1920 it was no more than 55 percent. This trend led Stein and Wright to state sardonically that "those who believe in the inexorable continuation of mathematical curves may comfort themselves with the indication that the [cost of the] structure itself will disappear in favor of site costs and appliances, some time after 1970."[45]

But there were other factors that contributed to the shifting costs of construction. Land and capital also played a central role in the high price of houses. If speculation created a displeasing physical environment, it was precisely because it continuously inflated costs. In fact, speculative profit constituted the one variable that could make a significant difference in the price a consumer paid for shelter. In the early 1920's, Wright had proved that a 1 percent reduction in the interest rate on mortgages would result in a 15 percent reduction in the total amount of money a person would pay for a house. Moreover, "not even the most drastic economies achieved by skimping on construction costs," Wright concluded, "could produce savings in rentals or in ownership charges equal to those to be derived from the slower rate of amortization resulting from stable financing."[46] For Wright and other members of the RPAA, the web of private financial interests was the main obstacle to cheaper housing and better patterns of community development. Without a stable pool of capital and without a curtailment of profits, savings attained through "scientific" construction would most likely be lost to increased land values and credit charges. The housing problem was once again shown to be one of capitalization.

THE formation of the RPAA in 1923, historian Roy Lubove has written, "signified a sharp break with traditional housing and planning objectives in the United States."[47] Members of the RPAA challenged the physical and social form of both the American city and the American suburb, and they spoke out against the patchwork plans offered by housing reformers and urban planners who contented themselves with technical solutions proposed by engineers, transit experts, and private real estate brokers. They harshly criticized speculative investment which inflated housing costs while it crowded the landscape. Mumford, MacKaye, Stein, Wright, and Ackerman presented their arguments with a sense of urgency because they perceived an "impending breakdown of metropolitan civilization"—and, shortly, of the emerging suburban environment as well—a breakdown that could be avoided by a more intelligent use of twentieth-century technology. The "arteries" of transportation in the congested cities were "clogged," Stein observed, and it seemed "inevitable that the end of this gradual clogging of movement" would be an outward migration of population. But the suburbs were "no escape": "they merely trade the disadvantage of congested and inadequate homes for inadequate and congested transportation. And soon the city is upon them." The only solution, for the RPAA, resided in a rational, systematic approach based upon garden city principles, a plan that would limit the amount of profits, people, and congestion in each city, and foster a process of environmental planning and experimentation.[48]

Mumford described the difference between the RPAA and other professional planners in the following manner. "The change [the RPAA advocates] consists in doing away with land-gambling, usury and the business of creating paper values: the fresh start [it envisions] is a matter of using the auto and radio and giant power to assist in creating new centers of life and culture, called garden cities." It was this same spirit that later enabled Wright to see Radburn as an experiment in "the full coordination of all processes of land development, house planning and community organization by sympathetic technicians as well as those trained in handling social and political problems under a single and coordinated process."[49] "Community planning" became one of the key terms in the organization's vocabulary, distinguishing the RPAA's unique brand of regional planning from more conventional ones. Thus—for example—to members of the association, streets were not simply traffic arteries designed to facilitate commercial and industrial growth; they were part of a complex communication and distribution network, the lifeblood of the community that had to be built in relationship to the rest of the urban and rural organism.

The RPAA's harsh critique of the American urban environment, and those who sought to reform it, did not prevent the association's ideas from receiving an adequate airing. As an expert organizer, Stein was able to garner the support of important political figures, including Governor Alfred E. Smith of New York. We have seen that in his position as chairman of the New York State Commission on Housing and Regional Planning he supervised a skilled research team, enjoyed access to the news media, and forged direct ties to some of the nation's most respected and powerful citizens. The RPAA's principles were thus to gain a respectability through association that the organization could not have nurtured on its own. Moreover, many of the RPAA members were talented writers (Mumford, MacKaye, Chase, Stein, Ackerman, and Wright). Even readers disagreeing with their arguments had to be impressed with the compelling style of their presentations. If nothing else, the RPAA members made good copy (in two senses) for relatively staid professional journals. Besides, each of them had gained a good deal of recognition in his or her chosen field. Indeed Stein and then Wright, as previously noted, chaired the American Institute of Architects' Committee on Community Planning, a position from which each was eminently able to communicate the ideas of the RPAA to his fellow professionals.

And in 1925, the RPAA hosted the International Town, City and Planning Conference in New York City. The conference was dedicated to the theme of the garden city and regional development. Ebenezer Howard attended. So did Patrick Geddes and the English planners Barry Parker and Raymond Unwin, who had been responsible for the site plan at Letchworth and thus for the transformation of Howard's diagrams and vision into the first garden city. Unwin also had engaged in a great deal of research on alternatives to traditional urban patterns of growth. His pamphlet "Nothing Gained by Overcrowding" illustrated that substantial savings could be attained in utility costs and roadways if housing density was confined to twelve units per acre, an argument which inspired Wright in his studies of cluster housing and undoubtedly served as one of the underpinnings of the "Radburn idea." During their stay in America, European garden city advocates joined members of the RPAA in Netcong, New

Jersey, to exchange ideas, to reaffirm each other's commitment to the garden city, and to learn New England folk songs and dances—symbolic expressions of regional values, charm, and significance.[50]

A short time before this meeting, Benton MacKaye met with Robert Bruère, the education editor of the reformist magazine *Survey Graphic*, to discuss the event. Bruère suggested that the RPAA arrange for a special issue of the *Survey* dedicated to regional planning and the two men hastily put together an outline which was forwarded to Mumford, who agreed to edit the collection. When the RPAA articles were first presented to the editor-in-chief, Paul Kellogg, he rejected them because he said the collection pertained to ideas, not the concrete facts which his social work journal normally dealt with. But the two English garden cities of Letchworth and Welwyn were facts, and so were partially responsible for changing Kellogg's mind. On May 1, 1925, the *Survey Graphic* published its "Regional Planning Number" with articles by Stein on the inherent social danger of unchecked metropolitan growth; Wright on group housing; Chase on waste in our transportation system; Ackerman on the destructive quality, yet sacred appeal, of the nation's capitalist financial schemes; Mumford on the history of migration in this country and a forecast of future demographic patterns; and MacKaye on ecological planning. The issue contained both the quintessence and breadth of the RPAA's vision of regional growth, and it illustrated the organization's ability to work in the realms of theory and practice at the same time. As one historian has recently written, "the *Survey Graphic*'s 'Regional Planning Number' presents a harmonious composition about the condition of urban life and a program for change. Its critique of metropolitan civilization and description of an alternative regional system based on new technologies and social institutions convey the 'essential thought of the RPAA.'"[51]

At the same time the RPAA was shaping its planning philosophy, other professional planners were fashioning a different type of regionalism. Between 1921 and 1929, the migration to American cities varied between 400,000 and 1.1 million annually.[52] Most cities were unprepared to absorb the waves of migrants which flooded them. Thus the population spilled over into the hinterlands beyond their political boundaries, which meant that the city's problems were no longer confined to the city's limits. To combat those problems, commissions, such as the Port Authority and Triborough Bridge Authority in the New York metropolitan region, were established. Each was charged with a single responsibility, usually directly connected to the region's infrastructure—for example, transportation, sewage disposal, water supply, or parkland. Contrary to the RPAA's sense of what was necessary, these "public" authorities rarely, if ever, tried to control urban population growth or to curtail speculative profits. Indeed by planning and financing the construction of the infrastructure as they did, they helped to further the concentration of people in the cities and to advance their dispersion into the suburbs.

As one critic has observed, regional planning need not be synonymous with the creation of such public authorities, as it appears to be in the United States. What made regional planning a potentially useful tool was its ability to coordinate the complex, but interrelated, factors of community development. By assuming single responsibilities, the public authorities actually stood in the way of such a comprehensive approach. "We display a certain lack of thoroughgoing conscientiousness," claimed planner Alfred Bettman, a tangential RPAA member, "when we claim as regional planning accomplishments, the special planning work of these regional or metropolitan boards which have to do with only one type of public utilities or improvements, such as transit or parks. In fact, . . . if the planning of the park system of a region or any other single type of utility may be treated as independent of the planning of the other utilities and amenities of the region, then there is no need for general planning."[53]

The purpose of these agencies conformed to the basic definition of regionalism applied by most planners. "Regional planning," George Ford, a prominent leader in the new discipline, proclaimed, "usually differs from city planning in the relative area of ground covered." G. Gordon Whitnall, one of the guiding forces behind the formation of the Los Angeles County Planning

Commission in 1920, envisioned an 800 square mile region (including 400 square miles within the boundaries of Los Angeles itself) urbanized into one solid mass. To underline this goal, the secretary of the Los Angeles Commission claimed that "the purpose of Regional Planning" is "to weld" the metropolitan area "into a unity of metropolitan consciousness and action." Thus regionalism, in the minds of most professional planners, represented a rational program to accommodate continuous population growth. From this perspective, regionalism was no more than a geographic extension of city planning.[54]

The RPAA's program and definition of regional planning would thus not be the hallmark of the planning profession during the 1920's. Rather, the Russell Sage Foundation's Regional Plan of New York, written under the direction of Thomas Adams, the most respected planner of his time, would serve that purpose. Adams began his career as the first secretary of England's Garden City Association at the turn of the century; he also served as manager of Letchworth and was a founding member and president of the British Town Planning Institute. Adams was therefore well versed in garden city principles and considered himself a disciple of Howard. But in his package of proposals to cure the ills of the New York metropolitan region, he offered the garden city as one small element, not the focal point, of the overall plan. Indeed, the proposals outlined under Adams' direction bowed to the trend toward metropolitan growth and tried to strive for improvements only within that pattern.

The Regional Plan of New York captured the spirit of planning in the 1920's. The project cost $1 million dollars and took a decade—from 1921 to 1931—to complete. It produced ten illustrated volumes of material, detailing the physical, social, economic, and political state of affairs in the New York metropolitan region, including discernible trends, and outlining proposals to solve the problems facing the area. Topics included, for example, major economic factors in metropolitan growth and arrangement; population, land values, and government; wholesale, retail, and financial districts; highway traffic; transit and transportation; public recreation; buildings, their uses, and the spaces about them; neighborhood and community planning; and physical conditions and public services. Thus prodigious in its research, no detail proved too insignificant for its inspection; thus comprehensive in its approach, it nevertheless accepted the landscape as a commodity and assumed that development would take place according to the forces of the private market; thus mindful of twentieth-century technology, it reviewed the influence of existing political institutions and determined that the suburban trend would continue.[55]

The RPAA had always recognized the need for compromise and flexibility in its tactics. But this did not apply to its ultimate aim: to the organization's abiding belief in Howard's garden city or the notion of balanced regional growth. To at least one member of the RPAA, Mumford, it appeared that Adams had succumbed to the forces that were responsible for the problem. Equally important, Mumford believed Adams had abdicated the essential role of the planner as an educator, whose responsibility was to present alternatives to existing patterns rather than accept those trends as inevitable. As early as 1925, Mumford criticized the Regional Plan of New York as "an attempt to promote better living conditions by costly plans for more traffic, higher buildings, increasing land values, more intensive congestion." He often compared the massive document to another regional plan for New York, drafted by Wright for the Commission of Housing and Regional Planning (to be discussed in the following chapter), and proclaimed that "these plans stood symbolically at opposite poles: one assumes that technical ability can improve living conditions while our existing economic and social habits continue; the other holds that technical ability can achieve little that is fundamentally worth the effort until we reshape our institutions in such a way as to subordinate financial and property values to those of human welfare."[56]

But it was not until 1932, when the project was completed, that Mumford criticized it bitterly, as a document that reinforced conventional patterns of growth. Moreover, he maintained that the plan was contradictory in it solutions. By trying to obtain universal political support, it provided solace to speculative developers and garden city advocates alike. But Mumford maintained that despite its tone of neutrality and objectivity the plan "drift[ed]" toward centralization and overintensive suburban development. By confining the area of study to a forty mile radius of New York City and estimating that the area would have between 21 and 29 million people by 1965, he concluded, the planners were promoting the current trend toward metropolitanization. According to Mumford, Adams thus had accepted the speculator's myopic vision of growth. And since he concentrated on remedies which could be effected immmediately and within the parameters of well-established financial schemes, the plan did not challenge the existing economic system, one of the fundamental sources of the problem.[57]

Although Mumford's attack was particularly harsh and ignored some areas of agreement, it sprang from a consistently held perception of the role of the planner. In 1927, Mumford had written, "if the city planner prepares for growth in the existing metropolitan areas his plans will tend to accelerate growth; if he anticipates the grouping of population into new centers, and prepares for a minimum expansion of our big cities, his plans will serve all communities in a state or region, and they will tend to curb the congestion and expansion of metropolitan districts. In short, the attitude of the city planner, the great industrial organization, and the public authority towards the future, is one of the prime factors that determine the future."[58] Five years later, in 1932, Mumford criticized the Regional Plan of New York for the same reasons.

Adams returned Mumford's ascerbic remarks in kind. He characterized his critic as an "esthete-sociologist, who has a religion that is based on high ideals, but is unworkable." Adams argued that political compromise, not Mumford's rigid adherence to gardent city principles, was the only sensible approach to the complexities of planning in a democratic society. Finally, he claimed that Mumford was indicting the Constitution, not the New York Regional Plan, by suggesting that private property was not sacred and that the perceived virtue of speculative profit could be debated in America's capitalist society.[59]

The metropolitanism of Adams and the regionalism of the RPAA were thus grounded in "irreconcilable differences."[60] The gap between Adams and Mumford indicated the enormous distance the RPAA would have to travel to reach the level of influence of more conventional programs for regional planning. The association had entered the debate over American land use policy in the 1920's, but for the RPAA—despite its influential contacts—to enter the decision-making process as a significant force would have required dramatic alterations in the nation's political and economic structure. Without such changes, the RPAA's vision of garden cities for America would compete badly with visions accepting or even embracing conventional methods of finance and development.

Toward a Regional Plan 4

The Garden City would preserve something of the outdoors within reach of the urban districts. But this is tame. We need the big sweep of hills or sea as tonic for our jaded nerves—And so Mr. Benton MacKaye offers us a new theme in regional planning. . . . He would as far as is practicable conserve the whole stretch of the Appalachian Mountains for recreation. Recreation in the biggest sense—the re-creation of the spirit that is being crushed by the machinery of the modern industrial city—the spirit of fellowship and cooperation.—Clarence S. Stein.[1]

The camp community is a sanctuary and a refuge from the scramble of every-day worldly commercial life. It is in essence a retreat from profit. Cooperation replaces antagonism, trust replaces suspicion, emulation replaces competition. An Appalachian trail, with its camps, communities, and spheres of influence along the skyline, should, with reasonable good management, accomplish these achievements. And they possess within them the elements of a deep dramatic appeal.—Benton MacKaye[2]

A plan of the State is not a thing to be willed into being by any one man or Commission or power. It is the result of many forces—physical, economic and social. Although it may rest on the unchanging physical conformation of the State, it is subject to constant revision as a result of changing habits and economic relations of men, and of their ability, through better understanding or invention, to harness nature to their need.—Henry Wright, Sr.[3]

THE Regional Planning Association of America never produced a complete text that explained its unique brand of regionalism, but two members provided particularly good outlines: Benton MacKaye in his 1921 description of the Appalachian project and Henry Wright in his 1926 report for the New York State Housing and Regional Planning Commision. Both documents serve to bring the RPAA's notion of balanced regional growth into sharp focus.

TODAY the Appalachian Trail is "primarily a wilderness foot trail" extending over 2,000 miles from Mount Katahdin in central Maine to Springer Mountain in northern Georgia. It is an impressive natural recreational reserve consisting of the "longest marked footpath in the world," providing hikers, backpackers, and campers with a taste of the primeval environment in the otherwise intensively developed eastern seaboard.[4] Despite persistent threats posed by housing and highway construction, the trail remains one of the notable achievements of the twentieth-century conservationist movement.

Its history begins with the publication of Benton MacKaye's article "An Appalachian Trail: A Project in Regional Planning," published by Charles Whitaker in the *Journal of the American Institute of Architects* in October 1921. RPAA organizer Clarence Stein, who met MacKaye through Whitaker's network of contacts, soon realized that MacKaye's proposal paralleled his own notions on regional development. A close friendship quickly evolved from their shared interests and ideals, a friendship of reciprocal respect and admiration that lasted for over fifty years. Throughout his lifetime, Stein rarely missed a chance to praise the broad vision of land use that framed the details of MacKaye's project. As early as 1922, he claimed the trail would provide an "opportunity for a new way of life and with it new types of communities."[5] When the RPAA was formed a year later, the organization voiced support for the trail project and MacKaye became one of the RPAA's most active members.

As indicated by the reference to "regional planning" in the title of his article, MacKaye conceived of the trail as more than a walker's route through the wilderness or a playground facility for the overcrowded northeast. The undeveloped Appalachian region of which it was to be the symbol and the spine would serve as a sanctuary for recuperation from the stress of urban life, where victims of "tuberculosis, anemia and insanity" could seek treatment in mountain "communities planned and equipped for their cure."[6] Most importantly, the trail project would lead to a redistribution of population by fostering a countermigration from the city to the countryside. Like other members of the RPAA, MacKaye was dismayed by the trend toward metropolitanization in the northeast, where the rural population had declined from 53 to 45 percent between 1900 and 1920 (as compared to from 60 to 49 percent throughout the nation). Most observers agreed that the imbalance would increase in the future, with the nation's larger cities continuing to grow at the expense of the rural hinterland.

To defuse this urban migration, MacKaye proposed to increase permanent employment in the Appalachian wilderness by developing industries that utilized the natural environment, and by rebuilding the historic role the Appalachians had played in the economic expansion of the northeast and in the nation as a whole before the overwhelming growth of the metropolis. Thus he presented the Appalachian project—a term that more aptly describes his plan than Appalachian trail—as a series of recreational, lumber, and farming communities connected by a wilderness footpath or walking trail. "The plan's "purpose,"

MacKaye wrote, "is to establish a base for a more extensive and systematic development of outdoor community life. It is a project in housing and community architecture."[7]

Although the creation of a trail from Mount Washington in New Hampshire to Mount Mitchell in Georgia was thus only one element in MacKaye's program, it received the most publicity, and he suggested that it be built during the early stages of the project in order to gain popular support for the entire plan. Moreover, as the RPAA pointed out, by serving as the backbone of the project the trail would emphasize that "industrial services are means and not final objectives." Or, as MacKaye wrote, "industry would come to be seen in its true perspective—as a means of life and not as an end in itself."[8]

The trail would be divided into sections, each under local control but tied to a federated system. It would be dotted with a variety of camps which, like garden cities, would be separated by green open space—not the cultivated fields of the rural environment, but rather the uncultivated majesty of the forest. Shelter camps for hikers would be constructed by volunteers. And community camps with a limited population engaging in "non-industrial" activities, such as educational and recreational programs, would be designed for the visitors. These community camps would be purchased and owned by the agencies responsible for the project and operated as comprehensively planned non-profit towns to avoid the pitfalls of speculative investment. Finally, there would be food and farm camps providing the agricultural bases for balanced regional growth, a pattern of land use "neither urban nor rural" since it would escape the "hecticness of the one, the loneliness of the other," and "the common curse of both—the high powered tension of economic scramble." MacKaye believed that the program would not only revitalize the region, but also serve as an example for alternative patterns of growth throughout many parts of the nation.[9]

MacKaye attributed the idea of the Appalachian project to his affiliation with the Appalachian Mountain Club between 1897 and 1912. Indeed it was during a six-week walking trip in the

White Mountains of New Hampshire with noted landscape architect and trailmaker Sturgis Pray that MacKaye was first struck with the idea of a long distance hiking trail as the spine of a regional plan. But his lifelong friend, Lewis Mumford, claims that the inspriation was probably derived from his boyhood "expeditions" into the countryside around his home in the quaint village of Shirley, Massachusetts. It was there that he learned the joy and wonder of solitary walks through nature, and lessons of life which only the wilderness could teach. As he matured, MacKaye grew more firmly convinced that only by preserving such primeval environments from the encroachments of nineteenth- and twentieth-century progress could that personally gratifying experience be shared by his fellow countrymen for generations to come.[10]

MacKaye eventually realized that his desire to preserve the primeval environment could only be achieved by a comprehensive concern for the total environment—a concern that would take into consideration the "development and redevelopment" of natural, residential, and industrial resources within a region.[11] Although the Appalachian project was formulated without any knowledge of Patrick Geddes' writings, it did conform to the Scottish intellectual's emphasis upon "geotechnics—the applied science of making the earth more habitable."[12] MacKaye's call for the conservation of natural resources and the preservation of the natural environment, as well as the importance he placed on commodity flow from resource to consumer in a balanced primeval, rural, and urban landscape, was central to Geddes' philosophy. When the two men met, at the Hudson Guild Farm in 1925, there was immediate camaraderie and a mutual understanding of each other's interests and principles. MacKaye later expressed his appreciation of Geddes in his desire to entitle his 1928 book *The New Exploration: A Philosophy of Geotechnics*. But the newness of the word geotechnics compelled others, most notably Mumford, to urge him to change the subtitle to something more familiar. As a result, *Regional Planning* was ultimately chosen.

MacKaye's philosophy was clearly illustrated in the creation of the Appalachian Trail. The footpath was pieced together by the Appalachian Trail Conference, which consisted of a federation of small private groups that had previously worked as distinctly independent wilderness societies stretching from New England to the Carolinas. Many of the footpaths were laid out by hundreds of private individuals and groups and then brought into a regional network by the Conference, which served as both directive force and clearing house for the undertaking.[13] That the trail was constructed largely through the efforts of volunteers not only confirmed MacKaye's suspicion that the government was uninterested in such projects but also reflected his unshakable belief in personal commitment as a means of "self-expression" and in cooperative effort as a means of developing the human spirit.

The importance MacKaye saw in permanent camps did not begin with the Appalachian project. As a young forester at the turn of the century, MacKaye quickly realized that one of the ways to preserve the wilderness would be to secure, in the undeveloped regions, permanent employment opportunities based on the area's natural resources and beauty. This would prevent social evils that accompany depopulation of the countryside (largely due to lack of jobs), and the inefficient, often destructive, exploitation of land by private homesteading, mining, and forestry. MacKaye first spoke about these problems in a report to the Department of Labor written in 1919 in response to the problems of post–World War I unemployment. Its burdensome title, *Employment and Natural Resources: Possibilities of Making New Opportunities for Employment through the Settlement and Development of Agriculture and Forest Lands and Other Natural Resources*, belied the crisp and penetrating analysis MacKaye applied to a critical national problem.[14]

MacKaye firmly believed that the pattern of growth in the farming, forestry, and mining industries could no longer be left to the determination of the pioneer who served neither himself nor the larger society efficiently or wisely. Instead he urged that the expansion of primary industries be organized as a community effort. "Forest trees," he complained, for example, "have been treated not as wood plants to be grown and cultivated, but as wood deposits to be exploited."[15] The result had been a migratory labor force who experienced working conditions that prohibited a stable family life. Moreover, the random destruction of the nation's forests would eventually translate into higher prices as supplies dwindled. Thus the pioneer spirit—whether applied to forestry, agriculture, or community development—created a pattern of growth detrimental to both the producer and consumer.

A cooperative community response to this problem, MacKaye stated, would create the "opportunity of making a permanent living, of establishing a family, and of developing a career in some steady occupation."[16] The logic MacKaye used in his discussion of employment was similar to that of the RPAA's analysis of the relationship between a house and its community. Just as a home was increasingly dependent on the community of which it was an integral part, an employee in any number of jobs and professions was finding it more difficult to operate as an individual entrepreneur. MacKaye harshly criticized the Homestead Act of 1862 for assuming that all a settler needed was raw land without any improvements. He praised the Australian system of land settlement because, he claimed, it was "based upon the principle that the agricultural worker deserves an even chance with the manufacturing worker, and so the farm as well as the factory should be equipped before, and not after, operations begin."[17] Thus in Australia farm buildings, supplies, credit, markets, and even land clearance were all taken care of before the farmers arrived. The "ready-made farm" was an approach to land use and community settlement which MacKaye found more appealing and productive, as he believed it would save both human and natural resources and lead to a more rational plan for development.

Although condemning the principle of fee-simple title, MacKaye did not call for the public ownership of land (thus exhibiting the political restraint characteristic of other members of the RPAA). According to his proposal, the reclamation services and equipment supplied by the American government would be charged to each American farmer and paid off through long-term, low interest loans. Although such active government participation would be a significant departure from previous methods of development in the United States, the capital would be raised in ways conservative reformers could applaud, since the extension of credit meant that little public expense would be incurred—and, just as in other segments of the economy, the government would use its resources to promote private wealth.

MacKaye's Appalachian project was thus an expansion of the ideas he had first articulated in his report on employment and natural resources in 1919. Both programs were designed to draw people from the urban centers to the countryside by making "industries" in rural areas economically feasible, while at the same time preserving the wilderness. MacKaye did not envision metropolitan development within the Appalachian region. But it was within a few hours of urban areas, close enough to allow communication and interaction to take place between dwellers in dramatically different environments: city residents would have access to the mountains and families living in recreational and farming communities could travel to the city. The result would be a balanced urban and rural environment on a regional scale. It was with this larger geographical matrix in mind that MacKaye discussed balanced growth within the context of the Appalachian project. The mix, MacKaye felt, was essential for the vitality of any society. For him, it constituted the fundamental goal to be achieved by a regional plan.

THE environmental design outlined in MacKaye's Appalachian project was brought to an even higher level of sophistication in Henry Wright's 1926 report on the regional development of New York state.[18] Published as a product of Stein's Commission on Housing and Regional Planning, the report stands forth as the clearest, and most comprehensive, documentation of the RPAA's regional vision. MacKaye did a good deal of the preliminary surveying and economist George Soule collaborated in the preparation of the text. But Wright was primarily responsible for its assumptions and conclusions.

Wright began by contending that New York state faced a double-edged, reciprocal problem: the concentration of people in urban centers was matched by the depopulation of the countryside. Within the past forty-five years, back to 1881, 5.7 million acres of farmland in New York had been withdrawn from cultivation as millions of families flooded the cities. And, although sparsely settled farm villages created certain social problems, the consequences of the state's changing demography were most pronounced in the increasingly overburdened urban centers that could not meet the demands created by an incessant flow of migrants. Echoing a complaint often voiced by the RPAA, Wright noted—that for example—the "staggering cost of needed rapid transit facilities is met by sacrificing schools, parks, and playgrounds and even this offers no relief."[19]

He observed that the late eighteenth and early nineteenth centuries had been periods when "the population was widely distributed over the whole state." Thus, between 1790 and 1840, the population of New York increased almost tenfold—from 350,000 to 2,400,000—but the inhabitants did not congregate in a single area or region. Instead they settled on farmland throughout the state and built "scattered local industry" (such as saw mills, tanneries, and grist mills) that formed a "part of the economy of the farm." The dispersion of population during this era led Wright to proclaim that "the whole period to 1840 was characterized by almost complete non-centralization, with small, self-sufficing communities scattered throughout the state—each raising its own food and manufacturing the greater part of its own necessities." In effect, Wright had depicted the natural evolution of a garden city pattern in New York state during the early nineteenth century.[20]

But this idyllic landscape was soon disrupted by a complex array of forces that exerted an enormous influence on the state's growth patterns. Between 1840 and 1880, which Wright labeled Epoch I, both the urban and rural areas developed at an enormously rapid pace. The creation of a state-wide transportation network, first of canals and then of railroads, not only opened up fertile western land for settlement but also made manufactured goods produced in urban centers like New York City marketable over a wide area. The polynucleated pattern of self-sufficient towns was transformed into a design where towns and regions contributed a specialized product or products. And indeed the entire state of New York became but one part of a more complicated web in the emerging national economy. For example, before 1850, intrastate commerce on the Erie Canal was more important than interstate commerce. After 1850, the reverse was true. "The cities of New York State and those in neighboring states," Wright argued, "became the factories for the whole country. The State as a whole changed from a self-sufficient unit to a specialized part of a highly complicated economic empire."[21]

The changes thus wrought by new modes of transportation were compounded by other new advances in technology. Between 1870 and 1880, steam surpassed water as the most important source of power. This made larger machinery possible and led to vast increases in productive capability, "forcing industry to seek wider and wider markets, and to fetch its raw material greater and greater distances." It also meant that factories had to be located near the coalbeds that were the ultimate source of steam power, or preferably along a canal or railroad to facilitate both the production and marketing of the manufactured goods. Thus steam power tended to reinforce the trend toward the concentration of population. By 1875, then, the Hudson Valley, representing about 20 percent of the state's total area, contained half of the state's people. New York City alone experienced a tenfold increase in population between 1820 and 1860, as the number of residents rose from 120,000 to 1,200,000. In 1840, New York City represented only 16 percent of the state's population; by 1880, its percentage had climbed to 38 and the end of its astonishing growth was not in sight. In fact, migration to the nation's largest city was proceeding at ever-higher rates.[22]

Despite such rapid change and dislocation, however, Wright maintained that during Epoch I the state had not yet undergone "the complete breakdown of the independent economic units." This occurred in Epoch II (1880–1920). It was during this second stage of development that "the city became the dominant organism, supplemented by the specialized farm."[23] No longer did rural and urban areas both grow at phenomenal rates; rather, as the city grew it seemed to sap the strength of the countryside. The statistical evidence for the change was startling. Between 1830 and 1850, every county in New York enjoyed an increase in population; between 1850 and 1920, more than half the state's counties experienced a decrease in population. After 1860, the shrinkage in rural population was so significant that fewer people resided in villages of fewer than 2,500 in 1920 than in 1820, while a smaller number of people lived on farms of any kind than was the case in 1810. As a result of this vast internal migration, improved land was abandoned at a rate of 100,000 acres a year between 1880 and 1920.

By 1920, the state's eleven largest cities, each with a population of 50,000 or more, had accounted for 86 percent of the state's population increase over the previous seventy years. Not surprisingly, New York City led the way in this rapid process toward urbanization: by 1925, the city had 6 million residents or 53 percent of the state's population. Thus the trend that began in the early 1800's, and accelerated over the course of the next century, radically transformed the physical and social landscape of New York state during the short span of four generations. "In 1840 the typical citizen lived in a small and almost self-sufficient rural community, about 500 of which were scattered all over the state," observed Wright. "At the end of the second epoch the typical citizen dwelt in the industrial center, he worked in a factory or an office with ever growing hordes of fellow employees and with automatic machinery always increasing in complexity."[24]

The nineteenth-century landscape was now, as we have seen also in Chapters 2 and 3, being transformed by new modes of transportation and new sources of energy. For Wright, electricity and the automobile were just as revolutionary in their potential consequences as steam and the railroad had been in the early nineteenth century. Whereas increasing concentration had been characteristic of previous epochs, decentralization of population and industry was now possible, as well as the enrichment of farm life, through a network of transportation and communication facilities that could reach out over a large land mass. Along with other members of the RPAA, Wright believed that the nation was at "the threshold of a period in which a strongly marked new trend [would] be established."[25]

This new process of decentralization, which Wright called Epoch III, would not be directly comparable to the pattern of dispersion that had existed in the nineteenth century (prior to 1840). As a result of its historical and natural advantages, the Hudson Valley would remain New York's most valuable and attractive region. Despite the advent of motor transport, railroad trunks would still be an essential component of the transportation system and an integral factor in the state's future growth patterns. But Wright insisted that balanced regional development was now possible. With the terrible social and economic costs generated by the concentration of population in urban centers Wright, like his RPAA cohorts, concluded that dispersion would be inevitable, as an increasing number of residents who could afford it would flee the city. And if properly coordinated, a comprehensive plan could direct this migration into a pattern of orderly and balanced regional growth.

Wright's detailed analysis of demographic changes in New York state conformed to the RPAA's broad vision of regionalism, placing fundamental stress on the natural environment and the state of technology as the principal ingredients shaping patterns of development. At the conclusion of the report, Wright argued that the best regional plan would be governed by the "physical contour and distribution of resources."[26] He reiterated this sentiment numerous times: "A regional plan really almost plans itself: it is merely the rational acceptance and control of the natural conditions of the environment."[27] MacKaye echoed this romantic perception when he boldly stated that "regional planning is a new approach to political economy . . . the approach from the viewpoint of the map."[28] The one obstacle standing in the way of the realization of this vision, according to Wright and other RPAA members, was (once again) the nation's method of financing real estate development. In the words of the organization's harshest critic of American capitalism, Frederick Ackerman, speculative investment created "a complicated web of inflated values and capitalizations which involve the necessity of growth and concentration."[29] The RPAA, in direct contradiction to conservative thinkers, contended that the influence exerted by speculative investors on potential twentieth-century land use patterns inevitably interfered with the "natural" evolution of the landscape, thus creating serious social problems through the misuse of technology.

Wright's analysis of the historic evolution of the New York landscape was a direct application of general theories that had been developed by his friend Mumford, who in 1925 had described broad demographic patterns in the United States in terms of "migrations." In one of the seminal articles on regional planning, "The Fourth Migration," Mumford had argued that there were three distinct periods of migration in American history, each tied to a particular mode of transportation and source of energy.[30] The first period, prior to the Civil War, corresponding to Wright's first epoch, was shaped by the covered wagon and water power. It was characterized by the clearing of land west of the Alleghenies and the opening up of the entire continent for settlement. The second migration, corresponding to Wright's second epoch, propelled by the railroad and steam power, resulted in desperately overcrowded urban centers, where the city, defined "solely as a place of work and business opportunity," failed to provide laborers with the basic amenities of a decent life. As Mumford stated, "if the first migration denuded the country of its natural resources, the second migration ruthlessly cut down and ignored its human resources."[31] Beginning in the 1890's, America experienced a third migration, marked by an extraordinary acceleration of demographic trends found in the second migration. Metropolitan domination resulted with the nation's largest urban centers monopolizing all economic, social, and cultural activities. Financial organizations, such as banks and insurance companies, superseded industrial establishments as the compelling forces behind metropolitan growth. These institutions utilized the most advanced techniques in communication and transportation, as well as sophisticated advertising campaigns, to create both national markets and national centers to augment their power.

But Mumford believed that in the post–World War I period the nation was at the dawn of a fourth migration based on the potential for change found in the use of the automobile and electricity. As we have seen, Wright was to refer to this same image of the future as Epoch III; and indeed MacKaye too was to present a paradigm similar to Mumford's in *The New Exploration* of 1928. Instead of "migrations" he employed the term "folk flows," but his periodization and analysis were akin to Mumford's despite the differences in terminology. His use of the word "flow" was very deliberate: it suggested a continuous process subject to changing conditions. Thus the RPAA vision was firmly based on assumptions developed by Mumford—assumptions which were in many respects modified applications of Geddes' theories.

It should be no surprise that members of the RPAA praised the twentieth-century engineer. Ackerman in his characteristic Veblenesque style called for a "technocratic society" and in the early 1930's formed the Continental Committee on Technocracy;[32] Chase often spoke about how the engineer could tame the "wild horses" of speculative growth and depression;[33] MacKaye referred to the engineer as "the modern explorer" who "does not create his own plan" but "discovers nature's plan; he reveals a hidden potentiality which nature's laws allow."[34] For the RPAA, it was the engineer's apolitical, scientific approach which would enable society to take advantage of opportunities afforded by nature and the potential for social improvement created by technology. Such an unshakable belief in technology has, of course, been one of the major themes in American history, and at no time was this belief stronger than in the 1920's. But unlike other intellectuals of their period, members of the RPAA believed that significant political changes within the existing structure would be necessary before the fruits of technology could be enjoyed by all. Only non-speculative technological development serving in the interest of human values would prevent the machine from destroying both our social fabric and natural environment. The question was no less significant than that.

Yet, although members of the RPAA realized that technology could never be separated from politics, they rarely insisted that revolutionary political change would be necessary to create a new age for American society. Nor, to the dismay of subsequent critics, did the group willingly plunge into the whirlpool of established political debate and organization. The political position of the RPAA was similar to its stance on the garden city. The immediate restructuring of our society, like the immediate construction of a complete garden city, was viewed as an impossible task. Operating within the restraints of the existing political system could never be avoided. The path to reform could only be cleared by education and rational discourse. This did not mean that social advances were impossible. "It may be," Mumford wrote, "the under terms acceptable to our present financial interests no effective planning can be done within the metropolitan district, and no solution in the interest of public health and welfare and amenity and the good life generally is possible. But this is no reason for evading the problem itself or for hiding the essential facts with illusory hopes and false promises. One of the immediate needs of a fundamental survey is to delimit those problems which can be handled immediately, those which can be dealt with by current methods once public opinion and official authority have been educated sufficiently, and those which cannot be handled at all until there is a complete reorientation in our civilization."[35]

The reformist impulse of the RPAA was long on principle and short on strategy. Members of the group articulated a clear perception of the type of society they wanted to see built in America, but preferring not to participate in formal political organizations, they rarely presented a precise political strategy for achieving that goal. This dilemma, however, never obscured the idealistic vision they held of a balanced and harmonious American landscape fashioned to a human scale, a vision most clearly presented in MacKaye's Appalachian Trail project and Wright's plan for the regional development of New York state. Although the Appalachian Trail was eventually completed, neither MacKaye's nor Wright's proposal ever served as a comprehensive blueprint for regional growth in America: they are thus glimpses of "the neglected vision of the RPAA," testaments to both the strengths and weaknesses of the organization's attitude toward reform.[36]

Toward a Regional Plan

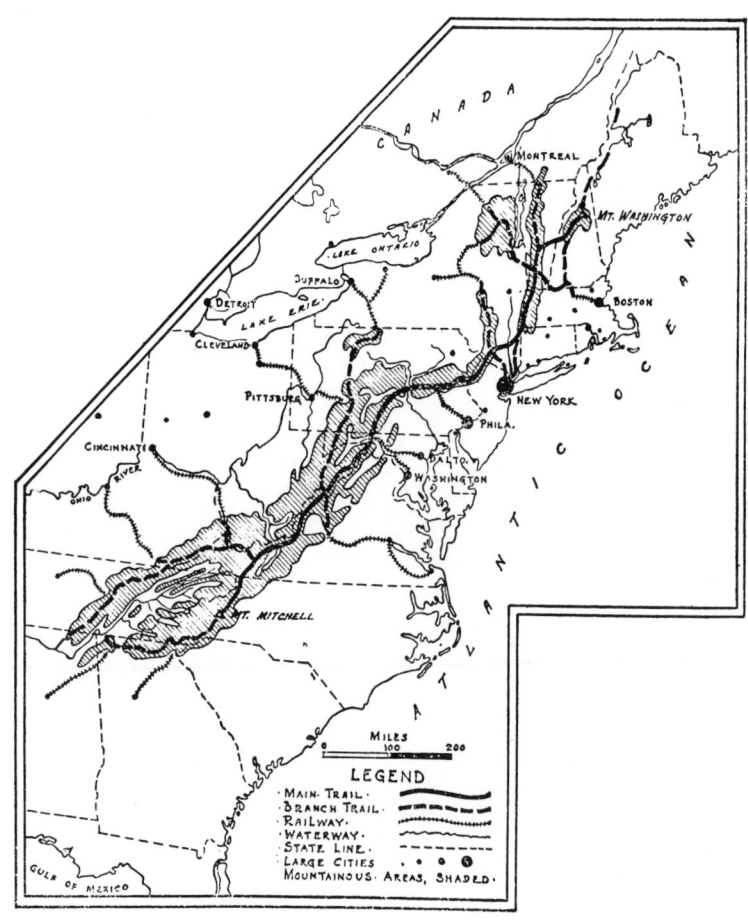

The Appalachian Trail: a project in regional planning, serving as the backbone of MacKaye's plan for balanced regional growth along the eastern corridor of the United States. With farming, timber, and recreational communities envisioned for the Appalachian region, it would provide a counterpoint to the urbanized Atlantic seaboard. Courtesy of the American Institute of Architects Archives, Washington, D.C.

The Appalachian Trail: a wilderness footpath of vast recreational and aesthetic value, but shorn of its original regional context. Courtesy of the Appalachian Trail Conference Archives, Harpers Ferry. W. Va.

Top: Wright's Regional Plan for New York, Epoch I (1840–1880): small, economically independent towns widely distributed throughout the state. Water served as a major source of power; canals and horses served as the prime means of transportation. The natural evolution of balanced regional growth. Courtesy of the Cornell University Archives, Olin Library, Ithaca, N.Y.

Bottom: Wright's Regional Plan for New York, Epoch II (1880–1920): the concentration of population along the Mohawk and Hudson River Valleys. Steam replaced water as the major source of power; railroads replaced horses as the prime means of transportation. The result: excessive metropolitan growth and regional imbalance. Courtesy of Cornell University Archives, Olin Library, Ithaca, N.Y.

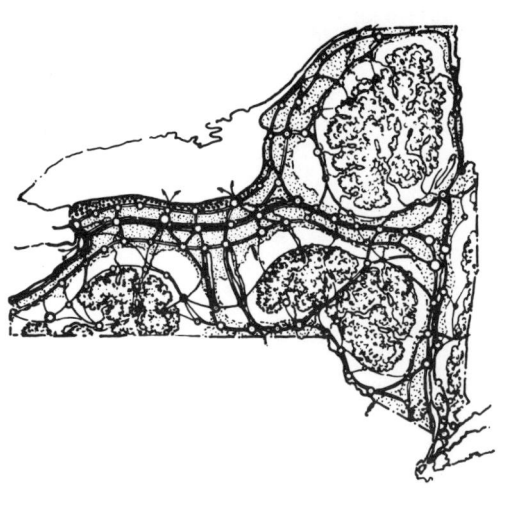

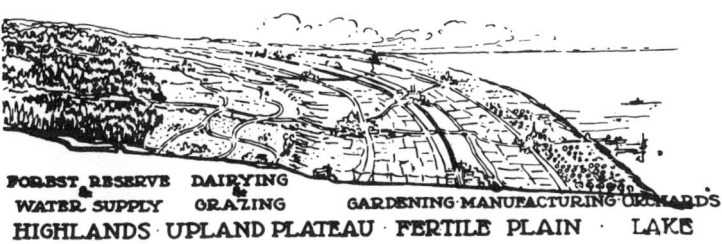

Top: Wright's Regional Plan for New York, Epoch III: future patterns of balanced regional growth based on the automobile and electrical power. Wright's optimistic forecast—"a more effective utilization of all of the economic resources of the state and . . . the most favorable development of acres especially adapted to industry, agriculture, recreation, water supply and forest reserve." The result: a return to balanced regional growth characteristic of the mid-nineteenth century. Courtesy of Cornell University Archives, Olin Library, Ithaca, N.Y.

Bottom: A Vision of Regional Growth for New York: applying Geddes' "valley section" to the state. Allowing the natural environment to determine the contours of development. Courtesy of Cornell University Archives, Olin Library, Ithaca, N.Y.

The Six Percent Solution   5

The building of homes has in the past been looked upon as an enterprise conducted like any other business in which the element of speculative profit has been the compelling force. Until this situation is changed it will be impossible to rebuild the tenement areas which continue throughout the years to be a menace to the health and the morals of the country.—Alfred E. Smith, Governor of New York[1]

It is absolutely necessary to convince the investing public that limited dividend companies can be conducted on a business-like basis, are absolutely safe investments, and at the same time, that when properly managed, they can accomplish very real improvements in housing and living conditions.—Alexander Bing, President of the City Housing Corporation[2]

[The City Housing corporation has] sold a good product at a fair price. There is a great deal in the policy of Henry Ford in achieving quantity production by selling a good article at the lowest price commensurate with a reasonable price per unit.—Lawson Purdy, Secretary of the Charities Organization Society[3]

101

TO conduct its experiments in community development, the Regional Planning Association of America needed a reliable financial base. Conventional sources of capital were out of the question, given the association's condemnation of speculative investment and its desire to construct moderately priced homes. And capitalization through public funding was equally doubtful in the face of the government's reluctance (indeed its principled objections) to engage in housing and community development projects. The method of financing best suited to the RPAA's reform impulses then was limited dividend investment that placed a ceiling on the rate of return on stocks and bonds, thus eliminating the specter of speculative profits without fundamentally altering the economic system. By depending on the good will and common sense of investors, limited dividends might clear the way for the development of a "peaceful path to real reform."

In 1924, less than one year after the formation of the RPAA, Alexander Bing created the City Housing Corporation (CHC) as "a limited dividend company organized to build better homes and communities." It was the product of twelve months of research conducted by Bing, Stein, and Wright into questions of site planning, construction, and financing. Dividends were limited to 6 percent by the charter. Investors were encouraged to participate in "a sound conservative business operation netting a fair return."[4]

The CHC's efforts, especially after the success of its first experiment at Sunnyside, received unanimous approval. New

York's Governor Alfred E. Smith praised the company for "courage and initiative" and concluded that it offered the "greatest possible value in aiding the movement for better housing." *New Republic* editors commended the CHC for not being a charitable organization: "Beneficiaries pay their own way," they reasoned, "and the extra-dividends" in "increased human happiness, [and] better health and morals are beyond all calculation." Darwin R. James, president of the East River Savings Bank in Manhattan and chairman of the New York State Board of Housing, claimed the CHC "demonstrated the soundness of limited dividend corporations" and pointed "the way to a rational rebuilding program for congested tenement districts." The Reverend Charles K. Gilbert, the executive secretary of New York City's Social Service Commission, called the company's experiments "splendid achievements," adding that the CHC proved "public-spirited citizens can make their contribution to the relief of a critical community need as a safe business investment, yielding about as large a return as a conscientious investor ought to expect." The editors of *The Independent* saw "no good reason . . . why [CHC] activities cannot be duplicated elsewhere. Home Building," they warned, "is a necessity, and unless private capital is willing to undertake it at a fair return the State will sooner or later be forced into it."[5]

The chorus of praise greeting the formation of the CHC reflected the national mood in the late 1920's. In the post–World War I era, progressivism did not disappear; the movement simply lost its muckraking edge. The alliance between corporate America and liberal social reform—never as tenuous in the pre-war years as some historians have suggested—blossomed during the "prosperity decade" of the 1920's.[6] By the time Hoover was elected president in 1928, even the nation's harshest social critics marveled at the social contributions of America's corporate executives and institutions. "Big business in America," stated the noted muckraker Lincoln Steffens, "is producing what the socialists held up as their goal; food, shelter and clothing for all. You will see it during the Hoover Administration."[7] Writing just before the stock market crash, historians Charles and Mary Beard in *The Rise of American Civilization* described a litany of social problems that had attracted the concern of business leaders. Over the past twenty-five years, they estimated, businessmen had contributed over 2 billion dollars to programs for social welfare, civic improvement, legislation to curtail poverty, and the patronage of the arts. As a result, the Beards observed, the social environment in the United States "offered material subsistence for a life of the mind more varied and more lucrative . . . than [that offered in] any nation that had flourished since the beginnings of civilization in the Nile Valley." Although they admitted that the future was unpredictable, they concluded their history of America on an optimistic note, placing their faith, with that of the "undistinguished masses . . . in inevitable progress."[8] It was progress that had apparently been secured under the direction of corporate America.

As founder and president of the CHC, Bing was very much like the individuals whom he encouraged to purchase substantial shares of its stocks and bonds. Like his brother Leo S. Bing, a fellow trustee, Bing acquired his fortune by purchasing land along Fifth Avenue in Manhattan at a cheap price just before the elevated railroad was removed during the second decade of the twentieth century. After the "el" was dismantled, the area became a fashionable place to live, and the Bings took advantage of the increased demand by constructing luxurious high-rise apartments. Profiteering on the speculative market, they both amassed sizable personal fortunes. Then, during World War I, Bing served on the government's labor board, applying his administrative talents to the national war effort rather than to the construction industry. His wartime experience instilled within him—as it had in other benevolent capitalists—a desire to pursue socially worthwhile activities after the Armistice, and in the early 1920's nothing in New York City appeared to be more important than building moderately priced houses. With his proven expertise in real estate development, Bing's choice was a logical one. In response to his own personal convictions and his friend Clarence Stein's encouragement, then, he organized the CHC with the sole purpose of building "homes and communities for people with small incomes." By offering $100 shares, Bing hoped to attract middle income groups into the company;

he even conducted an advertising campaign targeted to teachers, social workers, and others in the same salary range. But the large scale community development he envisioned required the active support of wealthy capitalists—friends and associates of Bing himself.[9]

Those appointed to the CHC's board of directors exemplified the often-praised alliance between the business community and social reformers, the organization's very structure and membership thus embodying the belief that profit and humanitarianism were compatible. The board included, in addition to Dr. Felix Adler and the other men mentioned in Chapter 2, Dr. Richard Ely, the progressive educator and economist who organized and directed the Institute for Research in Land Economics and Public Utilities; Eleanor Roosevelt, whose husband was then serving as governor of New York; and philanthropic capitalists John G. Agar, William Sloane Coffin, and V. Everit Macy—individuals who had not only displayed an ability to make millions of dollars, but had also exhibited a desire to contribute lavishly to charitable activities. Other trustees included Leo Bing, Charles S. Bird, Jr., Thomas C. Desmond, Douglas L. Elliman, Frank Lord, John Martin, Mrs. Joseph M. Proskauer, and Robert E. Simon.[10] The CHC's wealthy board members viewed social and political involvement as a by-product and responsibility of personal wealth—and assumed as benevolent capitalists that their private wealth could be used to meet the nation's pressing social problems without jeopardizing their own economic and social status, or the political structure upon which those were based. The limited dividends paid by CHC stock did not represent a radical departure from the existing system. It was simply perceived as a way of curbing its worst and most counter-productive tendencies.

Bing's appeal to investors was simple. You are placing your money in a "sound and social project," proclaimed the sales campaign literature of the CHC. All surplus capital will be directed "first to building up a safe financial reserve and second to experimentation and research in town planning and housing construction."[11] Thus he called upon prospective stockholders to engage in a benevolent project that would generate a modest, but secure and profitable, return. "We can appeal to our stockholders and to the public for their further support," Bing wrote in the first annual report of the CHC, "confident in the ability of the company to produce a fine community of moderately priced homes with unquestioned safety to investors in the project."[12] It was thus a delicate balance of profit and humanitarianism that Bing offered to other benevolent capitalists, hoping that they would find it attractive.

BY the 1920's, semi-philanthropic private companies were not new to the American landscape, especially in the housing industry.[13] As early as 1854, the New York Association for the Improvement of the Condition of the Poor (AICP) sponsored a program to build a "model tenement" in Manhattan that would provide adequate but affordable housing for laborers by limiting the investment return to 6 percent. The experiment proved a dismal failure, as the tenement degenerated into one of the worst pocket slums in the city. The AICP soon abandoned the project, selling the building in 1867.

The lack of success experienced by the AICP may have discouraged others from participating in limited dividend companies, but it did not destroy the idea. In the late nineteenth century, Brooklyn philanthropist Alfred T. White once again sought to prove that decent housing built for the working class could provide a good return on investment. "Neither White nor his contemporary housing reformers were radical, toying with imaginative reconstructions of the social and economic order," historian Roy Lubove has observed in *The Progressives and the Slums*. "Their aim was more modest—to provide safe, comfortable, and even pleasant housing for low-income groups within the framework of the capitalist-profit system."[14] The program for social reform advocated by White formed a link in the historical chain leading to the organization of the CHC fifty years later. White's model tenements attracted the attention of a number of charitable organizations, including the Children's Aid Society, the AICP, and the State Charities Aid Associations. His projects were hailed by observers as proof that the economic system could provide "well-ventilated, convenient, and agreeable" housing for the working class.[15] Like Bing—who was to follow in his path—White hoped that an alliance between social reformers and powerful capitalists would lead to a dramatic transformation of the urban landscape.

Between 1878 and 1890, then, White financed the construction of over 500 units in three separate projects. His tenements were substantially better designed than those constructed speculatively. The Riverside Buildings, for example, the last of his apartments, were built two rooms deep and were well ventilated, covering only 50 percent of their lot, when the New York tenement law—one of the most progressive in the nation—permitted 65 to 70 percent ground coverage, with a maximum of 90 percent coverage for a corner lot. But despite White's efforts, only well-paid wage earners could afford his rents, which, ranging from $7.10 per month for a single room on a ground floor to $15.60 for a three-room apartment, necessitated an annual wage in excess of $500. White's experiments could not resolve the housing problem for the seasonally or marginally employed worker, and thus the small number of units his company constructed did not begin to meet the needs of tens of thousands of New York's laborers.[16]

White's program suffered from the economic problems that would continue to plague semi-philanthropic private companies throughout their history. Large investors could find more lucrative and less troublesome investments in areas other than housing. The vast majority of investors in real estate development, small entrepreneurs (as Sam Bass Warner demonstrated in his case study of "the process of growth in Boston" during the late 1800's), had no desire to place their limited financial resources into model tenements returning a maximum 5 to 7 percent when they could derive a 15 to 18 percent profit from conventional methods of housing construction.[17] Benevolent capitalists like White, gentlemen reformers who hoped to devise a program that would complement, rather than alter, the existing capitalist structure, thus often found themselves in an untenable economic position. They were competing against builders and investment companies that possessed neither the inclination nor in many cases the financial ability to limit their profits; and without a lid placed upon profits, moderately priced housing capable of providing shelter for the poor was out of the question. Then too, White's managerial talents were not matched by those who tried to emulate him; and, moreover, as prices rose it became increasingly difficult for limited dividend companies to keep their rents within the range of even the well-paid laborers for whom White had been able to build houses. Edith Elmer Wood, one of the nation's more astute housing experts during the first half of this century, was to conclude that "none of [White's] imitators equalled his record. Either high standard, low rent or high dividend was sacrificed to a greater or less extent in every case."[18]

Nevertheless, White's experiments spurred a flurry of limited dividend construction in the late nineteenth century, as a host of semi-philanthropic companies was organized to attack housing problems in the nation's largest cities, mostly in the northeast. The Astral Apartments built by Pratt Institute in the Greenpoint section of Brooklyn, and apartments funded by the New York Tenement House Building Company and Boston's Improved Dwellings Association, all adopted White's basic principle of "philanthropy plus five percent"—placing a 4 to 6 percent ceiling upon the investment return. In the *Eighth Special Report to the Commissioner of Labor* (1894), the noted housing reformer and staunch advocate of investment philanthropy Elgin R. L. Gould optimistically reported that his investigation of housing conditions in America, and especially his study of model tenement construction, had proved "that proper housing of the great masses of working people can be furnished on a satisfactory commercial basis."[19] Warning in the same report that "if the solution of the [housing] problem is to depend upon philanthropy alone, . . . very small progress can be made, he added that "if city dwellers are to be better housed, better housing must pay."[20] In quest of that elusive goal, in 1906 Gould helped to create and then became first president of the City and Suburban Homes Company.

The history of this limited dividend company, the most successful in the nation's history, epitomizes that of the semi-philanthropic housing movement. The company originated from a conference conducted by the AICP, the agency responsible for the nation's first model tenement in 1854. The directors and officers included a list of New York's most respected reformers, many of whom had been previously involved in the housing problem: Alfred T. White, Felix Adler, and the muckraking journalist Jacob Riis all served on the board of the City and Suburban Homes Company. In a cooperative effort, like the CHC's during the 1920's, the enthusiasm displayed by such reformers was supported by the financial assistance of wealthy entrepreneurs: Cornelius Vanderbilt; Charles S. Smith, a former president of the New York Chamber of Commerce; and George W. Young, the president of the U. S. Mortgage and Trust Company were also directors of the company.

More often than not, such capitalists exhibited a fleeting enthusiasm. Investment dollars would never equal the initial expressions of support.[21] Nevertheless, in 1926, nearly two decades after its incorporation, the City and Suburban Homes Company owned almost 3,000 residential units in Manhattan, including apartments for blacks and a hotel for women. The tenements represented an investment of over $6 million and housed more than 11,000 people. Indeed the company served as the landlord for over 50 percent of all New York tenement dwellers who resided in semi-philanthropic structures.[22]

But City and Suburban Homes' successes were relative: successes only when measured against the abysmal failure of the vast majority of semi-philanthropic housing companies. Between 1870 and 1910 there were twenty-five different groups in New York City engaged in eighty-nine model tenement projects housing 3,588 families or approximately 18,000 people. During the same period of time, speculative builders in the city constructed about 27,100 tenements sheltering 253,510 families or over 1.25 million people. Thus only .06 percent of the tenement units built in New York during this thirty year span were financed by limited dividend companies concerned with creating well-built, moderately priced housing. In the years after World War I, that trend continued unabated. In New York City, where, as Edith Elmer Wood noted, the limited dividend concept "received much more attention than anywhere else in the country," investment philanthropy produced accommodations for about 6,000 families: this equaled a paltry 1 percent of the total number of housing units constructed by private developers in the nation's largest city. Thus model tenements never became a visible force anywhere in America, not even in the northeast where the need for low cost housing was most acute and the political and intellectual climate was most receptive to the idea.[23] In the post–World War I era, the limited dividend concept remained but a faint symbol of hope that the economic system could satisfy the housing needs of all citizens, especially the need for decent shelter among society's poorest members.

THUS when the City Housing Corporation was organized in 1924, the trustees had little reason to turn to the past as a source of encouragement. By 1910, over two-thirds of New York City's population had lived in multi-unit dwellings, yet even there, within the nation's largest city, individuals like White and Gould had remained a distinct, though vocal, minority. Outside the northeast, such social reformers remained virtually unknown. Just as few Americans could appreciate the distinctive urban environment of New York at the turn of the century, fewer still had understood the need for limited dividend construction companies. But the dismal history of limited dividend companies did not dampen the optimism of Bing and his associates. In many ways, they believed that they were at the threshold of a new period in history.

For not only was the business community expressing a sincere concern for the welfare of others, but the liabilities of unchecked speculative development had been forcefully illustrated—at least in the nation's largest cities. Before World War I, annual housing production in America stood at 400,000 units, a rate sufficient to replace housing stock that had been destroyed as well as to satisfy the housing requirements generated by yearly population increases. Much of the housing built for the poor was of inferior quality, but at least an adequate number of units had been constructed to meet the absolute minimum needs of the population.[24] In 1919, on the other hand, the volume of housing construction in America was only 58 percent of the pre-war level despite the enormous demand exerted by returning soldiers, and in 1920, it plummeted to 37 percent.[25] That translated into a critical housing shortage in New York City. One housing reformer estimated that that city alone required 50,000 new units to make up for the wartime lull in construction—and, as we saw in Chapter 3, by 1919 housing experts were estimating that the nation as a whole was experiencing a shortage of 1 million units. But the private contractor, despite dramatic increases in rental fees, was not responding as might have been expected to those market conditions. Inflated costs coupled with difficulty in obtaining credit and deflationary expectations made realtors reluctant to build houses expensively which they would later be able to construct more cheaply. Thus, for the builder, the scarcity of housing did not seem necessarily to mean higher profits, and the law of supply and demand seemed temporarily ineffective. For the renter, however, the theory of the market place held true. In 1916, the vacancy rate in New York City had been 5.5 percent, a figure that most observers agreed was high enough to protect renters from exorbitant fees; by 1920, the rate had fallen to one-third of 1 percent. It had become a seller's market. The housing shortage thus resulted in higher rents and overcrowded living quarters.[26]

Housing the poor, unskilled worker in America had always been a problem. New York City had led the way in seeking a solution, with the passage in 1867 of the nation's first tenement law. Never adequately staffed, however, the health and housing commissions charged with enforcing that and later ordinances faced a task beyond their resources. And now in the post–World War I period, the problem of providing quality housing for the poor had been joined by the problem of providing a sufficient quantity of housing for all citizens—except the wealthiest segments of society, who still managed to give contractors an attractive 15 to 20 percent return on their investment. As New York's Housing Committee observed, "it is essential to the health, happiness, industrial success and general welfare of every individual as well as the community as a whole, that all of the inhabitants of the state be afforded an opportunity to live in decent homes and in pleasant, healthful and attractive surroundings. Such opportunity is possible to a steadily decreasing minority."[27] Raising real wages sufficiently to meet the costs of housing would only result in an inflationary spiral of higher costs followed by higher prices. Thus the CHC hoped to contain the cost of construction by placing a lid on the rate of return for investment. It was a case of applying an old remedy to a chronic illness endemic to private speculative development. But Bing and other CHC trustees believed that an application of limited dividend principles could now have a noticeable effect upon the physical and social landscape. The experience of the post-war period had compelled those concerned with housing and social welfare to seek "new" solutions to correct the flaws of speculative development. Since earlier semi-philanthropic housing companies had been so uninfluential, perhaps, nothing seemed newer or more palatable than the program advocated by the CHC.

At the same time, reformers like Bing could point to recent publicly financed housing experiments in Europe and the United States as concrete examples of the practicality and benefits to be derived from new ideas in site planning and construction. As Chapter 2 noted, Holland subsidized housing both before and after the war, and, to encourage efficient wartime production, the British government had directed a national program for housing workers employed on the home front.[28] The United States had been much more reluctant to sponsor a federal program for housing, though the Wilson administration and eventually the Congress had acknowledged that a vital link existed between worker productivity and satisfactory housing. A severe housing shortage had been held responsible for the fact that the turnover rate in a Quincy, Massachusetts, shipbuilding factory skyrocketed to 354 percent annually during the early months of the war, while factories in Bridgeport, Connecticut, operated at 10 to 15 percent below capacity despite an enormous backlog of government contracts. According to a survey conducted by the Department of Labor, such deficiencies were characteristic of American industry at the outset of World War I. To counteract such hampering of the war effort on the domestic front the government had eventually, in 1917, created two agencies designed to stimulate housing construction—the Emergency Fleet Corporation and the U.S. Housing Corporation.[29]

Those first attempts by the American government to engage in housing construction represented a modest effort. Only a total of 176,000 units were completed during the eighteen months the agencies were in operation, and Congress chose to abandon the program soon after the Armistice. With few exceptions, political leaders never vacillated from the position, noted in Chapter 2, that the government had acted in response to a war emergency, rather than to take a first step toward a new housing policy. "This is not a peacetime enterprise on the part of the government," observed Secretary of Labor William Wilson. "It is being entered into by the government because the government conceives that it is necessary for the prosecution of the war."[30] Congressional hostility to publicly directed and financed construction was never more evident than in a 1920 report issued by the Senate Committee on Public Buildings and Grounds, which found the wartime housing agencies guilty of having built permanent rather than temporary homes. A number of Senators also argued that the corporations, had built better houses than the workers expected or needed. Thus the public housing corporations had exceeded the responsibilities they had been granted and in the process had burdened the nation with unnecessary expenses. "Congress certainly did not intend ... to enter into competition in architectural poetry with any nation or private organization," the Committee bitterly concluded. "We do not believe that this was necessary for the mechanics who were to be housed. They would not have complained of the color of the houses, or the curve of the dormer windows, or the 'orientation' of the blocks."[31]

Nevertheless, the efforts of the Emergency Fleet and the U.S. Housing Corporations had been hailed as a success by some of the nation's foremost housing reformers. Edith Elmer Wood claimed "it proved that government housing could be produced and administered in the U.S. without scandal, without the sky falling or the constitution going on the scrap heap."[32] When the

Senate decided to abandon the program immediately after the Armistice, reform groups such as the National Housing Association and the National Women's Trade Union League had urged the government at least to complete the projects which had been started. Lawrence Veiller, the nation's most noted progressive housing reformer and previously an ardent critic of publicly financed housing, joined the protest. Congress ultimately agreed to fund the completion of about two dozen projects—although suggestions to create a permanent housing research bureau within the federal government were never seriously entertained. Moreover, legislators voted to sell all government wartime houses at market value, rather than to transfer the communities to residential cooperatives as some critics had urged. Thus, the work of the Emergency Fleet and U.S. Housing Corporations became a brief episode in American planning history, more important for the influence it exerted on the planning profession than for the impact it had on public policy.[33] Clearly the war experience convinced some individuals that housing was a social problem requiring some degree of government involvement. This sentiment in part served as the impetus behind the creation of the CHC and gave it a chance for success.

But another important lesson had been learned from the government's involvement in war housing. The government's housing agencies had illustrated the benefits to be derived from large scale production and the use of experts, thus in effect showing that the principles of rationalization used in American industry could be used in land development. Few of the nation's political leaders could disagree with such assumptions. Bing, after the success of the CHC's first project at Sunnyside, Queens, in New York, wrote enthusiastically about his firm's accomplishment in just those terms. "It affords unmistakable proof of the value of a carefully reasoned and studied plan in low cost housing construction instead of 'hit or miss' methods which have been so universally followed in almost all large cities, it has demonstrated that the economies of large scale operation are as substantial in this field as in other industries, it has proved that scientific planning can provide such essentials as gardens and park space even in communities for families of limited means."[34]

These factors were lessons in land use first learned by the government's housing agencies in World War I. By applying them in the private sector, the CHC would bring the concept much closer to traditional American values. Equally important, the CHC's rational approach to land use gave the company a method of community development that corporate leaders could appreciate. "It is becoming increasingly evident," wrote Harry E. Ward, the president of American Irving Exchange, "that the problem of providing adequate housing facilities in our great cities for people of limited means requires the application of scientific methods."[35] For this reason, he voiced staunch support for the housing experiments conducted by the CHC.

Thus Bing and his associates designed a strategy of land use that paralleled the approach of large industrialists. Utilizing principles devised by corporate leaders Andrew Carnegie, John D. Rockefeller, and Henry Ford, substantial tracts of land would be purchased to take advantage of the economies of scale and to assure the execution of a comprehensive plan. In addition, carrying costs would be minimized by commencing construction soon after the land had been purchased, and a schedule would be devised to allow building to continue throughout the entire year, which would eliminate costly delays during inclement weather. As Bing stated to the stockholders in 1925, winter construction "produces economies and gives us the completed houses in the spring and early summer, the most desirable selling season."[36] All of this was part of a rational plan to guarantee the realization of the progressive vision of efficient production. The "moderate prices" charged for the company's houses would be "made possible by . . . large scale building operations, by employment of its own construction force almost uniformly throughout the year on one class of building, by its great purchasing power, and by a considerable saving in selling costs."[37] And, like any modern corporation, the CHC depended upon expert advice to improve production. The CHC established an advisory board "consisting of leaders in social work, in business and economic fields." Some of the nation's most prominent architects and site planners were placed on the board, including Thomas Adams; Otto M. Eidlitz, who had headed the United

States Housing Corporation; and Henry Wright, Frederick Ackerman, and Robert Kohn. The technical expertise of these individuals was complemented by the knowledge of social theory and organization of Richard Ely, Lawson Purdy, and pioneer social workers and community organizers such as Mrs. V. G. Simkhovitch and Lillian Wald. "Active management of the corporation," Bing contended, would be "in the hands of conservative, experienced and prominently successful administrators of real estate and real estate investments, of architects, housing and city planning experts, and of landscape architects."[38] Efficiency based upon technical knowledge remained paramount: but instead of automobiles or steel, the company was producing houses and communities.[39]

It was precisely this rational, systematic approach that had resulted in such lavish praise for American business during the mid-1920's. The "machine age" had produced an unprecedented "era of prosperity." To most observers, the nation's wealth was not necessarily being distributed more equally, but the economy was expanding so rapidly that everyone could enjoy a larger piece of the pie, and economists attributed this trend to technological advances which led to a rapid rise in productivity per unit of labor. Profits were increasing not because of any price rise, but rather because of increases in sales and productivity—or so America's corporate leaders proclaimed. In any event, corporate profits and the real wages of workers rose simultaneously, thus lending credence to the belief that the interests of capital and labor were the same. "Applied science and business organization," in the words of a respected American intellectual, "created widespread wealth in America."[40] Social and economic engineering administered within the context of capitalism were hailed as the key to the nation's success. Thus, as historian Arthur Schlesinger, Jr., has observed, "the imagination of the American capitalist and the ingenuity of the American engineer were never more apparent in the life of the people" than during the 1920's.[41] The executives of the CHC, hoping to apply the talents of these two groups to housing construction, anticipated a degree of success comparable to that apparently attained in industrial production.

Bing and many of his associates expressed confidence in the semi-philanthropic formula because they identified with the principles of the "New Era." History may have revealed a dismal track record for companies that endeavored to combine a commitment to social welfare with a desire for non-speculative profits. But the 1920's was viewed as a new dawn for American capitalism. Business leaders had expressed a sense of social responsibility. Not only had families like the Rockefellers, Mellons, and Sloanes contributed substantially to programs for hospital construction, libraries, and museums, but corporate leaders had also espoused the virtues of employee stock sharing, pension plans, and labor welfare programs. By combining the business community's public commitment to social service with corporate tactics based upon the rationalization of the production process, the CHC believed it could solve the housing problem. What capitalists and political leaders had found worrisome about the World War I housing experiments had been the government's direct involvement in construction, which they believed threatened the sanctity of private property. Investors providing private capital to builders at a limited dividend rate was one thing: allowing the government to build, own, and operate housing developments was quite another. The CHC, then, presented a formula that espoused the virtues of large scale development without assuming the perceived liabilities of government control. With the specter of public ownership eliminated, the CHC limited dividend concept conformed to a basic American tradition: it was a voluntary program of social reform that depended upon the good will and common sense of the nation's investors in the private sector. The experiments conducted by the company at Sunnyside and Radburn may have been hailed as displaying revolutionary approaches to land use and development, but in each case the company would achieve its revolutionary goals by "a sound conservative business operation." As a benevolent capitalist gesture, the program presented by Alexander Bing spoke to the spirit of the age.

Sunnyside Up 6

Sunnyside, a new community in the midst of the dismal city, an outstanding community of green garden courts—three-quarters of a mile of them—on the inside of normal New York blocks, usually cluttered with garages, sheds, or fences and seldom grassed or finished even for children's play-yards.—Henry Wright, Sr.[1]

Sunnyside Gardens proves that . . . private enterprise can improve standards without sacrificing reasonable profits, without sweeping government aid or subsidy, and without demoralizing the housing market.—Richard T. Ely, Professor of Economics at Columbia University[2]

Sunlight, fresh air, open space, opportunity for play, good house design—these are not the idle dreams of Utopians; [in Sunnyside] Mr. Alexander Bing . . . has shown they can be a sound business proposition.—Lewis Mumford[3]

THE Regional Planning Association of America's affiliation with the City Housing Corporation enabled it to achieve a rare combination of "theory and practice." The first attempt to build an experimental community to evolve from this relationship began in 1923, with the "Preliminary Study" on the Harkness tract, which was discussed in Chapter 3. But after that initial site in Brooklyn had proved unobtainable, Bing selected a much smaller tract of land on the border between Garden City and Queens: a tract which was to become a part of planning history as the location of the CHC's first practical experiment, Sunnyside Gardens. Consisting of seventy-six acres, the land had been assembled by the Pennsylvania and Long Island Rail Road Company between 1902 and 1906 to build a freight yard. When those plans were finally abandoned after World War I, the railroad company no longer had any use for the tract and placed it on the real estate market. In early 1924 the CHC purchased it for a total of $1.3 million or approximately $16,800 an acre ($.50 a square foot). Compared to the average price of $2,600 an acre the company paid for unimproved land to build Radburn in rural Fair Lawn, New Jersey, that price represented a substantial amount of capital, but it also represented a reasonable figure for valuable acreage "next door" to Manhattan's skyline.[4]

The site at Sunnyside Gardens met the same criteria which had been previously outlined in the "Preliminary Study" for the Harkness tract. The site was within a five-cent subway fare of Manhattan, and was only fifteen minutes from Grand Central Station. Proximity to New York City meant that Sunnyside itself would not have to provide those employment, recreational, and cultural opportunities afforded by the great metropolitan center, and, moreover, the planners would be able to tie their new community into the city's water and utility lines—factors that would reduce the cost of construction.

But, as the "Preliminary Study" also predicted would be true on the Harkness tract, Sunnyside's urban setting would limit the scope of the experiment. The community would have to be built within the frame of the urban grid pattern, or as Stein aptly described it, on the "cramped stage" of New York City.[5] Working within the existing urban design prohibited innovative site planning on the scale that both the RPAA and the CHC had envisioned. In the interests of greater flexibility, the CHC tried to convince the Borough Engineer's Office of Queens to relax certain zoning ordinances and to eliminate proposed streets that amounted to nothing more than dead-end alleys unnecessarily dividing the land into small blocks. Except for a few exceptions made along the northeastern edge of the proposed development, the office refused. The area freed when the streets were not built was a spacious one, subsequently used for grouping garages and for the construction of the Phipps Apartments in 1931.[6] "Elsewhere," as Stein asserted, "we were forced to fit our buildings to blocks rather than blocks to the living conditions, as we did afterwards at Radburn."[7] Most importantly, Sunnyside could do nothing to alleviate the problems of metropolitan growth. The success of the first CHC experiment depended on its proximity to the nation's largest city, and "a single housing region," the CHC readily admitted, "dependent on a big city for the occupation of its inhabitants, for schools, theaters and many other social agencies, does not solve the fundamental difficulties interwoven with the very existence of overgrown and unplanned centers of population."[8] The application of more fundamental garden city principles on a metropolitan and then regional scale would have to await future experiments.

Still, Sunnyside fulfilled many of the modest goals established for it by the CHC. Richard Ely described it as an "urban laboratory" out of which would come more ambitious experiments in the future. Although its houses were not cheap, Sunnyside's town planners and architects—Stein, Wright, and Ackerman—were able to produce well-constructed homes at prices which were substantially below those of other newly constructed houses built in New York City at the same time. Savings were achieved according to plan, by purchasing underdeveloped land at a reasonable cost (given existing market conditions) and by engaging, according to plan, in rapid construction to avoid expensive carrying charges. Building schedules were arranged, as we have seen Bing argue in Chapter 5, to permit year-round construction. In 1924 and 1925 only two weeks of work were lost due to inclement weather. (Such continuous employment for the construction workers, the CHC contended, also helped to boost worker morale and efficiency, since no one had to fear being dismissed once a particular job was completed. It almost epitomized a CHC management ideal: a steady wage was assured the worker within a plan for high productivity.) As a result of such planning, just over 1,200 units were completed in the four-year period between 1924 and 1928. Finally, by carefully planning public improvements, the company saved a good deal of money in the creation of the physical infrastructure. Streets and utility lines were not extended until a particular area was chosen as the next building site. Any facility therefore served a maximum number of units from the moment of completion, whereas haphazard and sporadic development often left streets and utility lines underutilized for many years after construction.

Building had begun in Sunnyside in April 1924, just two months after the land had been purchased. The desire to demonstrate alternative principles in land use in an initial small scale experiment, coupled with the need to avoid costly carrying charges, meant that "there never was time to study the plan of Sunnyside as a whole."[9] But that the site plan had to be hastily arranged did not make impossible Stein and Wright's introducing innovations in community design there. The theory and general blueprints for an open site plan with a substantial amount of common parkland had already been drawn, and all those involved in Sunnyside had utilized such basic principles while employed in the federal government's war housing agencies. The only difficulty at Sunnyside was to apply this general knowledge to a specific environment, while operating within the financial restraints imposed by the CHC and the residents for whom the company hoped to provide housing.

Thus, in Sunnyside, building coverage amounted to only 28 percent of the total area. The Tenement House Law of New York—which, as stated in the previous chapter, was one of the most progressive in the nation—permitted much more extensive coverage. Even large scale apartment complexes built in the mid-1920's as low cost model housing by private corporations, such as the New York Metropolitan Life Insurance Company, did not leave more than 50 percent open space on the site. In comparison, 72 percent of Sunnyside was designed for gardens and lawns.[10]

Through the employment of a series of cluster or row houses, the density at Sunnyside was made to average about twenty-seven families per acre. This was nowhere near the enormously high densities recorded in lower Manhattan since the mid-nineteenth century. But, on the other hand, it did not approach the maximum density of seven to fourteen families per acre common in middle class neighborhoods at the edges of the nation's cities, where lots measured a spacious 3,000 to 6,000 square feet. Sunnyside was set in an urban environment and it would be given an urban ambiance by economical rows of attached houses built along the perimeter of each block. But the planner yet hoped to demonstrate a practical alternative to the dreary and unhealthy gridiron city where city blocks were sliced into small, narrow lots (some only 25 feet in width and 100 feet in depth)— a scheme which resulted in a cityscape marred by long, dark alleys that shut out light and blocked ventilation.

As Wright had persistently argued during the previous decade, "the whole problem of decent planning is to get road frontage," and this problem could only be solved by abandoning the conventional lot line.[11] In Sunnyside, then, each house was given broad frontage and constructed only two rooms deep. Instead of pushing the design into the interior of the block, the designers turned the frame of the house ninety degrees and stretched it along the perimeter of the street. That "shallow

Garden Cities for America   124

construction" not only enabled each resident to enjoy ample fresh air and light but also left a large interior space at the center of each block. To satisfy mortgage requirements, each lot was deeded back to the center of the block, but the interior was preserved as common open space through forty-year easements placed on the deed. Unlike those in conventional subdivisions, then, the "backyards" in Sunnyside were not cut into individual private parcels to be covered by a mélange of fences, garages, and clotheslines. Instead the garages were grouped together and placed off to the side. Buildings encircling the open space were able to convey a sense of enclosure and human scale which enhanced the dignity of the development. Residents at Sunnyside enjoyed a small park outside their doors that could be shared with neighbors. The frame of the grid pattern confined the size of the park to a width of sixty feet, but it did establish the principle of common interior space. In Radburn the basic concept devised in Sunnyside would be implemented in the form of four- to six-acre parks laced through the core of the town's "superblocks." Nevertheless, Sunnyside's parks proved that "green commons in block centers can be developed even within the limitations of the characteristic American gridiron street pattern."[12] For this reason, the experiment in Queens not only represented a step towards the "Radburn idea," but also a remedy for the ills and crowded conditions endemic to the urban grid.

A Sunnyside house cost between $4,800 and $17,800. The homes were sold at prices which would pay overhead costs, meet carrying charges on vacant land, distribute dividends at 6 percent—and accrue a small profit as part of a policy to establish a revolving capital pool.[13] When the development's 1,202 units were completed, sales had generated a total surplus of about $300,000, a fact not many residents were aware of and one that was to serve as a bitter bone of contention during the confrontations between the CHC and Sunnyside families during the Depression.

The CHC hoped to accommodate the housing needs of families with annual incomes ranging from $1,200 to $3,500. Had they succeeded in doing so, the lower priced houses would have been within the reach of about 75 percent of all urban families. Through a variety of measures prices were kept at $10.50 per room, substantially below the minimum price of $15 to $20 per room in apartment houses being built at the time by speculative contractors. Sunnyside prices, nevertheless, were still too high for all but the skilled and professional classes which model housing of the late nineteenth century had accommodated.

A Sunnyside house or co-operative apartment with a 10 percent down payment cost a minimum of $42 a month or $504 a year to maintain, necessitating an annual family income of $2,500, an amount earned by only 40 percent of all urban families. Moreover, though the CHC had intended the monthly charge to cover all maintenance costs, including taxes, insurance, interest, and installment payments on principle, it soon discovered that it was economically unfeasible to incorporate heating and repair costs into the total price.[14] During the 1920's, Sunnyside's median family income was approximately $3,000. In the United States, two-thirds of all urban families earned less than that.

However, within the limits imposed by its prices, Sunnyside attained a varied demographic composition. In part, this was due to the liberal financing schemes devised by the CHC; in part, it was a result of its rents being at least comparatively cheap; and in part, it was a consequence of Sunnyside's experimental nature, which attracted highly educated people into the community. For these reasons, families who moved to Sunnyside enjoyed an environment of diversity not readily apparent from the price of its homes.[15]

A survey of residents conducted in 1927 when construction was nearing completion, for example, revealed that 116, or 20 percent, of the 566 responding heads of households were skilled or semi-skilled mechanics; and another 134, or 24 percent, called themselves either office workers or small tradespeople with moderate incomes. There were even a number of restaurant workers (18, or 3 percent), domestic servants (12, or 2 percent), and chauffeurs (5, or 1 percent), all adding to the community's demographic variety. The attractiveness of its homes and parkland, combined with its proximity to Manhattan, drew a large number of business and professional families to Sunnyside. Of those who responded to the survey, 182 residents, or 32 percent, were employed as businesspeople, and 99, or 17 percent, categorized themselves as professionals—including a sizable proportion of young artists, writers, and liberal intellectuals who were fascinated with the concept of a planned community and found Sunnyside an exciting and convenient place to live.[16]

Mumford resided there for eleven years; Charles Ascher, a noted real estate lawyer and the legal consultant for the CHC, also made his home in the community in the 1920's, as did a host of political activists who would serve as the nucleus of a strident community protest movement against the foreclosures and evictions that occurred during the Depression. "In the block where I lived," Mumford has recently reminisced, "there was a grocer's clerk who earned 1200 to 1500 dollars a year, and a physician who earned ten thousand—then a large salary. So this effort at an acceptable minimum in housing achieved something even more important; a mixed community, not the economically segregated kind that the higher costs of a well-planned middle class suburb demand."[17] The price of Sunnyside's houses may have precluded the degree of diversity sought by its planners and advocates, but, despite economic constraints, the community was inhabited by a rich cross section of families.

To accommodate the largest possible percentage of potential residents, the CHC undertook a number of financial experiments. Bing initiated a loan fund of his own which could be utilized by approved applicants to secure the difference between the 10 percent down payment required by lending institutions and the family's savings. No interest was charged on the loan and it could be repaid over a one- to two-year period. The company also introduced a single-mortgage payment system with a 10 percent down payment and a long-term amortization period of twenty-two years.[18] But in the 1920's, the CHC found it impossible to convince financial institutions to participate in a single-mortgage program. Without government guarantees, that method of financing required the extension of too much credit without enough equity—a risk banks and insurance companies were unwilling to take. In place of that arrangement a two-tiered mortgage system was devised, one more closely resembling conventional mortgage agreements of the pre–World War II period. The first mortgage, which involved a large down payment, varied between 50 and 60 percent of the purchase price and ran for a period of five years. Although the mortgage was usually granted by a large financial institution, the CHC guaranteed the home buyer a renewal for an additional five years if it was necessary. The second mortgage covered the remainder of the cost and had an amortization period of twelve to fourteen years. The CHC often co-signed these second mortgages or issued the loans independently (and thus became liable for any failure of payment by residents). The company then used the mortgages as collateral for issuing bonds that helped to broaden the company's capital base. For each resident, the CHC also served as a financial agent: thus the expenditures for mortgages, taxes, water bills, and insurance were incorporated into one monthly payment to simplify each family's financial payment responsibilities and record keeping. This scheme was later adopted in Radburn.[19]

Further, to assist potential buyers at Sunnyside, the CHC also built a substantial number of two- and three-family homes. For example, in the first section, completed in 1924, there were forty two-family houses and only eight one-family homes. The former allowed individuals who could not otherwise afford to purchase a home under the existing market conditions to do so by having a tenant defray a good portion of the costs, thus assisting in the payment of the mortgage. A two-family home priced at $9,350 would cost $102 a month to maintain, necessitating an income of $6,000 a year; but a landlord could receive as much as $75 a month for a four-room apartment, therein cutting net monthly expenses to less than $30. In the halcyon days of the 1920's, two-family houses appeared to be a viable solution to the desire for homeownership among moderate income families. However, when the Depression struck, those who purchased a two-family house found themselves in double jeopardy. Not only could they no longer afford their own monthly payments but the tenants on whom they depended also faced personal financial hardship. The idea proved to be so vulnerable that it was abandoned by the time Radburn was conceived.[20]

Finally, the CHC experimented with co-operative apartments. Again the intent was to promote ownership, rather than rental, among middle income families, a goal which grew out of the traditional American perception that private ownership produced greater care in property maintenance and repairs and more stability within the community—an attitude which reflected the conservative bias that often accompanied the innovative programs put forth by the CHC. The co-ops represented the lowest cost housing built in Sunnyside, and indeed, if they had been tax exempt, would have been the lowest cost housing constructed in New York City during the mid 1920's. A four-room co-op apartment was priced at $4,800. It required a $480 down payment and a $50 monthly fee which included the fixed charges of interest, taxes, water, and insurance as well as operating costs such as coal, electricity, general repairs, and the janitors' wages. For the down payment the resident received ninety-six shares of co-op stock at $5 a share, and as the mortgage was paid off each part owner was entitled to additional stock, all of which paid a maximum annual dividend of 4 percent.[21]

In comparison with the enormous success of Sunnyside's units in general, the co-ops did not sell well. Only 50 percent were purchased after an intensive six-month campaign. To help defray the expenses of maintaining the half-occupied buildings, the CHC agreed to pay rents on all unsold apartment units to the non-profit company which owned them, until they were purchased—a benevolent gesture which became an economic burden to the CHC. Finally, it was decided to rent the co-op apartments with the hope that the renters would eventually become owners. Sales, however, continued to lag behind those of non-co-op homes and apartments in Sunnyside. The experience led the executives at the CHC to conclude that the "co-operatives' best chances for success lie among a homogenous fraternal or racial group" such as existed in the Bronx apartments built by the Amalgamated Clothes Workers' Union for its members and the Paul Lawrence Dunbar Apartments, a Rockefeller project built for blacks in Harlem. With a diverse population, Sunnyside could not attain the solidarity that appeared to be a necessary ingredient for successful co-operatives in the 1920's. For this reason, the concept was not retested in Radburn.[22]

"Represented among the home buyers are the more stable groups that make up the mass of the city's population," proclaimed the Sunnyside ads put out by CHC. "Teachers, municipal employees, skilled mechanics, professional people, artists and writers are all to be found there."[23] Not only did these diverse families live in the same community, but they often lived on the same block. Stein and Wright placed different types of housing in one row so that owners of single-family dwellings lived next to apartment dwellers. It is interesting to note that this kind of site planning would not have been permissible if Sunnyside had been zoned for residential use. Only because it was designated an industrial area was no restriction placed on the mixing of building types. "In spite of speculative operators' fear of such indiscriminate grouping, and the zoners' preoccupation in keeping dwellings of similar type together," Stein later boasted, "we found this did not cause sales resistance."[24]

The architects claimed that by not segregating building types they created a more aesthetically pleasing environment as well as a more dynamic social setting; the latter, they believed, would evolve from the mixing of families with different incomes and occupations. Three-story apartments were placed next to two-story private homes: the varied roof line (which again would have been prohibited if Sunnyside had been zoned residential) gave "far more interest than could any amount of pattern, horizontal or vertical massing of windows, or lines of brick ornament."[25] But, most importantly, the physical layout enhanced the social activities which became the hallmark of Sunnyside. "The variety, spontaneity, and vitality of the residents' community activities at Sunnyside," Wright asserted, "arises from the variety of families living there, a variety possible only by virtue of the diversity in dwelling types."[26]

The common interior space at the center of each block necessitated political structures to deal with community activities taking place within them. Block associations were formed of residents who lived in the houses and apartments encircling the private parks. These associations were charged with the responsibility of monitoring social activities, as well as assuring the architectural integrity of the grouping. Representatives in the block associations turned out to be vigilant administrators. But the playgrounds and common open areas were found to be annoying and bothersome to some residents who insisted that the parklands interfered with their privacy. (To overcome such difficulties, the blocks developed after 1924 were divided into quadrangles, some of which were "intended for restful gatherings and quiet play" only.)[27] In addition to the common interior areas within the blocks, a three and one-half acre park was set aside for the entire community in the northeastern corner of the development. In 1926, the Sunnyside Gardens Community Association was formed and the CHC hired playground directors to organize community activities in the park. The association had five officials—two representatives of the homeowners, two from the CHC, and one neutral member. Funded by a one dollar monthly fee charged to each family, the association was responsible for general, community-wide activities, while the management of the interior space inside each block was left to the block associations. For example, a garden club, a children's club, and a co-op buying group were all created through the efforts of the Sunnyside Gardens Community Association, while matters such as lawn maintenance concerned the block associations.

To both residents and investors, the physical, social, and financial plan in Sunnyside remained an unquestioned success throughout the 1920's. First, the CHC had proved the viability of limited dividend investment—at least for the moment. Second, planners and architects Stein, Wright, and Ackerman had illustrated that innovative site planning could bring a good deal of open space and parkland even to the grid pattern. Third, the company had fostered a social plan that encouraged vigorous community spirit and citizen participation in recreational and cultural activities. To those who built and lived there, Sunnyside enjoyed a sense of beauty and neighborliness difficult to replicate in the private landscape of the nation's conventional cities and suburbs; and its residents seemed especially fortunate compared to those who lived in the adjacent Queens developments built at the same time. For CHC officials anxious to demonstrate their project's viability, Sunnyside's appealing qualities were confirmed by rapid sales and by the fact that over 50 percent of the last units, built in 1928, were purchased by friends and relatives of existing owners.[28] Yet, beneath the public acclamation was the disturbing reality that Sunnyside could not provide housing for the full spectrum of income groups. The community enjoyed social and cultural diversity, but only within the limits created by the relatively high prices of the houses.

Of the seventy-six acres originally purchased for the Sunnyside project, only fifty-five acres were developed. The remaining twenty-one acres of unimproved land were resold once the scope of the experiment had been determined. Largely as a result of the development at Sunnyside, the surrounding land increased substantially in value. The CHC was able to sell its excess acreage in 1926 for $1.62 a square foot, or nearly three times the amount the company paid for it: a profit of $646,786 was realized for land held less than two years. In effect the CHC had been the beneficiary of the speculative market which Bing and his associates saw as a major reason for the nation's urban problems; the company had taken advantage of rising land values in the same way as any speculative builder. The essential difference was that private developers chose not to limit the return on their investment and accepted a good portion of the profits as private income. In contrast, the CHC used the one-half million dollars attained in the sale of the excess land to establish a revolving capital fund to serve as the basis for the company's second project at Radburn, as Bing, Wright, and Stein had suggested might be done in the "Preliminary Study" for the Harkness tract. Thus the profit derived from the Sunnyside experiment provided a "nestegg" for the construction of the first real garden suburb in America.[29]

Despite the modest scale of the project, the CHC viewed Sunnyside as a successful prelude to a comprehensive program of garden cities for America. Indeed it seemed to confirm the company's belief that significant improvements in housing and community development could take place without a dramatic restructuring of the economy. Sunnyside "stands as a consciously successful demonstration of how much can be done to better housing conditions, provide garden and play space for children and put these advantages within financial reach of wage earners and other moderate income families," the CHC proclaimed, "all by the course of a sound, conservative business operation."[30] With the success of its initial experiment well documented and publicized, the company could embark on a more ambitious project in Radburn confident of its ability to advance garden city principles.

The Evolution of the Radburn Idea

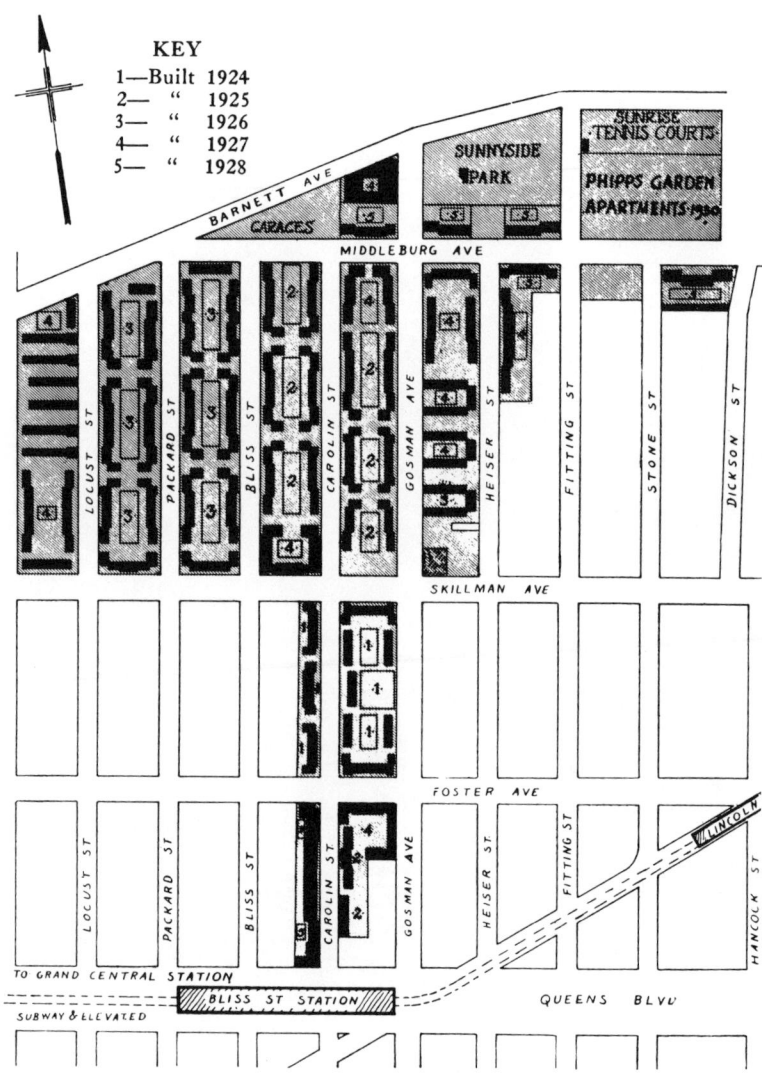

Opposite: General Plan for Sunnyside Gardens (1924): innovative site planning within the urban grid. Houses are stretched along the perimeter of the block while the center is preserved for common open space. From Clarence S. Stein, *Toward New Towns for America* (Cambridge, Mass.: MIT Press, 1973). Copyright Clarence S. Stein, reprinted by permission of The MIT Press.

Above: Interior Courtyard at Sunnyside (c. 1935): common space put to many uses—gardens, decorative flower beds, pedestrian paths, and quiet play areas. Courtesy of the Cornell University Archives, Olin Library, Ithaca, N.Y.

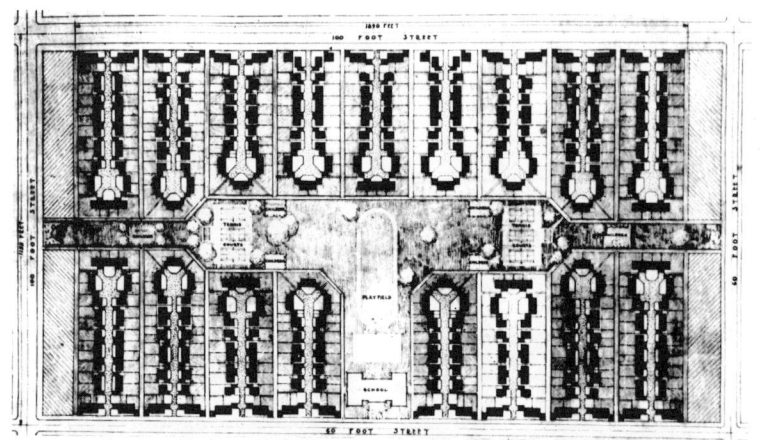
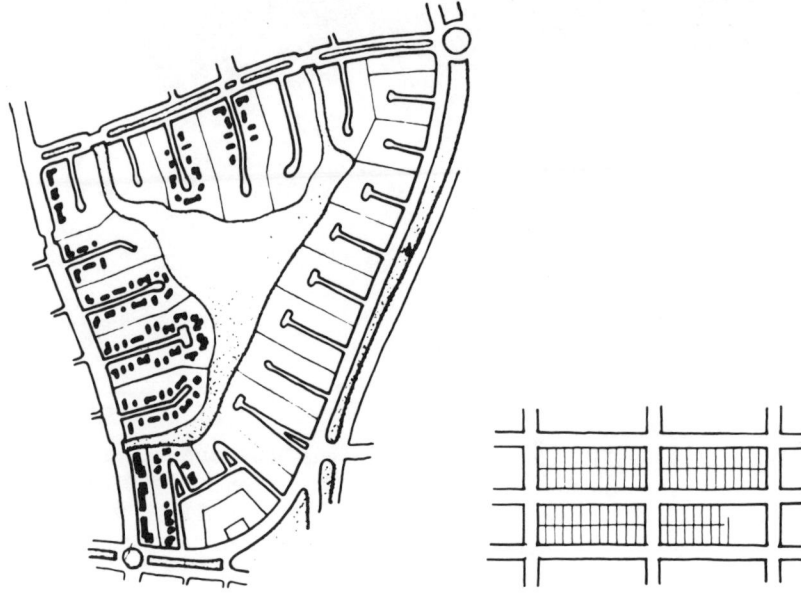

Opposite, top: The Birth of the Radburn Plan (1928): Stein credited the basic elements of the Radburn plan to Herbert Emmerich, a City Housing Corporation administrator, who in December 1927 rough-sketched a town plan with common parkland and cul-de-sacs on the back of an envelope. Emmerich's ideas were refined in the above theoretical depiction of the superblock drawn by Radburn's architects in January 1928. Courtesy of the Radburn Association Archives, Fair Lawn, N.J.

Opposite, bottom: The Radburn Superblock (1929): a core of open space surrounded by a network of cul-de-sacs or dead end streets. Compare to the urban grid: the conventional physical landscape in America, dominated by the street and private lot. Courtesy of the Radburn Association Archives, Fair Lawn, N.J.

Above: The Cul-de-sac (c. 1932): houses are clustered around a narrow dead end street that serves only the residents who live there. It forms part of a functional street system where each street's dimensions are determined by its role in the transportation system of the entire community. Courtesy of the Radburn Association Archives, Fair Lawn, N.J.

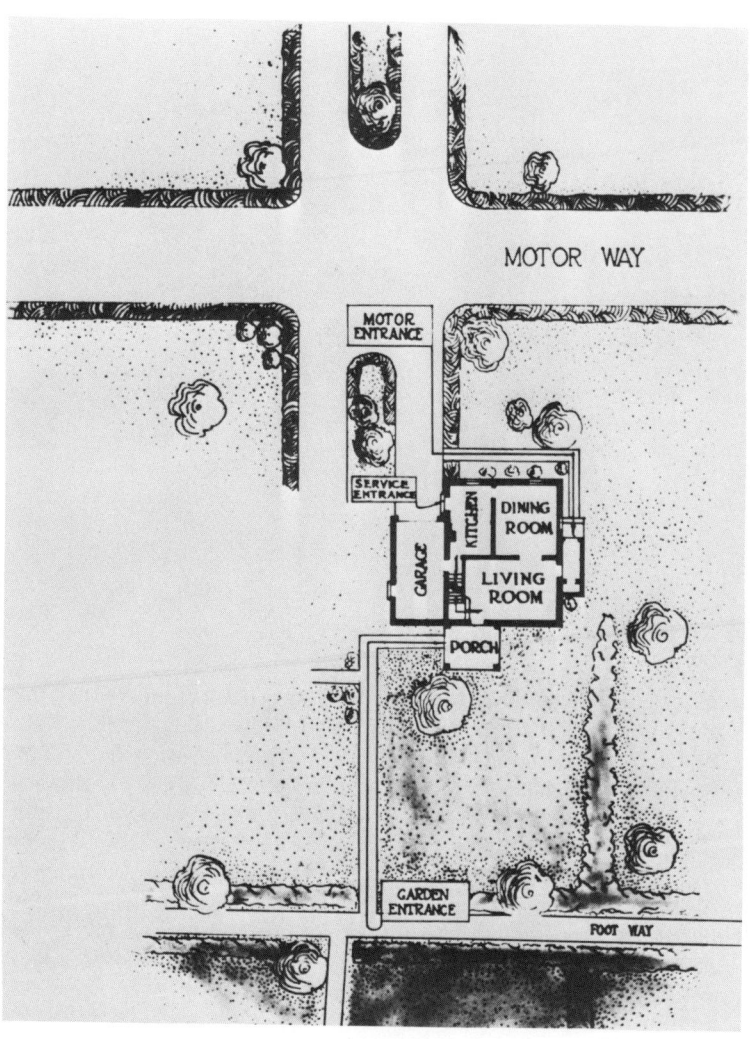

Turned-around Houses: the interior layout of each house is opposite from the conventional design—the living room faces the interior parkland and the kitchen fronts the cul-de-sac. Courtesy the Radburn Association Archives, Fair Lawn, N.J.

Top: A View of the Family Entrance (c. 1932): displaying many of the aspects of the Radburn idea—pedestrian walkways provide safety for residents; the interior green corridors give a sense of natural beauty and tranquility; and moderate population density is attained through the use of clustered housing.

Bottom: Radburn Architecture (c. 1932): notice how the architects varied the lot sizes, rooflines, compositions, and positioning of the houses to achieve an elegant diversity. On the opposite side of the family entrance is the cul-de-sac and driveways planned for the convenience of automobile drivers. Courtesy of the Radburn Association Archives, Fair Lawn, N.J.

Top: Howard Avenue Underpass (c. 1949): the enduring symbol of Radburn. The underpass insured a complete separation of pedestrian and vehicular traffic and justified Radburn's dual epithets—"a town for the motor age" and "a town for children." Courtesy of the Cornell University Archives, Olin Library, Ithaca, N.Y.

Bottom: Eye-level View of the Interior Parkland (c. 1932): an attempt to create a balance between private and community space. Courtesy of the Radburn Association Archives, Fair Lawn, N.J.

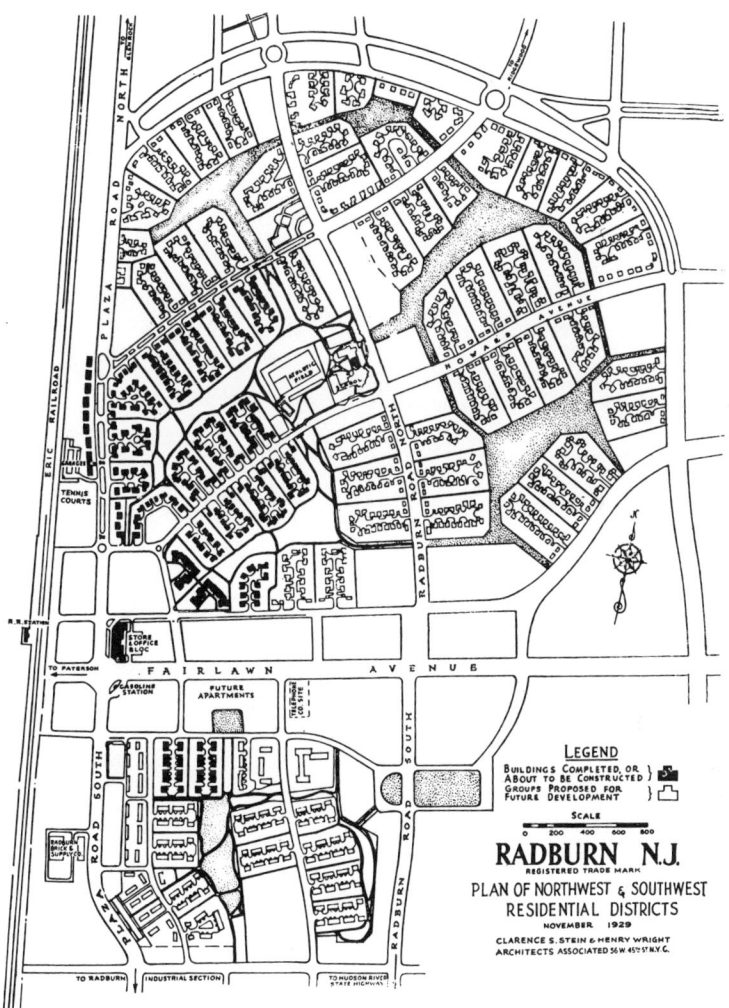

The Neighborhood Unit (1929): Radburn's answer to the faceless metropolis would contain 10,000 people and include an elementary school and a shopping center to achieve a degree of self-sufficiency. There is a striking similarity between Radburn's neighborhood unit and Howard's garden city ward. Courtesy of the Radburn Association Archives, Fair Lawn, N.J.

A Town for the Motor Age   7

A town built to live in—today and tomorrow. "A town for the motor age." A town turned outside-in without any backdoors. A town where roads and parks fit together like fingers on your right and left hands. A town in which children never dodge motor-trucks on their way to school. A new town—newer than the garden cities, and the first major departure in town planning since they were built.—Geddes Smith, on Radburn[1]

[Radburn] represents the first scientific effort that has ever been made to establish a community designed exclusively to minimize the danger of automobile accidents. Yet there were other things to consider. . . . It was the desire of the builders to create not only a [safe and sane] community . . . but also one . . . of beauty in appearance and the utmost in modern efficiency.—*The American Architect*[2]

Sunnyside Gardens and Radburn and the Greenbelt towns were but finger exercises preparing for symphonies that are yet to come.—Lewis Mumford[3]

IN 1927, the City Housing Corporation began to search for a suitable site on which to build its second experimental community. Company executives canvassed seventy-seven sites throughout the northeast, finally settling on a large tract of land in Fair Lawn, New Jersey, a small rural community in central Bergen County about fifteen miles from Manhattan. Fair Lawn was chosen because it was one of the few remaining places within the shadow of New York City's rising skyline to contain an extensive rural area, testimony to the fact that by the late 1920's a good deal of suburbanization had already taken place. But the town's expansive agricultural land was not the sole reason for the selection of the site. Only a single road (Fair Lawn Avenue) dating back to the colonial period bisected it, and no official road maps or zoning ordinances had been put into effect. The absence of formal land use procedures would facilitate innovative site planning. Moreover, the gently rolling, well-drained terrain was both attractive and easy to develop. Little grading would be necessary; and, because the land was not rocky, no heavy blasting would be required. The tops of the rolling hills, however, would provide excellent natural locations for community buildings.

The CHC hired a real estate company in nearby Hackensack to assemble this undeveloped land and to act as its agent. The firm was told not to reveal the plans of its client because, as Alexander Bing justifiably feared, any public knowledge about the large scale project would inflate land values and unnecessarily add to construction costs; therefore the land was purchased in secrecy.

Knowledge of the plans for the construction of Radburn never reached the farmers of Fair Lawn until the formal public announcement on January 26, 1928. Sales agents simply presented themselves as private, independent realtors interested in purchasing and developing small tracts of land. During a five-month period beginning in July 1927, the CHC thus assembled a parcel of land over 640 acres or one square mile in size. Purchased from forty-six individual owners, the plots ranged from one-quarter of an acre to eighty-eight acres. During the next three years, upon the suggestions of English architect and site planner Raymond Unwin, the company doubled its land holdings in Bergen County.

The large number of real estate transactions aroused the suspicion of Fair Lawn's residents. A rumor spread in the last half of 1927 that either the federal government or local political bosses were buying large tracts of land for some unspecified project. This suspicion pushed prices upward. Further inflationary pressure had been applied to land values with the beginning of the construction of the Hudson River (later renamed George Washington) Bridge and well-publicized plans for a state highway running east-west across Bergen County. Nor were truck farmers in Fair Lawn eager to sell their land: it was fertile, productive, and profitable. Farmers managed to produce two and sometimes three spinach crops each year, in addition to large quantities of other fresh fruits and vegetables. Proximity to New York City meant they could beat most of their competitors to that lucrative market. These excellent conditions translated into yearly gross incomes of $10,000 for some of the town's wealthier farmers.[4] Besides, the land had often been owned by the same family for several hundred years, and the present generation balked at giving up what they considered to be a part of their heritage, their roots. Herbert Emmerich, who managed the real estate department for the CHC, acknowledged the existence of these strong personal feelings when he publicly stated that "many of the deeds which have come to us show two or three transfers of the property in 100 to 150 years, and in a few cases go back to royal grants from Great Britain in colonial days."[5] For all these reasons—proximity to New York City, rising land values, and an affluent agricultural economy—the CHC paid an average price of $2,600 per acre or $.10 per square foot—still, however, a reasonable sum when one considers that land several miles to the east in Englewood had skyrocketed to $5,000 an acre by the late 1920's.[6]

In all, then, about 1,300 acres or two square miles of land were purchased at a cost of $3.3 million. Plans specified that Radburn was to be built on one-half that total area, after which Bing planned to resell the excess land at a substantial profit, just as the company had done in the first experiment at Sunnyside, to establish a revolving capital fund to finance the construction of its hoped-for series of garden cities. The community's boundaries were drawn at Saddle River on the east (the word Radburn, coined by Charles Ascher, means Saddle River in Old English), the Erie Railroad on the west, and the townships of Glen Rock on the north and Saddle River on the south. The Old Mill, dating back to the colonial period and now a part of the Bergen County Park System, was to serve as the grand entranceway into the city, symbolizing the planners' concern for nature and leisurely activities.

Radburn was to be nothing less than America's first garden community, another significant step advancing the principles of Ebenezer Howard. But even at the initial planning sessions held at the Hudson Guild Farm in Netcong, New Jersey, it was apparent that Radburn would compromise a number of Howard's basic ideas. Although acreage purchased in Fair Lawn could house between 25,000 and 30,000 people, the protective greenbelt—an essential component of the garden city—was abandoned during the early stages of discussion because of the cost and difficulty of acquiring sufficiently large tracts of land near the nation's largest metropolitan center. Members of the RPAA realized that Radburn's site, with an expressway along the northern boundary and a fairly narrow strip of parkland on the eastern edge, provided an insufficient buffer from the onslaught of suburbanization sure to occur on the adjacent land. Built on its one square mile of land without the five-mile greenbelt recommended by Howard, Radburn would lack the physical definition and the rural-urban balance basic to a complete garden city, which, in Howard's model, was a relatively self-contained community incorporating agricultural, residential, commercial, and industrial facilities. The absence of a greenbelt around Radburn not only left that area open to development; it also jeopardized the production of foodstuffs on it. The members of the RPAA also realized that it would be difficult to attract industry to a new community. They chose Radburn in part because of its proximity to New York City's large market and they set aside ample space for industrial development. But, as we shall see shortly, they overestimated the strength of Radburn's geographic location and found themselves unable to build a strong industrial base.

In his model, Howard included housing for a wide range of income groups so that each garden city would be a microcosm of the larger society. But in conferences leading to the construction of Radburn, it soon became evident that the community would not be able to accommodate a large spectrum of the population. As Clarence Stein lamented, "if the poorly paid workers were admitted into the garden city, the industry that used them would have to subsidize the workers' houses or advance their wages; there was no other way of providing them with the barest minimum of good houses unless the garden city duplicated the very conditions that it existed to escape from."[7] The housing standards and the number of community facilities the RPAA proposed in America's first garden community would price the working class out of the housing market. In January 1928, when the CHC announced that it would finance the construction of Radburn, Bing still hoped that skilled laborers and craftsmen would be able to purchase Radburn houses. But their prices during the first year ranged from $7,900 to $18,200, more than twice the average price of an American house in the late 1920's.[8] Indeed the lowest priced house in Radburn cost almost 70 percent more than the cheapest Sunnyside house. The additional high cost of maintaining a home in Radburn meant that the community would contain affluent business executives and educated professionals, and the first survey of Radburn, conducted in 1933, showed that indeed 87 percent of the men had some college education and almost all of them held white collar or professional positions. Thus the social composition of Radburn hardly resembled that depicted by Howard in his portrait of the garden city, and it even marked a step backward from the degree of diversity attained in Sunnyside.[9]

To maintain the integrity of the site plan and to prevent speculative development, Howard called for the municipal ownership of land and for a system of leaseholding rather than private mortgages. Through a program of long-term rentals periodically adjusted to reflect rising land values, he believed, the "unearned increment" obtained through individual speculative investment could be translated into a "collectively earned increment" to benefit all city residents.[10] But the sacred tradition of private homeownership in the United States prevented this scheme from being transferred to Radburn. Except for the apartment units, houses in Radburn were sold individually rather than leased by the construction company or a private realtor, while the common interior parkland was held in trust for the community by the Radburn Association, an "extra-municipal government" organized to conduct the town's political affairs. Thus the backbone of the Radburn plan—the park—was protected from private speculation and development and preserved for the benefit of the entire community. But the method of attaining that goal was rooted in the American experience more than in Howard's ideas. The restrictive deeds established in the romantic nineteenth-century suburbs of Roland Park, Maryland, and Llewellyn Park, New Jersey, and in the pre–World War I planned community of Forest Hills, New York, served as the precedents for Radburn's political structure.[11] The use of such traditional methods of real estate development instead of the potentially revolutionary concept of public ownership placated potential investors and homeowners—as it had done in Sunnyside.

Thus the experiment at Radburn failed to conform to several of the basic tenets of Howard's garden city. Since Radburn lacked a greenbelt, it was vulnerable to suburban sprawl, and since it failed to attract industry, it could never achieve the economic and social balance at the heart of Howard's reform measures. Despite these serious compromises, Radburn adhered to enough garden city principles to differ substantially from other residential developments throughout the country. "We committed our share of mistakes," Charles Ascher, the author of Radburn's land use covenants, recently admitted, "but everything was planned."[12] Howard's emphasis on rational, systematic development in contrast to the haphazard, incremental growth found in most cities and suburbs remained at the center of the "Radburn idea." Just as Howard had advocated, the site plan at Radburn was designed to limit the population to between 25,000 and 30,000 people. Even before Radburn was conceived, the RPAA concluded that an American garden city should not have more than 50,000 residents because, in the words of Stein, a larger number of people would "complicate and heighten the costs of any city life."[13] The RPAA feared that without a lid on population growth Radburn would suffer from the same problems that plagued conventional suburban developments. And since Howard concluded that each community should stop growing at a predetermined point, the RPAA realized that the success of the garden city movement depended ultimately on a patterning of land use that extended beyond the design and construction of one town. As a single community built within the metropolitan landscape of northern New Jersey, Radburn would not fulfill Howard's plan for decentralized, polynucleated growth. Thus Radburn, like Sunnyside, was approached as but another step toward a comprehensive garden cities program.

RADBURN'S special place in the history of urban planning is based on its physical site plan and particularly on its unique system of handling pedestrian and vehicular traffic. Advertised as "the town for the motor age," Radburn became the first planned community to consider the automobile as a vital part of the American way of life, but one that should not be permitted to dominate the landscape.[14] Twenty years after the construction of Radburn, Stein, one of the community's chief architects and site planners, stated that "the Radburn idea" sought "to answer the enigma, how to live with the auto," or perhaps more precisely, "how to live in spite of it."[15] Thus the architects of Radburn "never thought well of the automobile." But as one historian has recently stated, they "realistically assessed the role of the car in American society and came to the determination that only through planning with the automobile in mind could it be controlled."[16]

To overcome the problems created by the automobile required a radical rethinking of the relationship among homes, streets, gardens, paths, parks, neighborhoods, and highways. A new functional relationship among these elements was attained through the creation of the "safetyhurst or superblock," Radburn's basic unit of construction.[17] Whereas the predominant grid or checkerboard pattern in a traditional residential or commercial environment consisted of 200 foot by 600 foot rectangular blocks, the planners of Radburn created a "superblock" which was circumscribed by a roadway that directed automobiles around, rather than through, the community, thus providing an interior area ten to fifteen times the size of conventional American city blocks—one 1,200 feet by 1,800 feet, unencroached upon by vehicular traffic. Instead of the inefficient, unsightly maze of garages and alleys that characterized a good portion of American residential development at that time, the open space in Radburn was set aside for common interior parklands averaging four to six acres in size. This design, foreshadowed at Sunnyside, represented an attempt to link the parks and homes directly without inhibiting the flow of automobile traffic. A system of pedestrian walkways connected the houses to the interior parkland, and underpasses and overpasses between the superblocks permitted a complete separation of vehicular and pedestrian traffic. The site plan thus protected the pedestrian from the dangers presented by the automobile and freed the automobile driver from the inconveniences created by the pedestrian. As Benton MacKaye noted, "Radburn was the first town to be planned on the assumption that through motor traffic must be completely separated from the communal aspects of the environment." He believed that if this functional separation was created and maintained, both roadway and town could become safer and more beautiful.[18]

Radburn was to remain protected from, but not entirely impervious to, vehicular traffic. Express or arterial highways would connect it to other towns; secondary or connector roads would tie together the six superblock units formulated as a part of its original plan; and, finally, service roads or cul-de-sacs would provide its residents with direct vehicular access to their homes. Such a plan prevented the roadway from dominating the environment and thus becoming the most significant factor in the town's future development. Since the roadways were planned to serve distinct purposes, they could vary substantially in width: indeed the cul-de-sacs or dead-end streets were as little as twenty feet wide, which was more than adequate for the limited use they would receive. Such preplanning of the functional street system enabled the designers of Radburn to limit road area to only 21 percent of the development, instead of approximately 35 percent as in conventional American subdivisions. As Stein summarized it, "the greatest difference between the old method of city planning and the Radburn method is in regard to the road plan. In the old, it dominated; at Radburn it serves."[19] That accomplishment led the *New York Times* to editorialize that Radburn represented "the first deliberate attempt to harmonize the rights of the pedestrian and of the motorist."[20] In a more dramatic assertion, Mumford later proclaimed that Radburn was "the first major departure in city planning since Venice."[21] The danger and congestion caused by increasing dependence on gas-driven vehicles was emerging as a fundamental problem in twentieth-century America, and the nation was at the same time increasingly emphasizing leisure and recreational activity. Radburn, with vehicular traffic controlled and no home more than 400 feet from either the parkland or a major roadway, promised and provided safe accessibility both to the automobile and to the natural environment. No wonder a positive response was elicited from the planning profession.

Slotted into the edge of the superblock, each cul-de-sac in Radburn was lined with ten to eighteen houses, creating a ratio of seven homes to an acre—almost twice the density of that in conventional suburban developments. The homes were situated on small parcels of land, averaging about 4,500 square feet or roughly one-tenth of an acre. Clustering these homes together and laying out fewer, smaller, roads preserved a good deal of land within the superblocks for common interior parkland without reducing street frontage. Of the 149 acres ultimately developed as part of Radburn, 23 acres (about 15 percent of the total area) consisted of green open space to be shared by the entire community. The money saved due to a 25 percent reduction in the space usually required for streets and utility lines provided the capital to construct and landscape the common parks. This fact led Henry Wright, Sr., one of Radburn's chief site planners, to conclude that "these parks come to us for almost nothing—merely the price of the virgin land—because [they] do not have to be served by sewers, water, gas and all sorts of things, as they would have to be if the street ran along in front of them."[22]

Although almost half of the homes in Radburn were single-unit dwellings, they were not, then, erected on typical quarter- or half-acre building lots. Since design preceded subdivision, Radburn could never have been built if conventional zoning ordinances had been in effect in Fair Lawn during the 1920's. Such laws, which typically divided the land into a set of identical lots, would have precluded cluster housing. Instead of platting the land as an initial step, the planners of Radburn began by creating a pleasing relationship among the houses to be erected along each cul-de-sac. Once they positioned the houses, they determined the size and shape of each lot. By reversing the conventional planning process, the Radburn architects and site planners freed themselves from the restraint imposed by rigid geometric patterns and permitted themselves to experiment in innovative methods of land development. Various types of housing—single-unit, semi-attached, row, and multi-unit dwellings—could all be incorporated into the original design of a single superblock to avoid the one-dimenstional quality common in conventional American suburbs of detached, single-family homes. The uniqueness of the Radburn plan startled Fair Lawn's part-time tax assessor, and it took a good deal of coaxing to convince him of its merits. "None of our houses fitted his types," recalled Charles Ascher, "and our cockeyed scheme of street layout with cul-de-sacs upset him completely."[23]

To create an attractive diversity of housing, as well as to save space and money, about 50 percent of the houses in Radburn were either attached or multi-unit dwellings. By varying the roofline, color, composition, and texture of each house (from brick veneer to clapboard to stucco to shingle), the designers of Radburn developed a diverse residential environment. The variety was created not despite the construction of row houses but because of it. Through the use of such simple but effective techniques, the architects of Radburn's attached houses avoided what they considered to be the montonous appearance of row houses in places like Philadelphia and Baltimore. Moreover, the construction of varied cluster housing provided the opportunity to overcome the conformity symbolized and encouraged by a suburban development that carved the land into identical lots.

To reduce the impact of the automobile upon the residential areas even further, each home was given two entrances of equal importance—one on the cul-de-sac, designed for the delivery of goods and services, and the other on the pedestrian walkway or parkland, intended for leisurely recreational use. "At Radburn we have abolished the backyard and made it the front yard," wrote Louis Brownlow, the municipal consultant to the CHC. "We have tried to do away with the back door and we are building houses that have no backs, but have two fronts."[24] This idea was most clearly expressed in the floor plan of a Radburn house: unlike that of the conventional American house, the interior design of a home in Radburn was turned "outside in." Rooms for family use and sleeping, which had traditionally fronted the street, faced the walkways or parkland. Utility rooms, such as the kitchen, overlooked the noisier, less aesthetically pleasing cul-de-sacs, instead of the backyard. In other words, the "integrated framework" created a house with "two faces" looking out at two views of which "the one is paved, the other mainly green. They fit together like fingers on two hands," Stein suggested, "but they never overlap or interfere with each other's activities."[25] Each entrance, like each roadway, was thus developed within the context of a comprehensive site plan to serve a specific function.

All these design elements—the superblock, the specialized highway system, the common interior space, the complete separation of pedestrian and vehicular traffic, and the turned-around houses—were devised to direct the residents' attention away from the street and toward the parkland. The institutions and facilities basic to any community were all to be accessible via the pedestrian walkways within the park. The designers of Radburn did not believe that the physical structure or layout of a community determined social values, but they were convinced that the site plan was not a neutral force. Whereas the grid pattern dominated by the automobile frayed the social fabric of American communities, the parkland constructed in relationship to educational, civic, and commercial centers would generate an atmosphere conducive to neighborliness and cooperative effort. "Small neighborhoods are essential for eye-to-eye democracy," Stein proclaimed in *Toward New Towns for America*, an autobiographical account of his professional career. "This is basic, not only for local contentment, but for national freedom and world-wide security."[26] The sentiment and the social values expressed in this statement shaped the Radburn idea. For those who designed Radburn, its site plan was to provide the potential for creating a face-to-face village atmosphere in a modern industrial society.

To that end the "neighborhood unit" concept was utilized—a scheme of community growth articulated by planner and social worker Clarence Perry as an outgrowth of his personal experience in the Russell Sage Foundation's pre–World War I project in Forest Hills, New York. Perry gave the most detailed outline of his ideas in 1929, in volume seven of the Regional Plan of New York.[27] He argued that parks and playgrounds should comprise at least 10 percent of a neighborhood's total area and that commercial facilities should be located at the edge of the neighborhood within easy access of each resident's home. Wherever possible, the street system should route traffic around rather than through the community so as to provide a safe and pleasing environment, especially for youngsters. Most importantly, Perry maintained that the size of a "neighborhood unit" should be determined by the number of children (and therefore the number of households) needed to support an elementary school. Perry estimated that 1,500 students would be the maximum number. This meant that each neighborhood unit would comprise 4,000 to 7,000 people—a figure close to the target set for Radburn, which, originally designed as a community for 25,000 to 30,000 residents, was divided into three neighborhoods of from 5,000 to 10,000 residents each. Thus the family, and specifically the children, were the focal points of Perry's concern in devising his scheme, as they were to continue to be for Radburn's developers, who proudly advertised Radburn as a "town for children."[28]

In the simplest terms, the Radburn neighborhood unit could be described as two superblocks, each with a radius of no more than one-half mile. But conforming to Perry's principles, the size of a neighborhood unit was actually dictated by the number of children required for an elementary school, which would not only serve as an educational facility for children but also as a cultural center for adults. A high school—symbolically located at Radburn's highest point of elevation—was envisaged as the institution that would bind the entire community together. Just as the church provided the nexus for community activities in an eighteenth-century, colonial New England town, so was the school in twentieth-century Radburn designed as the focal point of neighborhood development. As another tool facilitating community interaction, the school provided the forum where residents could exchange their ideas and interests. To this end, the high school was to contain an auditorium, gymnasium, library, and perhaps even a small museum, opened to all citizens of the town.

"At Radburn, the neighborhood idea formed the basis of the town plan," as Stein later wrote in an unpublished manuscript.[29] The intent of those responsible for Radburn was to create a design that would meet the new complexities confronting twentieth-century America while providing a firm foundation for the social and economic amenities characteristic of a strong community. They realized that the town would have to contain a sizable population to fulfill these goals. But the neighborhood unit was viewed as the basic element upon which to build the community. It was hoped that Radburn's ultimate size and unique physical form would enable residents to exhibit the friendliness of a small village without succumbing to parochialism; and to enjoy the social diversity of an urban center without suffering from anonymity.

From the outset, Radburn was designed as a semi-autonomous town incorporating residential, recreational, commercial, and industrial facilities. As noted above, it was originally hoped that a sufficient number of industrial and commercial establishments would move to Radburn to provide employment opportunities for a sizable portion of the town's residents. The southern corner of the town, located along the Erie Railroad and at the edge of the proposed state highway, was designated a manufacturing district. Companies moving into this area would have to pay an assessment fee beyond conventional property taxes in order to defray the cost of municipal programs and services. Thus non-residential property use would not only advance the RPAA's and the CHC's town planning principles, but also strengthen the financial status of Radburn itself.

But despite vigorous efforts, a manufacturing district never materialized because industrialists saw Radburn as more of a risk than an opportunity. "We learned," Stein recalled long after construction in Radburn had ceased, "that industry lives in the present."[30] When the community opened in May 1929, the Erie Railroad was only a minor line not connected to any major trunk; the George Washington Bridge was still under construction and not scheduled for completion until 1931; and plans for Bergen County's state-financed highway (ultimately Route 4) were just being drafted. With inadequate transportation facilities, the CHC found it difficult to convince industry to move to Radburn. New Jersey Bell Telephone and the American Radiator Company were the only two corporations of any consequence to establish offices in the community. Even if the Depression had not struck just five months after the first residents arrived, it still would have been difficult under the circumstances to establish a strong industrial base for the community. Conceived as a relatively self-contained city, Radburn soon emerged as a "satellite town" that would depend on the nearby metropolitan area for most of its employment opportunities. The economic collapse of the 1930's destroyed even that limited vision. With 1,500 people (a figure that grew to 3,000 after World War II), Radburn became a small, residential section—one of a sprawling web of dormitory suburbs extending throughout Bergen County. The CHC recognized this situation as early as 1930, when it advertised that the 7:52 train could get a commuter to his New York office by nine o'clock.[31]

Radburn planners had also called for a matrix of commercial establishments to service the needs of the residents. A cluster of stores was planned for each neighborhood unit and a large regional shopping center was to be built on a tract of land along the proposed state highway. In line with the planners' approach to the construction of the entire community, a great deal of research and planning went into these commercial areas. The neighborhood shopping centers were designed to stand at the edges of the superblocks at least one within one-half mile of each home. Since all stores were connected to the pedestrian pathways, an adult or child could walk to any one of them without crossing a street. As in the residential environment, such focus on the safety factor did not render the designers oblivious to the automobile. Along with the Country Club District in Kansas City, Radburn had the first shopping center equipped with off-street customer parking, and was thus a precursor of the present day malls that have spilled across the American landscape since the 1950's. But within the context of the Radburn idea, the shopping center was to play a much different role than its descendents do in contemporary American society. It was to be built within the fabric of an overall plan for community development—not as an afterthought that simultaneously confirmed and fueled suburban sprawl. Connected to the pedestrian walkway while at the same time easily accessible for automobile drivers, the local stores in yet another way followed the example of the Radburn house. The retail facilities would "face the park; be within walking distance of each resident's home; provide space for the auto without permitting it to dominate the environment; and be safe for children." In short, the "scientific method of community store planning" would follow the basic principles of the Radburn idea.[32]

By not allowing the automobile to impair Radburn's physical and social fabric, the community's site planners minimized the automobile's impact without ignoring its significance. The landscaped parks at the heart of the superblocks would provide residents with a sense of spaciousness and proportion, and a fluid relationship between architecture and the natural terrain. "The green center" would create a serene stage that facilitated a communal spirit, while it protected an individual's privacy. These values were conveyed in the following panorama of Radburn's parkland, painted by Stein. A resident "may stroll quietly across the green. He passes children at play or on the way to school. He glimpses gay crowds around the swimming pool or walking there in bathing suits. He sees elderly folks talking in the sun or shaded by trees that have been there twenty years or more. It is a peaceful escape from the hazards of the motor age."[33]

But Radburn was not a "town for the motor age" only because it restrained the potential damage automobiles could inflict upon a community. There was another, more subtle reason. Radburn's designers proposed to utilize the techniques of industrial production, perfected in the manufacture of cars, and to apply them to real estate—or, more precisely, to community development. Thus scientific management, large scale production, and extensive research were all central to the implementation of the Radburn idea. These principles had been advocated by urban planners in the United States since the late nineteenth century, but rarely for the same purpose as they were in Radburn. Those who built "the town for the motor age," as we have seen, were not solely interested in rationalizing metropolitan growth so as to make it more efficient; nor were they simply concerned with cleaning up unsanitary conditions that had been the worst side effects of rampant urban development. Rather, they were charting the way for a new pattern of land use: for the development of a physical and social landscape that would focus on the family, and especially the child—not the real estate speculator—as the major concern. By curtailing speculation and thus creating stable communities, planners like Stein and Wright hoped to create an efficient method of community production that would promote both family and friendship.

It has often been pointed out that the architecture in Radburn was unfailingly conservative. Despite the experiments of the bauhaus in Germany and forays into prefabrication in both America and Europe during the 1920's, neocolonial motifs dominated the design of Radburn houses. Thus the "new city form" blueprinted for Radburn was not matched by innovative architecture. However, neocolonial architectural themes did not stand in contradiction to the revolutionary principles of the site plan. Indeed the architecture complemented the landscape. For in the final analysis, the untraditional physical form of Radburn was intended to promote and preserve traditional values of family, kinship, and community spirit. These values could undoubtedly be expressed through modern architecture; but perhaps they were more clearly conveyed by traditional designs.

RADBURN—like Sunnyside—provided practical experience, or field work, necessary to explore the RPAA's theories in practice. "The main point to remember is the experimentation of our group," Mumford has emphasized, "our willingness to make small mistakes instead of plunging into bigger ones."[34] This spirit of experimentation enabled Stein to reflect upon Radburn as "a splendid adventure: a voyage of discovery in search of a new and practical form of an urban environment to meet the actual requirements of today. This exploration opened up and charted the way—no matter how limited the settlement remains."[35]

Although Stein thus asserted that Radburn was "a revolution in town planning," he readily admitted that "none of the elements that make-up the Radburn idea was completely new."[36] The use of common interior parkland and cul-de-sacs in the English garden cities of Letchworth and Welwyn provided an immediate example for Radburn's site planners; indeed Stein and Wright visited those English communities on a "special investigation trip" before planning Radburn. And as Radburn's designers often pointed out, the Radburn plan was not dissimilar from the campus greens found at universities such as Oxford, Cambridge, and Harvard. In Central Park, built in Manhattan in the mid-1800's, the noted landscape architect Frederick Law Olmsted, Sr., also created an environment where people could enjoy the complete separation of pedestrian and vehicular traffic. Indeed the separation of pedestrian and vehicular traffic had been successfully accomplished in Venice, centuries before Henry Ford mass produced the automobile. Stein also went so far as to suggest that the Dutch had devised a modified superblock when they settled New Amsterdam at the tip of Manhattan during the sixteenth century. Recent American planning innovations were closely studied prior to the construction of Radburn. Houses oriented toward a parkland were used successfully at Sunnyside Gardens. In the 1920's, a functional U.S. highway system was in its initial stages of development: Westchester County in New York State had constructed a small network of limited access parkways, and New Jersey had designed cross-county thoroughfares, like railroad lines, to bypass towns and admit traffic only at certain locations.[37]

In Radburn, however, all of these concepts were synthesized and broadened into a new environmental design. The common interior space in an English garden city had been the size of a small courtyard and its primary purpose was to create a tranquil retreat for residents; in Radburn, the parkland was expanded in size and purpose into the backbone of the residential environment, not only protecting it from the automobile but also serving as the stage for a comprehensive social program. The specialized highway system constructed in the United States during the 1920's was rarely sophisticated enough to do more than distinguish parkways and expressways from ordinary city streets; in Radburn, the planners applied Benton MacKaye's notion of a "highwayless town" and "townless highway."[38] Instead of reinforcing the conventional methods of development, Radburn's intricate functional street system, designed in relationship to residential areas and open space, contained the potential framework for a new pattern of land use in America.

Thus Radburn struck a responsive chord among urban planners because it synthesized many of the concerns and ideas which the profession had expressed for the past two decades. "Radburn stands out," one planner observed, "because it is the first tangible product of a new urban science ... that seeks to make places of man's habitation and industry fit the healthy requirements of his daily life."[39] A similar reaction led Thomas Adams, perhaps the most noted urban planner in the United States during the 1920's and, as we have seen, the general director of the Regional Plan of New York, to praise Radburn as "the most forward step in town planning in America." The community, he said, "exemplifies ... an ideally planned place to live."[40]

Both the RPAA's commitment to regional development and its self-conscious experimental approach were basic to the evolution of the Radburn idea. Any study of the history of the community must consider those two aspects of it to understand its full dimensions. The Radburn design, with its superblock structure and its strict attention to the problems created by the automobile, marked a significant departure in the history of American urban planning. But the parkland, forming the core of the superblock, constituted only a part of what architectural historian Walter Creese has referred to as the "internal green," which itself is only one element of a comprehensive program for balanced regional growth. The Radburn idea, not only as a basis for a physical construct but also as part of a larger social and regional program, can only be understood through a study of garden city principles, or what Creese calls the "external green."[41]

Studying its distinctive site plan and strong sense of community, planners have long praised Radburn's technical achievements as ends in themselves. But for those who devised the "Radburn idea," the site plan was a means toward an end: it was in Mumford's words a "finger exercise preparing for the symphonies that are yet to come."[42] Radburn, lacking a regional pattern of development, was destined to turn into a conventional suburb with a distinctive site plan. Instead of providing an alternative to traditional suburban development, the community was consumed by the process of land use its planners sought to change. Translating the Radburn idea into a tangible community form even on a small scale was a difficult task, one that often would be hindered by the traditional values of the residents and the day-to-day concerns of Radburn's administrators.

Pioneering in Suburbia 8

Radburn's Early Years

I'm not too fond of what we did at . . . Radburn; but whatever it was, the important accomplishments were social rather than technical.—Henry Wright, Sr.[1]

To make participation in the activities the result of interest and desire alone, to give all members of the family equal opportunity to avail themselves of selective choice, to make such choice available from as widespread a field of activities as might be possible, and by reasonable family contribution, to provide for the organization and development of such activities as are of interest to its people are the aims of the community plan.—Robert Hudson, Radburn's first recreational director[2]

If you want to own a lot of spacious private property, then Radburn isn't the answer. But if you like a place which is at the same time busy and safe for children, where you don't have to spend all your time driving around, and where you have beautiful parks and great public amenities, then it's dandy.—George Sporn, long-time Radburn resident[3]

THE national publicity accompanying the construction of Radburn did not apparently affect the families who purchased homes or rented apartments in the community. The first residents may have realized—or, as one early homeowner aptly put it, had "an impression"—that Radburn was experimental in nature.[4] But for most of these families, Radburn represented neither a first step toward a solution to America's chronic housing problem nor a fundamental element in a dramatically new vision of regional development. Instead, it was valued as a new home in what promised to be an attractive community setting and an excellent place for affluent young couples to raise children. "Being out of the city was what appealed to us most when moving to Radburn," recalled long-time resident William Elbow in a statement echoing the sentiments of his contemporaries. "I don't think there was anything else that was a prime mover in our thinking. . . . My wife was pregnant and we wanted to start a family in that kind of environment rather than the city streets."[5] As Robert Hudson, the community's first recreational director, stated, "people do not come from distances away because of Radburn. Rather they come because they have business connections in the metropolitan area and need a desirable place to live, where they and their families can enjoy the amenities of life that are not found in all suburban communities."[6] Thus early residents were drawn to Radburn for the same reasons that suburbanites of the late 1920's moved into other burgeoning communities at the edge of the nation's large urban centers: Radburn promised a pleasant environment that all members of the family could enjoy.

Radburn homes also contained all the modern conveniences. Equipped with ash chutes, underground garbage containers, accessible coal bins, modern bathrooms, up-to-date kitchens, and spacious basements, the houses provided a degree of carefree maintenance unavailable in older homes. Conforming to the widespread American sentiment that "new is better," Radburn, in this respect, also expressed the prevailing belief in technology, a key cultural attitude in post–World War I society. The significance of Radburn's supplying these seemingly mundane items should not be underestimated. As vehicles for more leisurely lifestyles and symbols of a high social status, the conveniences constituted selling points that the CHC—vitally concerned with protecting its investment for both economic and social reasons—was not about to ignore.[7]

The CHC was also responding to the American homeowner's increasing awareness that houses were "more than places to sleep and eat." Thus Radburn not only provided domestic conveniences associated with a new, modern home, but also offered a wide range of community services that suburbanites were coming to expect from the neighborhoods in which their houses were set. As we have seen, the schools, shopping centers, and recreational facilities in Radburn were built within walking distance of each home, not in an incremental fashion but rather as part of a comprehensive plan. And the park, an increasingly important part of the environment in the emerging suburban landscape, was created as the centerpiece of the Radburn community. Appealing to the values of Radburn's prospective homeowners, the CHC rarely failed to emphasize the importance of parkland. "To be complete, and provide fully for family life and growth, a home must be more than four walls," the company reasoned in its advertising campaigns. "And no matter how attractive a house may be, it will fall short of present day requirements if its location does not offer recreation and play facilities for children and adults."[8]

In many ways, as the Introduction suggested, Radburn's designers hoped to democratize the social amenities found in the elite, wealthy country clubs and suburbs built during the 1920's. In the decade following World War I, the automobile first exerted a significant impact on the American landscape: car registrations rose dramatically from 8 million in 1920 to 23 million a decade later.[9] One of the many consequences of this was the proliferation of elegant country estates, expensive homes built for America's most renowned citizens and by the nation's most respected architects. Another consequence was the creation of country clubs, the popularity of which, especially in areas like Weschester County, just north of New York City, led the well-respected professional journal, the *Architectural Record*, to devote regular features to discussions of their style and influence. Situated amidst the natural beauty and splendor of the nation's wealthiest suburbs, the country clubs amalgamated a set of social institutions that had evolved from the lifestyles and physical land use patterns made possible by the automobile. The clubs linked the residents of expensive, but isolated, estates to a larger community setting composed of homogenous groups of corporate executives, political leaders, and well-paid professionals. Thus just as the country estates would have been inconceivable without the automobile that made long distance commuting possible, the social life generated by the clubs also depended upon cars and roadways.

And by generating a strong sense of community in the face of an increasingly privatized landscape, the country clubs were also confronting a problem that Radburn's planners believed to be central to twentieth-century community development. This concern is clearly conveyed in architect Michael Mikkelsen's portrait of the Riverdale Country Club, one of the numerous prestigious clubs located on the lower Hudson and frequented by the enormously wealthy families of Cleveland H. Dodge, George W. Perkins, and George B. Cortelyous. "The [club] building," Mikkelsen explained, "in addition to providing for recreation, was to serve as a community center, where something of the spirit and the functions of the early New England town meeting might be revived."[10] Thus the technical advances which made these institutions possible were more of an opportunity than a threat to Americans of power and wealth. The automobile in particular provided the framework for an environment that would balance the desire for privacy with the need for social interaction. With business firms located in the city and residential retreats in the countryside, private cars supplied the lifeline linking the pleasures of a rural environment with the business and social amenities of an urban center.

When architect A. Lawrence Kocher suggested that the country house in the 1920's could be thought of "as an urban residence set down in a rural park, and made accessible by convenient motor and electrical transportation," he was describing a landscape similar to the one envisioned by Radburn's site planners.[11] Open space, a commodity too expensive for most municipalities to purchase in large quantities, would be an important part of the Radburn plan. And the recreational and leisurely activities that could take place within a cheerful natural environment would be extended to American families who possessed neither the wealth nor status of the Rockefellers, Carnegies, or Mellons. But Radburn's planners sought to devise a landscape that would not consume the same amount of space as the business–country estate–country club axis. Indeed they hoped to create a rural-urban environment within one relatively self-contained community.

Moreover, instead of a tightly knit, elite social structure, Radburn's planners desired to build a town that would be a microcosm of the larger society, in terms both of age and income distribution. Yet, as we shall see shortly, its expensive homes, formal community setting, and highly organized social activities made Radburn a thoroughly upper middle class community. At bottom, it was the cost factors, rather than a cultural bias, that determined the nature of the Radburn community. Market conditions simply made houses in Radburn too expensive for the majority of Americans. "Who will live in the garden houses of Radburn?" asked Geddes Smith, one of the public relations officers for the CHC. "Clearly a house selling at $7,000 or a little less is beyond the lower paid silk workers of nearby Paterson. No miracle is promised here," he warned. "The wage earner at the bottom of the economic scale is still unprovided for. At such wage-levels industry must lift its workers before the town planner can do much for them. There is, however, no reason why a family with a total income of say $2,500 should not be able to make a 10 percent down payment on a Radburn house and carry the upkeep and an amortization."[12] But as prices escalated in the late 1920's, even this modest goal proved elusive.

Radburn thus never attained the elite social status of a Westchester country club, an outcome the planners wanted to avoid; but, to their dismay, its demographic composition did resemble that of other wealthy suburbs that took shape in northern New Jersey during the same period. Since the least expensive home in Radburn cost a minimum of $70 a month to maintain, a Radburn family's income had to be in excess of $4,000 a year—and for many homes at least $5,000 annually.[13] This excluded 90 percent of all urban families from Radburn's housing market.[14] Since the lowest priced houses ($7,900) cost substantially more than the cheapest houses (not including co-ops) in Sunnyside ($4,800), Radburn could not match the demographic variety attained in the CHC's first town planning experiment. Thus Radburn was not an enclave for senior corporate executives, like a country club, but it did become a town of upper middle class executives and professionals: engineers, salesmen, managers, bankers, lawyers, and architects made up its occupational profile. A survey in 1934 revealed that 71, or 19 percent, of 366 employed persons in Radburn (the sample constituting 75 percent of the entire working population) classified themselves as salespeople; another 32, or 9 percent, were self-employed businesspeople; 37, or 10 percent, called themselves junior executives; 32, or 9 percent, were office or store managers; and 49, or 13 percent, worked as bankers, accountants, insurance agents, or stock brokers. Thus 221 Radburnites, or 60 percent of the community's responding heads of households, had ties to business in at least mid-range executive positions. There were also 64 respondents, or 17 percent, who were employed as engineers and 40, or 11 percent, who were teachers. The remaining proportion of Radburn's working population had assorted occupations, ranging from architects to publishers. No one in the survey described himself or herself as a skilled or semi-skilled worker, and only 12 people, or 3 percent, categorized themselves as clerks. This narrow occupational spectrum gave Radburn a homogenous quality characteristic of affluent, upper middle class suburbs.[15]

The degree of success Radburn residents had acquired in their professions was to some some extent a function of their age. In the early 1930's, Radburn was a distinctly young community, a characteristic common to new towns and particularly to new suburban developments. The average age of male residents was a fraction over thirty-five and the median age of women was thirty-three. Advertised as a "town for children," Radburn's demographic statistics gave validity to this aspect of the CHC's sales campaign. Twenty-eight percent of Radburn's population in 1934 was between the ages of one and five.[16] It was yet another kind of homogeneity.

But the homogeneity of the community was most clearly revealed by the educational background of those who moved into Radburn. At a time when less than 6 percent of the American population received college degrees, a remarkable 87 percent of the men and 75 percent of the women in Radburn had attended college. The educational background of the residents was correlated with the types of high status occupations prevalent in the community, which helped to solidify the shared values enjoyed by the families. "The whole town reflects the college influence," wrote Robert Hudson, who as recreational director was also in charge of the town's educational programs during the 1930's. "In fact, Radburn often reminds one of a college campus or peoples' campus."[17] Indeed, in its social plan, Radburn became more of an experiment in continuing education for college educated adults and their families than one in alternative community patterns.

Added to all this was the fact that 77 percent of the population were Protestants. Thus, in all, Radburn's demography in the early 1930's emerged as something quite different than its planners had initially envisioned. Indeed Radburn assumed the one-dimensional quality of the conventional American suburb, a social landscape which its planners detested. With 70 percent of the community's employed population commuting to New York City each weekday morning, Radburn became a dormitory suburb similar to those sprouting across northern New Jersey's landscape during the 1920's.[18]

Since the residents rarely thought of themselves as participants in a model experiment designed to reshape the nation's conventional pattern of community development, they were usually pleased with Radburn. For most families, the community functioned well. It gave them the opportunity to express their personal values and interests in an harmonious social setting. For the town's administrators the question was not how to get families with different incomes and educational backgrounds to live together harmoniously, but rather how to build a dynamic environment that well-educated young families interested in culture and sports would find fulfilling.

In the early 1930's, Radburn was a beehive of activity. The inventory of facilities available to the 1,500 residents—impressive even by today's standards—included approximately twenty acres of parkland, two swimming pools, four tennis courts, four ball fields, three playgrounds, five basketball courts, an archery plaza, and two summer houses.[19] Youngsters from the ages of two to eighteen enjoyed an array of recreational activities organized by professional athletic directors. (In line with the CHC's emphasis on the value of trained experts, most of the recreational staff was hired from the National Recreation Association, the professional organization for recreational workers.) There were nursery schools, "tot lots" (small playgrounds), and a whole range of craft and sports activities. During the summer months, children enjoyed a well-organized and well-staffed day camp program. In winter, the after school hours were filled with activities ranging from ballet to basketball.

But in Radburn, community activities were not relegated to children. For adults, the community provided courses in psychology, music appreciation, current events, and American and English literature; seminars and workshops on nutrition and childhood development; an amateur theater group and a chorus; bridge tournaments; craft lessons; and a host of recreational sports programs. Even a conversational French study group existed during Radburn's early years, an example of a self-improvement course that reflects the extensive educational background common to Radburn residents. "Radburn offers more than merely comfortable homes," the CHC proclaimed as a major part of its advertising campaign. "It offers a new freedom for play and recreation to adults and children alike."[20] The company defined freedom in a way that struck a responsive chord among Radburn's prospective homeowners: it was presented and perceived as liberty to pursue recreational and cultural activities. In the jargon of contemporary sociology, the designers of Radburn had tailored an excellent "environmental fit" by creating a physical and social environment that catered to the values and interests of the community's residents. From the 1934 survey, it is clear that most Radburn residents actively participated in the offered programs. Of the 336 families who responded, only 11 or slightly more than 3 percent did not participate in any community activities, and only 10 percent of them confined their participation to recreational as opposed to cultural events.[21]

The recreational and cultural programs for the adults were conducted largely by the Citizen's Association, an organization formed two months after the arrival of the first residents. Created as an "open forum" to discuss "matters of common interest to the neighborhood," the Citizen's Association had eighteen subcommittees, most of which were primarily concerned with social activities.[22] "We tried not to be paternalistic," explained the first town manager, John O. Walker, in defense of the highly structured community plan. "The citizens were left to pursue activities that were of interest to them." Nevertheless, Walker admitted that the Citizen's Association did try to harness and organize the "spontaneous demand" expressed for recreational and cultural programs.[23] To facilitate community interaction, each new household was given a list of activities: its members were asked to place one check next to the activities in which they had some interest and two checks next to those in which they had particular skill. Largely on the basis of this questionnaire, one particularly significant because it epitomized a kind of community engineering based on extensive data collection and analysis, the community arranged its wide spectrum of activities. The amount and kind of attention given to details of the social programs thus corresponded to that which had been given to details of the physical environment. A rational, systematic approach to both physical and social planning—more than the long list of activities offered to Radburn residents—distinguished the community from other affluent suburbs developed in the late 1920's and early 1930's. Charles Ascher was right: in Radburn "everything was planned."[24]

"We tried to get people who fit together," John O. Walker recently stated in reminiscing about Radburn's early days: similarities in backgrounds and interests were promoted in order to protect the community's solidarity.[25] Ironically, the homogeneity the formulators of the Radburn idea wanted to avoid was perceived as a common good by the town's administrators, and so—like so many other Radburn ideals—the social ideals upon which the community was to be founded were not applied to the landscape. The community's Protestant cast has been mentioned. Although Radburn followed no explicit policy of discrimination against Jews, in the first years of the town's existence only two Radburn families were Jewish, and one of these families, of a mixed religious heritage, practiced both Judaism and Catholicism. To create what they saw as a congenial environment, realtors hired by the CHC discouraged Jews—as well as blacks—from moving into Radburn, a policy which met with approval or indifference from the town's financiers, administrators, and residents alike. Shared values and experience, not economic and ethnic diversity, were considered important attributes for a smoothly functioning, attractive community.[26]

THROUGH the Citizen's Association, Radburnites had direct involvement in determining the types of activities to be incorporated as part of their recreational and cultural program. But they did not enjoy the same level of participation in the political structure of Radburn, where crucial financial decisions were made. To conduct the community's political affairs, including devising a budget, the Radburn Association (RA) was formed by the CHC in April 1929, one month before the first residents moved into the community. Described as a "private" or an "extra-municipal government," the RA was a "non-profit, non-stock" corporation designed to service the needs of the residents and to oversee the parkland deeded to it in trust by the CHC.[27] Specifically, the Declaration of Restrictions enabled the RA "to fix, collect and disburse the annual charges" levied against the property; to "maintain the necessary community services, parks and recreation facilities"; and to protect Radburn's architectural integrity from "thoughtless or inconsiderate purchasers" who could "destroy the harmony or spoil the plan by building structures inappropriate in design or location." As a political institution, the RA was given broad powers "to administer, interpret and apply the restrictions." In short, it was charged with the responsibility to determine community policy, which it did largely through the disbursement of funds that remained "wholly" under its "absolute discretion."[28]

Those revenues were to be derived from an assessment fee based upon the property tax. According to the land use covenants, the fee was not to exceed 50 percent of the total borough tax, which residents were also obliged to pay. The basic scheme devised for the Radburn Association was not new to public administration in the United States: the concept had been utilized in planned communities well known within the profession—places such as Roland Park, Maryland; Palos Verdes, California; and Forest Hills, New York. But each of these communities had established a set fee. After studying how the scope of activities in Forest Hills had been seriously hampered by the inflationary spiral of the post–World War I period, Radburn's planners decided to make the assessment a percentage of the property tax so that the RA's revenues could fluctuate with changing economic conditions.[29]

"The [Radburn] Association has been organized on the model of the best modern practice in municipal government," each resident was told in a summary of Radburn's protective restrictions. Quite simply, this meant that the RA's structure parallelled the progressive era's council-manager political structure. The organization consisted of a president and nine trustees, corresponding to a mayor and council, whose policies were to be administered by an appointed manager, corresponding to a city manager, chosen by the board "solely on the basis of his executive and administrative qualifications." The by-laws explicitly stated that neither the manager nor any trustee "need . . . be an owner of the property."[30]

In place of the council-manager system of elected representatives, the Radburn board of trustees "included public spirited citizens of New Jersey experienced in municipal and community affairs and officers of the CHC familiar with the plans for the development of Radburn."[31] Among those selected by the CHC for the RA were Mrs. Henrietta Hawes, a northern New Jersey resident and a leader in women's civic groups throughout the state; Bertram Saunders, a respected planning official from Paterson who became the Association's first president; Dr. John Carlisle, active in reform movements in northern New Jersey; and Spaulding Frazer, a Newark attorney who had served in Mayor Thomas L. Raymond's progressive administration. The company also placed a number of its own executives and consultants on the roster: in addition to Bing, the corporation's president, the board contained the CHC's legal consultant, Charles Ascher, and its vice-president and general manager, Herbert Emmerich. Louis Brownlow, a recognized international expert in the field of public administration and a CHC consultant, was selected as the first vice-president of the Association. Of the initial nine board members, only Brownlow lived in Radburn and he came to the community not simply as a resident but rather to assume his duties as a salaried company consultant. John O. Walker, who had worked with Brownlow in Knoxville, Tennessee, was made the first town manager of Radburn, where he lived and worked during the community's initial eight years of development.[32]

The purpose of the administrative plan was obvious: to protect the financial investment and community plan that the CHC had devised not only for the benefit of its stockholders but for Radburn's residents as well. The company's approach to political affairs was consistent with its overall approach to community development. Whether the CHC was analyzing the development of the physical site plan, architecture, or recreational program the use of experts, experienced at their work and conversant with the most efficient techniques available, was deemed essential if the best plans were to be drafted and implemented. Afraid that the resident farmers of Fair Lawn neither appreciated nor understood the Radburn experiment, Bing and other CHC executives refused to depend on the established municipality to enact the company's plans. To place the plan for America's first garden city community in such inexperienced hands—leaving possible hostility quite aside—would jeopardize the success of the project. At the same time, the company was distrustful of Radburn residents who, it believed, had insufficient expertise in political administration. The CHC did not isolate itself from the public. For example, both the company and the RA board of trustees welcomed citizen reaction to the budget, and the annual December public meeting to discuss budgetary matters was usually well attended, two to three hundred residents often turning out. But the company carefully protected its right to render independent political and economic decisions concerning life in Radburn: although they could express their opinions, citizens exercised no formal authority in drafting the final budget, Radburn's financial matters remaining the unchallenged province of the Radburn Association.

The CHC did not conceal Radburn's political structure from either prospective homeowners or investors. Indeed the executives expressed their pride in what they considered to be a progressive approach. Charles Ascher, the architect of Radburn's political plan, echoing the themes of the progressive era, declared that the residents would be "assured of a disinterested, impartial and experienced management during the development years."[33] And in a similar vein, the City Housing Corporation explained in its advertising brochures that "the company owes its beginning to a group of men and women who sensed the civic and social need for a scientific attack on the problem of providing better communities and houses for the average family."[34] Radburn's developers were not motivated by a desire to protect themselves from Radburn grass roots power, or from some Fair Lawn version of the corruption often characteristic of local politics in America. Just as Radburn's political structure expressed the corporate, liberal belief in a scientific, rational

Garden Cities for America   180

approach, so its ultimate intent expressed the social liberal's belief in education. Progressive reformers like Bing were convinced that political education must precede power—in Radburn's case, not only to protect the CHC's investment but also to assure that, as Ascher had promised, the community would operate smoothly during the critical stages of its initial period of growth. As some critics have charged, this was a form of paternalism. But it was a benevolent paternalism consistent with the CHC's approach to Radburn as an educational experiment—one not only teaching valuable lessons to investors and developers but to the development's residents as well. Indeed, looking through the eyes of the Radburn Association's trustees, the community resembled a Hull House for the professional middle class. Just as Jane Addams had provided an environment to socialize the immigrants and to teach them what to expect when they went out on their own, the Radburn Association was formulated in part as an institution that would gradually introduce the residents to the problems of community administration.

But although the CHC hoped the residents would eventually assume political control over the Radburn Association, the company set forth neither a timetable nor a procedure for the accomplishment of that transformation. The first special meeting to discuss the problem of citizen representation was held in June 1930. Not until a decade later, however, would residents attain majority control on the board of trustees, and not until 1948, more than ten years after the CHC went bankrupt, would the board consist entirely of Radburn residents.[35] Even as the residents gradually gained political control, the board insured its own continuity and stability by selecting the nominees to replace members who left and by choosing officers from its own ranks. The organization's by-laws, enacted before the first residents arrived, could not be altered without extraordinary difficulty for twenty-year periods. Changes had to be submitted five years before the twenty-year expiration date and approved by 50 percent of the residents. Amendments could be nullified if anyone owning more than 20 percent of the property—namely, the CHC—protested in writing without then being overruled by seven of the nine trustees and 50 percent of the residents. On the other hand, a policy decision rendered by the board could only be defeated through a referendum supported by at least one-half of the residents. Thus the broad powers and insularity of the board made Radburn something less than the participatory democracy which in earlier chapters we saw its architects and planners envision. In Radburn, direct representation always took a back seat to efficient, centralized decision-making.[36]

"We recognized the self-perpetuating quality of the board," one early resident of Radburn recently remarked, "and we accepted it."[37] This sentiment was reiterated by the majority of Radburn's early homeowners. Both the residents and developers identified with the ideas of rationality, efficiency, and systematization associated with the progressive era of the early twentieth century. It doubtless helped that, since Radburn was never incorporated as an independent municipality, residents of the community were also citizens of the borough of Fair Lawn, New Jersey, where they were obligated to pay taxes and had the right to vote and to hold office. Thus the Radburn Association's assumption of responsibilities as a management corporation did not completely prevent the residents from having local political affiliations, and a substantial number of Radburnites became active in Fair Lawn politics. Moreover, despite the limitations placed upon participation in the RA, Radburn provided several forums where residents' suggestions and complaints could be heard. Throughout the year, the president of the Citizen's Association, who was elected by the residents, served as an ex-officio member of the RA board. Although not entitled to vote, he could voice residents' complaints directly to board members. And, finally, Radburn in the early 1930's was a small, homogenous community consisting of fewer than 500 families. Although he was not required to do so, Manager Walker resided in Radburn and was in constant communication with the residents, welcoming new families, keeping them informed of community programs, listening to their complaints and responding to their suggestions. In administering the policies of the board of trustees, Walker, as an appointed executive, may have been protected from the wrath of an irate citizen's vote, but he was undoubtedly sensitive to a neighbor's scorn.

Thus the administrative success of Radburn in terms of the residents' satisfaction with the political process did not necessarily turn on the principles of efficiency and rationalization which the RA expressed and which the community indeed respected. Rather, the face-to-face contact between Walker and the residents may have been a good deal more than partially responsible for the harmonious relationship that existed between the board and those who lived in the community. How population growth would have influenced attitudes toward the Radburn Association is difficult to gauge, but undoubtedly it would have placed additional strains on Radburn's political structure, which in principle and practice emphasized efficiency at the expense of democratic participation. If Radburn had grown to a town of 25,000, Walker would have been unable to provide the informal, personalized service which helped to compensate for the limited formal access residents had to the political process.

Resident satisfaction was also fostered in that the trustees and manager realized that the Association's regulations must be administered within a flexible framework of common sense. Ascher warned that it was important not to make the restrictions appear to be too ironclad, because such a rigorous policy would frighten prospective buyers and lead to dissension within the community. Thus although the Radburn Association had the right to sue for a violation committed against its by-laws, only one lawsuit was filed in the first twenty years of Radburn's history, the case involving a resident who had built an obtrusive addition to his house without the permission of the RA's architectural committee. There were fourteen months of litigation. The trustees first hesitated to act and then seized on an offer from the defendant that affirmed the principle of control but, in fact, begrudgingly accepted the undesired addition. The incident led Ascher to admit that testing a private sanction is "slow, expensive and uncertain," and that harmony in Radburn had been maintained "more by explanation, mediation, and adjustment of differences than by police action."[38] Once again personal interaction—in this case, more than legal precedent—was the source of the community's success.

Beyond the legal and financial difficulties it posed, the CHC feared that direct community control on the residential level might be oppressive. For the majority of families in Radburn, as in most suburban communities, the protection of property values and the maintenance of their homes were primary concerns. Access to the larger political process and democratic tolerance are interests which may have been overshadowed by the basic, traditional desire to protect and promote the attractiveness of the private domain. In Sunnyside, the company had discovered that the resident-controlled block associations overseeing external changes in the environment were for such reasons much stricter than the company had intended: residents who failed to keep their gardens up to community standards were reprimanded by representatives from the block association for very minor infractions and mistakes, and local control often became an excuse for an annoying interference with a person's privacy. The CHC wanted to establish a citizen's forum in Radburn, but without reprovoking the minor, but irritating, incidents which flared periodically in Sunnyside.[39]

To avoid the problems found in Sunnyside's small block associations, which contained several hundred people, the Citizen's Association in Radburn was designed to represent up to 10,000 people. That would introduce greater diversity into the citizen's group and alleviate some of the pressures that had accompanied the small, highly personalized structure existing in Sunnyside. In fact, Radburn's Citizen's Association did not engage in the kind of rigorous policing characteristic of some of Sunnyside's block associations, although the value and liabilities of a very large citizen's group were never fully explored in Radburn because the community has never grown beyond 3,000 residents. Another thing, however, is clear: although the Citizen's Association had the potential to mobilize the political concerns of the community, it never did. Its authorized powers were restricted, and most of its energy was devoted to the creation of committees that planned and directed the residents' leisurely pursuits. Expanding the democratic base among middle class homeowners determined to protect their land values and the status of their community would not necessarily have the same effect as expanding worker participation in the management of industry. In Radburn, there are indications that the trustees of the Radburn Association were more willing to pursue community-oriented policies than the residents would have been if placed in positions of power. Originally, for example, the Radburn assessment fee was designed to supplement municipal services and beyond that to provide programs which the local government of Fair Lawn could not or would not provide: residents enjoyed additional police protection, a private library, street lighting, and other social amenities unavailable to the citizens of the borough of Fair Lawn. The Radburn Association, however, hoped that as the borough further suburbanized, such responsibilities would be assumed by the municipality, thus releasing Radburn funds for what they considered to be more progressive programs—programs which reveal the breadth of their social vision.[40] For example, they ultimately envisioned the creation of a community health organization to be financed from the assessment fee. In addition, John Walker spoke about establishing an institute for adult education within the town, to be built up around a group of resident professors and scholars from throughout the New York metropolitan area. In many ways, early Radburn residents expected less from the CHC and the Radburn Association than those organizations were willing to give them. The town's administrators and financiers were neither dismayed nor apprehensive about the Radburn Association's financial condition, compared to its ambitious plans, until the full strength of the Depression was upon them. Indeed at one point when finances were strained, Walker recommended borrowing money. In his estimation, "it was fair to charge against later residents the excess cost of organizing the [Radburn] Association's many activities at this early date when the [size of the] community did not necessarily warrant such undertakings."[41]

But the residents had less romantic visions. For the majority of them, the business of the community was to create and maintain the active, carefree lifestyle of a country club—a refuge from the tensions of the business world, a place where cultural and competitive activity could take place on a friendly basis among others who enjoyed similar values and interests—not to promote communal experiments in health and education.

While the Radburn Association dreamed of unique health and educational programs in the future, the homeowners expressed concern for the cost of existing facilities. The assessment fee for an average Radburn family in the early thirties was about $2.16 for each $100 of assessed valuation, or $22 a year.[42] For that family, the fee represented a tax, one that translated into a wealth of appreciated and valued services, but a tax which was nevertheless a burden most were determined to keep light. Even during prosperous times, Radburn was never able to cover its expenses from the revenues derived from the assessment fees. During the first five years of its existence, the community received a combined subvention of over $30,000 from the CHC and the Carnegie Foundation. In characteristic fashion, the CHC's motivation was both philanthropic and entrepreneurial. The board of directors, led by Bing, was determined to provide facilities and programs that the company had promised in its advertisements; in fulfilling this pledge, it hoped to improve the quality of life found in the conventional American suburb. By contributing these grants the CHC made the community a more attractive place to live, while at the same time providing a concrete demonstration of the benefits to be derived from a comprehensive social and physical plan: thus both Radburn houses and the Radburn idea would be easier to sell, and perhaps, if successful, Radburn would serve as a model for subsequent development. As for the Carnegie Foundation, it was interested in exploring, as well as promoting, educational programs for young adults who were no longer affiliated with any college, and Radburn with its college educated population provided an excellent laboratory for that type of investigation. But the CHC and Carnegie Foundation grants did not free the Radburn Association from debt. Each year the community discovered its expenditures exceeded revenues by at least $4,000.[43] Executives of the CHC realized that the Radburn Association would have to deal with certain administrative costs regardless of the inefficiently small size of the Radburn population, and that if the town's characteristic activities were to be sustained, in the future, the residents would have to assume their full expense. Without a self-supporting financial structure, Radburn's social programs eventually would be dismantled.

None of the visionary programs ever moved beyond the initial stages of discussion. For one thing, financing a community-wide health insurance program or the offering of a comprehensive curriculum for educated adults depended on a large population. By 1933, the Depression had aborted the growth of Radburn. Only 462 families resided in the community during the mid-1930's. Radburn's growth then was stymied at 1,500 people until after World War II. Thus it never had a sufficient population to support programs of the magnitude envisioned by the town's planners. And, in the dark days of the Depression, neither the residents nor the administrators could justify the cost of such programs when, like other towns throughout America, Radburn could barely find the capital to keep vital services in operation.

THE early residents of Radburn, like many of the first families who move into a new community, would affectionately refer to themselves as pioneers. But they were not nineteenth-century pioneers seeking homesteads in the wilderness. Radburnites were part of an emerging breed of twentieth-century upper middle class professionals moving into suburban homes within the shadow of the nation's metropolitan centers. These people shared similar goals: a lifestyle emphasizing recreational and leisurely pursuits; a community providing a stimulating, yet safe, environment for children; a home containing all the modern conveniences that would prove to be a wise investment. These considerations outweighed concerns over the non-representative nature of Radburn's political structure; and, as long as those responsible for managing Radburn's affairs fulfilled such requirements, Radburnites expressed satisfaction with their community. Social and political elements of the Radburn idea, such as the desirability of a heterogeneous population, were antithetical to both the administrators' and the residents' definition of the good life. Instead of as an experiment leading to a new social order, Radburn's resident pioneers cherished their community as the realization of the American dream and, more specifically, as a suburban community tailored to the needs of affluent, young professionals with children.

The way Radburn was "lived in" did not completely contradict the planners' ideals, but it was only a partial fulfillment of their vision. "Perhaps the real importance of Radburn," an historian has recently written, "rests in its ability to become the synthesis of the obvious and the desirable."[44] But what the planners defined as desirable was not necessarily desirable to the residents. More importantly, the planners and managers of Radburn were caught in a vortex of contradictory impulses of their own—the desire to create a participatory democratic community with the need to protect their investment in an experimental real estate venture; the vision of heterogeneous neighborhoods with the knowledge that homogeneity is often a prerequisite for community interaction; plans for extensive social programs with an awareness of increasingly restrictive financial conditions. The transformation of the original physical and social plan during Radburn's early years of development reveals a great deal about the nature of "community" in America, and shows planners trapped by conventional forces and values—even as they sought to change them.

A Bankrupt Vision 9
Radburn, Sunnyside, and the Depression

The depression has created a very difficult situation for many Sunnyside residents and for the City Housing Corporation. It has been a hard time for both. We believe that we have recognized our social obligation in our treatment of home owners in distress to the very utmost of the financial ability of the company.—Alexander Bing[1]

God protect us from philanthropists—against commercial swindlers we can protect ourselves.—B. Ginzburg, resident of Sunnyside[2]

Perhaps one difficulty is that limited dividend housing is neither fish, flesh, nor fowl—it's not straight public housing, nor is it cooperative housing nor commercial housing.—Loula Lasker[3]

THE City Housing Corporation entered the Radburn project a well-heeled company, and its prospects in light of its previous success at Sunnyside appeared even brighter. By 1928, Sunnyside had provided the CHC with a substantial capital pool, national recognition, and a large base of supporters—including John D. Rockefeller, who loaned the corporation $5 million. When ground breaking ceremonies took place at Radburn, the CHC enjoyed assets of $4 million and had been permitted to capitalize stocks at an additional $3 million. With these substantial resources, Bing and other company executives were confident that Radburn would be as successful as Sunnyside.[4]

The initial momentum generated by the opening of Radburn carried it through the first years of the Depression. Since the steep economic slide had not yet reached affluent upper middle class families, the community did not show any effects of the stock market crash during the winter of 1929–1930. In response to brisk sales and in an attempt to keep carrying costs at a minimum, the CHC was building quickly. Before the end of 1929, 170 single-family homes, 10 two-family homes, and a group of garden apartments containing 92 units had all been constructed.[5] On the first anniversary of Radburn's opening, the town contained 202 families and housed 587 people. The rapid growth prompted the *New York Times* to editorialize that "if Radburn hasn't already received the Census Bureau's prize for the fastest growing community, it ought to be awarded without further delay."[6] Radburn's distinctive character not only as an experimental "town for the motor age" but also as an affluent dormitory suburb was rapidly emerging. Officials of the Erie Railroad, which connected northern New Jersey to Manhattan, added two more trains to the Radburn line—for a total of seven—in order to service the large percentage of commuters who lived in this small town and worked in New York City.[7]

In July 1930, the CHC laid plans for the construction of 115 new dwellings. Sales during the previous month had bolstered the company's confidence. In June 1930, more homes had been sold in Radburn than in any single month during the previous year. The rapid sales led *Business Week* to conclude that Radburn was immune from the Depression since the dismal state of the economy had "had practically no effect upon" the community's growth.[8] To most observers, Radburn's success was testimony to the town's intelligent site plan and the progressive financial scheme devised by the CHC. Cul-de-sacs, interior parkland, and pedestrian walkways had made Radburn "automobile-proof"; and the limited dividend concept, which placed a 6 percent lid on the return for its stocks and bonds, seemingly rendered the community "depression-proof."

But the praise was premature. Indeed if accountants had scanned the CHC's financial records, they would have come to a different, far less optimistic, conclusion. The last time dividends had been paid from the company's earnings was 1929. Even though sales remained brisk at Radburn in 1930, dividends were paid out of the surplus accumulated in previous years. The depletion of funds was so swift that the company experienced its first deficit in 1931, and it never again turned a profit. As the Depression deepened, its devastating effects eventually reached into the pocketbooks of upper middle class American families and thus depleted the town's pool of potential buyers. In 1931, only sixteen units were built, despite the opening of the Hudson River (George Washington) Bridge linking Manhattan to northern New Jersey. In 1932, only eleven more units were added, and in the next year just ten houses were built, as the CHC struggled unsuccessfully against the precipitous economic decline. By 1933, all construction had ceased.[9]

As the Depression worsened, the CHC found itself in an

untenable position in Radburn—and in Sunnyside as well. The financial scheme that received so much praise in the late 1920's proved to be an unexpected trap once the full force of the stock market crash had been felt throughout the nation. More than other more conventional developers, the CHC depended on continuous expansion to assure its success; and retrenchment for it meant not only the loss of contracts for housing construction but also the shattering of a vision of comprehensive community development. As explained in Chapter 4, a good portion of the capital for the construction of Sunnyside and Radburn was derived from the sales of stocks and bonds—all pegged to a maximum 6 percent return on investment. The bonds were secured through mortgages held by homeowners and issued or guaranteed by the CHC, which co-signed the contracts. Since these mortgages served as the collateral for the stocks and bonds, a family's failure to pay not only made the CHC liable for payment but also jeopardized the company's primary means of capitalization. Thus the company was balanced on the point of a potentially unstable economic pyramid. The continual payment of the mortgages was not only necessary to generate working capital that had been advanced to the homeowners, but was also required to retain the confidence of its stock and bond holders.

During the "prosperity decade" of the 1920's, the company broadened its economic base by appealing to potential homeowners and philanthropic investors alike. John D. Rockefeller's $5 million loan (which he vaguely hinted might turn out to be a subvention) was one philanthropist's charitable gesture. When the CHC guaranteed first mortgages, large financial institutions—such as Equitable Life Assurance and the Irving Trust—began to provide substantial amounts of mortgage money to prospective homeowners in both Sunnyside and Radburn. But when the CHC pyramid collapsed in the early 1930's, investors demanded their money just at a time when families no longer possessed the financial resources to pay either their first or second mortgage payments. In 1934, caught between hard-pressed homeowners and its investors, the company declared bankruptcy and requested relief in the federal courts under title

77B of the federal bankruptcy law, newly created by the Roosevelt administration to deal with the epidemic of business failures sweeping across the nation.

The CHC sought to build stable communities. In the absence of dramatic political change, any attempt to achieve that goal required continual economic expansion: thus success could only be attained in an environment conducive to speculative development. During an era, like the 1920's, of continual economic growth and inflated land values, an adequate capital fund could be sustained for a moderately successful town planning movement based on CHC principles. During a period of economic turmoil, it would be impossible for such a company to wait out the financial storms. In later years, Bing would attribute the company's failure to the fact it had "gone too quickly and spread (itself) too thin."[10] Given the CHC's need for large pools of capital and the company's desire to build a series of complete communities, it is difficult to conceive what alternative paths to social reform might have been taken. Indeed the CHC was more closely wedded to the larger economic system than even the conservative but socially minded Bing would have chosen to believe. Instead of an independent alternative to traditional patterns of development, his financial program appears really to have been made possible by capital derived from inflated land values and expanding profits—its successes thus a by-product of speculative development.

The Depression soon unravelled the cordial relationship existing between the Sunnyside and Radburn residents and the CHC. Bing and the board of trustees had viewed potential residents more as clients in a social welfare agency than as consumers purchasing homes from a real estate agent. The company donated parkland to the community that could have been used for additional development; it granted substantial sums of money to generate extensive social activities; and besides co-signing first and second mortgages, Bing established private loans for families who wanted to purchase homes at Sunnyside or Radburn but were unable to obtain adequate mortgages from conventional lending institutions. Indeed, in the early years, the CHC tried to instill a sense of community beyond the expectations of most residents: company officials, not homeowners, promoted innovative community programs.¹¹

By 1933, however, the CHC was rapidly retreating from its commitment to social experimentation. As revenues declined, it sought to cut expenditures as a means of remaining solvent. But its residents, facing personal financial ruin, just at that point began to demand more assistance from the company. And, ironically, the CHC had unwittingly built the framework for a bitter confrontation between itself and its residents by creating and supporting a number of forums where a protest movement could be mounted. It had provided the tools that allowed residents of Sunnyside and Radburn to speak out against the Depression more effectively than other citizens who lived in conventional neighborhoods and communities suffering from the same financial strain. But the nature of the protest in each community was largely a result of its demographic composition. The way the tools were used did not depend upon the physical and social plan that had been forged but was rather a function of the type of individuals each community had attracted.

THE Depression sent out its first shock waves in October 1929, but its impact was not felt in Sunnyside until 1932. For those three years, the stock market crash and the nation's ensuing economic problems amounted mostly to a topic of conversation for most Sunnyside residents. Indeed homes could still be sold for a substantial profit, and the majority of residents believed that they were building up valuable equity through their mortgage payments. But by 1933, the situation suddenly changed. Most Sunnyside residents discovered they could no longer avoid the dislocations that had severely damaged the foundations of the rest of society. The average family income in Sunnyside fell precipitously from $350 per month in 1928 to $174 per month in 1933. Over 10 percent of the families reported they had no income at all and just under 30 percent claimed they were earning less than $100 per month.¹² With personal savings declining rapidly, nearly one-half of the homeowners in Sunnyside were in legal jeopardy of losing their homes. Foreclosures became epidemic as families, who were convinced in the late

A Bankrupt Vision   195

1920's that economic security and advancement would continue indefinitely, faced personal financial ruin. As one observer stated, "with respect to moderate finance charges, low carrying costs and security of possession, the plan controlling Sunnyside Gardens goes far beyond ordinary real estate practices; yet it, too, has proven inadequate in the face of the depression."[13]

Although the same desperate events were unfolding throughout the United States during the mid-1930's, Sunnyside was one of the few places where the situation was not accepted passively. In response to the foreclosures and threats of evictions, the Sunnyside Home Owners Committee was formed. The social interaction the CHC had fostered had generated a type of community spirit the company never anticipated. Out of a total of 564 homeowners, over 300 belonged to the committee, and they eventually set their sights on the CHC: the meeting halls previously used for nursery schools, garden clubs, and play rehearsals became the forums for protest rallies against the CHC and the lending institutions, now cast in the role of villains who had duped unsuspecting homeowners for the financial gain of their directors. ("Sunnyside," one angry citizen wrote, "was glorified speculation, which charged all the traffic would bear and ploughed profits into Radburn until the bubble burst.")[14]

"The Sunnyside folks had no stronger case than the hundreds of thousands of little 'homeowners' throughout Queens," observed Stein. "But they were organized: they were a community that had experience in working together through its association which was started and developed by the company that the citizens finally fought."[15] Or, as another sympathetic observer put it, "by a turn of fate, under stress of hard times, the community spirit thus fostered became the seed for the owners' organization once the strike was on. The common greens and meeting places were put to collective and then to to rebellious use."[16]

When financial problems among Sunnyside residents first became apparent in 1932, the CHC responded by making special arrangements with individual homeowner. It reduced rental fees; it cut the prices of homes and waived mortgage payments—not as a general policy, but rather in response to the specific needs and problems of each resident. To alleviate the personal financial burden faced by many residents, the company advanced interest payments on first mortgages which it had previously co-signed: the CHC spent over $45,000 for this purpose, assisting more than 200 families.[17] It also reduced the principle and rate of interest on the second mortgages. Finally, Bing urged bondholders to waive interest payments until the Depression subsided. Seventy-five percent of the investors consented to this request. But the dysfunctions in the economy were systemic and could not be solved on an individual basis. Thus the antidotes administered by the CHC could not begin to check the rampant economic ills inflicting the nation. Moreover, these humanitarian gestures further jeopardized the weakened financial condition of the CHC. By 1933, it was over one-half million dollars in debt; by 1934, as has been noted above, it was bankrupt.[18]

Facing their own financial ruin, Sunnyside residents displayed little sympathy for the plight of the CHC. In 1933, the Sunnyside Home Owners Committee requested "blanket relief" for its members, asking for a temporary moratorium on amortization payments and a permanent reduction in interest rates and principle. It argued that property values had declined so dramatically over the past four years that the price Sunnyside residents were paying for their homes was no longer indicative of current market values. Thus permanent adjustments had to be made. To deal with this situation on an individual basis, as the CHC was attempting to do, side-stepped the overwhelming dimensions of the problem, they argued, and failed to provide adequate relief to the majority of residents who desperately needed it.

Bing's response to the committee's requests revealed the tenuous position of the CHC. Since the company had guaranteed many of the first mortgages, it could not agree to a moratorium on mortgage payments or a reduction in principle and interest rates without the consent of the lending institutions that had issued the contracts, and therefore controlled their terms. As the banks and insurance companies scrambled to preserve their diminishing capital reserves, they were not about to free a group of residents from their financial obligations. Moreover, second mortgages had been granted to secure a bond issue. To forego payments on this obligation would have jeopardized the CHC's ability to fulfill its legal responsibility to its investors. As the company tumbled into bankruptcy, it had no choice but to urge residents to continue monthly payments according to the terms of the contracts signed during the prosperity of the late 1920's. "Otherwise," as one observer maintained, "they were doomed to foreclosure and the community into which the company and residents had put so much hope and effort would be disrupted."[19] As the Depression deepened, Bing tried to summon the cooperative spirit that was a crucial part of the company's formula for success before the stock market crash. As a pointman in this semi-philanthropic financial scheme, he was the beneficiary of a great deal of praise in the late 1920's; now in the depression decade of the 1930's, he became the object of scorn and distrust. The corporation he had established to "build better homes and communities for people of moderate incomes" was ridiculed as just another slick, speculative real estate company out for a fast buck.[20]

Instead of heeding the advice of the CHC, residents of Sunnyside became more militant. The committee, gaining additional support from the homeowners, continued to demand a comprehensive solution to the problem. It asked that the original 6 percent interest rate for mortgages be cut in half; for a moratorium on foreclosures; for a cancellation of all unpaid fees; and for a 95 percent cut on the face value of second mortgages to reflect the precipitous decline in land values.[21] These demands threatened the investment made by the CHC's stockholders, who were also suffering from the effects of the Depression, and who were no longer enjoying the luxury of engaging in semi-philanthropic ventures. In the face of declining profits, the banks and insurance companies issuing the mortgages refused to reduce interest rates or place a moratorium on any payments; and the stockholders, including benevolent institutions such as the Russell Sage and Hofheimer Foundations, formed their own committee—to protect their investments in Bing's troubled company. Thus squeezed between the urgent demands of the homeowners and the creditors, the CHC could offer little comfort to either. Bing's limited dividend corporation was being victimized by its own creation.

As the situation deteriorated, the hard-pressed homeowners—to the company's dismay—heightened the confrontation yet further. In February 1935, members of the Sunnyside Home Owners Committee went on strike: over one-half of all families in the community stopped paying their monthly mortgage fees.[22] Throughout 1935, accusations were continuously hurled as the residents picketed the offices of the CHC and refused to make any payments until their grievances were redressed. Sunnyside families petitioned Governor Herbert H. Lehman of New York and President Roosevelt to investigate the "extortionate rate of interest charged by powerful institutions." They accused the CHC and Equitable Life Assurance (which held almost half of the first mortgages in Sunnyside) of harassing strike leaders by leaning on them, for payment, with more zeal than on other less politically active families who were also delinquent. As a symbolic gesture, the committee invited notable political officials, including Eleanor Roosevelt, Governor Lehman, and New York Senators Robert F. Wagner and Royal Copeland to the eviction of a Sunnyside family. The invitations were in Old English lettering and embossed on fine stationery, as for a wedding or some other gala occasion.[23]

In April, the residents challenged the legality of the CHC's foreclosures in the federal courts, arguing they had been deliberately misled by the company when they signed the mortgages. But they were rebuffed by the presiding judge, who stated that "he had little sympathy" with persons who tried to "put the squeeze on others to get out of their own obligations." When the homeowners demanded the right to participate in the reorganization of the CHC, a spokesperson for the bondholders denounced the Sunnyside committee as a "semi-communistic organization." In October, Equitable Life Assurance agreed to consider an interest rate reduction, but only after the arrears on the mortgages had been paid up to date. For the majority of Sunnyside residents, who had long since run out of money, this stipulation made Equitable's gesture a hollow one. Finally, in

November—nine months after the strike began—the bitter conflict culminated in a suit filed by the residents against the CHC's directors and advisory council. Among the defendants named in the suit were Alexander Bing, Eleanor Roosevelt, Arthur Lehman (the brother of New York's governor), Dr. John Elliot (the leader of the Ethical Culture Society), and Clarence Stein and Henry Wright. These socially minded individuals, who had thought of themselves as part of a spirited reform movement, were now caught in the vortex of an acrimonious legal battle, where they were denounced as selfish capitalists who victimized innocent, hard-working people.[24]

Filed by 269 homeowners out of a total of 600, the suit demanded $850,000 in damages from the CHC for fraud and misrepresentation. The residents claimed that the company had diverted $50,000 earmarked for park maintenance and community activities into its sagging bank accounts, as a way to shore up its revenues at the expense of Sunnyside families. Bing vehemently denied the charge and no proof was ever brought forth to prove the contention. The residents also claimed their houses were shabbily built. Experimental construction led to some problems, but indeed CHC representatives argued with justification that Sunnyside homes exceeded the quality of comparably priced houses built by speculative developers. Consequently, the quality of construction could not be used as a legitimate reason for a suit. In a more complicated accusation, the residents attacked the CHC for charging far more for the homes than they had cost to build, thus enabling the company to accrue more than a 6 percent profit. Bing responded by stating that the company never intended to sell the homes for cost. It planned to generate a modest profit from the sale of Sunnyside homes to be used as part of a revolving capital fund for subsequent developments. The CHC, he maintained, advertised itself as a limited dividend company. No ceiling was placed on profits, but a stipulation was made that only 6 percent of those profits would be given to investors—a promise the company had kept. Nevertheless, it is easy to see how bankrupt Sunnyside residents became incensed when they learned that a "semi-philanthropic" corporation enjoyed earnings beyond the limit which it had itself proclaimed was both fair and the key to improved housing for moderate income families. As a protesting resident put it, "God preserve us from philanthropists—against commercial swindlers we can protect ourselves."[25]

The suit did not confine the debate to the courtroom. Indeed the residents literally took to the streets to express their grievances, as foreclosure proceedings moved along the judicial path towards evictions. On December 4, 1935, the Sunnyside committee heckled Eleanor Roosevelt, as she entered the Hotel Commodore in New York City to address a luncheon meeting on the need to abolish slums. They issued her a summons to appear in court as a defendant even though she had resigned from the CHC board of directors in 1928. Throughout the winter, they vigorously protested the auction of foreclosed homes. The committee installed sirens above the homes of residents who were threatened with evictions so the community could be alerted when the police appeared. On January 26, 1936, six residents were arrested for disorderly conduct for refusing to leave the home of an evicted family after they had been ordered to do so by the sheriff. The family's furniture had been weighted with concrete to delay and annoy the authorities. While the level of confrontation in the streets edged toward violence, the residents lost the first round in their court battle. The judge ruled against the lawyer of the Sunnyside Home Owners Committee who had contended that the residents had been falsely led to believe that the CHC was a non-profit company.[26]

Throughout 1936, Sunnyside residents continued to battle the CHC and the lending institutions (such as Equitable). The "bulk of the striking homeowners," one observer wrote, "now asserted they had been fleeced by well-to-do people, who had 'pretended' to want to help improve conditions."[27] With mortgage payments withheld by the majority of residents (who could not have paid the monthly fees even if there had not been a strike), foreclosures proceeded in earnest. By June 1936, foreclosures had been processed in 227 cases, and 46 had been completed. An ever-increasing number of homes were repossessed and placed on the depressed market for resale. Four families, who refused to leave their houses or to make any effort to pay their mortgages, were physically evicted.[28]

These foreclosures stiffened the committee's resolve. Residents had lost their entire savings, as well as the five years of equity they had accumulated through mortgage payments. Indeed many residents remained as renters in houses that they had previously owned—houses that had been repossessed but not yet resold. For Sunnyside residents, the protest represented a legitimate right to redress serious grievances. They believed that they were fighting financial tyrants who were insisting that the victims of the Depression be held accountable for saving the system. It made matters worse in their eyes that those demands were presented by the CHC in the name of philanthropy. On the other hand, the planners and public officials who had been instrumental in the creation of this progressive experimental community were bewildered by the residents' behavior. For them, it indicated a surprising lack of understanding for the plight of the CHC—if not ingratitude and irresponsibility. In later years Stein lamented that the strike had revealed that "democracy is not necessarily grateful. It is often more strongly influenced by feelings or demagogues than by understanding or reason."[29] And Bing would attribute the Sunnyside protests to a small band of communists who were determined to discredit his enlightened financial scheme and community plan. At the height of the controversy, he proclaimed that the leaders had entered "into a conspiracy to wipe out the investment of generous people," and that attitude remained unchanged throughout his lifetime.[30]

THE Depression struck Radburn with the same degree of harshness as Sunnyside, but the response was different. On April 10, 1933, over 200 homeowners in Radburn petitioned the CHC for a moratorium on mortgage payments and a reduction in the interest rate from 6 to 4 percent. An ad hoc committee, "representing virtually the entire community," estimated that two-thirds of all homeowners had defaulted on payments. To avoid the imminent danger of wholesale foreclosures, it urged that immediate steps would have to be taken to alleviate the financial burden threatening nearly every family in the community.[31] But there were no violent confrontations between management and the residents. Harsh words were rarely exchanged and the committee never contemplated legal action against the CHC. Although faced with personal financial bankruptcy, the residents appreciated the enormous difficulties faced by Bing, and they identified with the plight of his company. Even after a fifty-year lapse in time, a number of early Radburn residents praised the efforts of the company to help families keep their homes during the Depression. Indeed they looked back fondly on these years as a time of sacrifice, cooperation, and community spirit that dissipated quickly during the era of post–World War II prosperity.[32]

Radburn families did not accept their fate with complete passivity, but the residents' attitude lacked the critical edge so prevalent in Sunnyside, where the Home Owners Committee effectively energized and directed the anguish felt by a majority of the residents. Radburnites, a large percentage of them engaged directly in business and corporate activity, as the occupational survey considered in Chapter 8 revealed, had a vested interest in upholding the integrity of the system. To speak out against the CHC would mean not only turning their backs on a company they respected but also directly challenging the values they had been taught to cherish—as was not so in Sunnyside, which, as was showed in the survey reviewed in Chapter 6, had a more diverse but generally less well to do population (and a number of radical political activists).

Radburn, during the Depression, fought not so much with the CHC as within itself and with its neighbors. Because of their backgrounds and status, the residents of Radburn were never warmly received by the inhabitants of Fair Lawn. "Fifty dollar a week millionaires" is the way those long-term residents of the area sarcastically referred to Radburnites.[33] In 1935, the uneasy coexistence between the two groups grew into a bitter controversy over the issue of the construction of a high school in Fair Lawn. With a keen interest in education, Radburn residents actively sought funds for a high school. They no longer wanted

A Bankrupt Vision

to send their children to nearby Paterson, where many believed their teenagers were receiving an inferior education. When Public Works Administration money became available during the Depression, the argument put forth by Radburn residents became even stronger, since the federal government would now assume most of the expense. But Fair Lawn residents saw no need for a high school and believed that any costs incurred by the municipality for such a project would be excessive: after a heated debate, the proposal was defeated in a 1935 referendum.[34]

To maintain the highest quality of education possible, Radburn families then decided to send their children to Ridgewood rather than to Paterson's East Side High School. Since educating their children was defined by Radburnites as a community activity, the additional tuition resulting from this switch was initially picked up by the Radburn Association. But Radburn was a community of young adults whose children had not yet become teenagers: in 1936, only twenty children were old enough to attend high school. Other residents soon objected to an additional expense from which few families benefitted. After a vigorous community debate, the residents of Radburn in a close vote recommended that community funds not be used for high school tuition, and, as a result, the program was discontinued. After 1937, if any family wanted to send its children to Ridgewood High School, it would have to pay the additional cost on its own. Only in 1938 was tension over the issue relaxed, when Fair Lawn voters reversed their previous decision and decided to accept Public Works Administration money for the construction of a high school. The building was not completed until 1943, just before the borough's postwar population boom.[35]

This debate over high school education reveals much about Radburn during the Depression. While Sunnyside residents battled the lending institutions, their counterparts in New Jersey fought more conventional and conservative fights. Amid the overwhelming economic problems of the 1930's, Radburn families spent a good deal of time arguing with one another over where to send their teenagers to school.

There was one issue on which the Radburn residents did come to question the policy of the CHC—representation on the Radburn Association, which had been given not to them but to "publicly spirited citizens of New Jersey" and employees of the company.[36] When Radburn opened in May 1929, only one RA board member lived in the community, and for the first decade of Radburn's existence the political structure continued to be controlled by those who did not live there. During Radburn's early years, as we saw in Chapter 8, this system aroused little hostility. In fact, it was accepted as an agreeable way of conducting political business. But toward the end of the 1930's, attitudes began to change.

In November 1938, a Special Evaluation Committee created by the residents issued a report which appraised some of the changes that had taken place during Radburn's first ten years of growth. The committee was concerned with re-evaluating community expenditures in the face of the persistent economic Depression, and it was interested in studying various aspects of the community plan now that it had become apparent that Radburn's size would be substantially smaller than originally envisioned. ("We look forward with confidence in the future of Radburn as a desirable place in which to live and raise our children," the committee asserted, "not to a city of 25,000 people as originally conceived, but to a community assured of orderly growth, retaining the virtues of smallness but at the same time reaching a size which will assist us to have the civic virtues we all desire.")[37] But the citizen committee's reiterated theme was the undemocratic nature of the Radburn Association. Although they conceded that the board of trustees "have carried on a well-conceived plan in a most conscientious and efficient manner," the residents were nevertheless disappointed by the limited input they had in the decision-making process. "The chief criticism of the Radburn Association plan," the committee concluded, "lies in the lack of a democratic process for securing ... representation, ... and the mystery and secrecy, unintentional to be sure, in the proceedings of the Board, which emerges into public view only once a year at the budget hearing."[38]

A Bankrupt Vision   205

The committee was thus careful not to demean the accomplishments of the RA; it commended the board for working in the community's interest, even though the majority of its trustees lived outside of Radburn. And its critique was only partially motivated by a principled desire for local control. But it contended that "Radburn had now come of age and should assume responsibility for the selection of its trustees and the proper functioning of the . . . Association."[39] The committee implied that it was perfectly acceptable for the CHC to retain control of Radburn's political structure while plans were still being carried out to build a town for 25,000 people, since the company had a legitimate right to protect its investment. But the CHC was now bankrupt, and the original plans had been scrapped. In an almost predictably hard-nosed, business-like way, the special committee based its findings on the situation in Radburn near the end of the Depression—not on an abstract allegiance to democratic principles.

Rather than to institute an abrupt change in policy, the committee sought to alter Radburn's political framework gradually. Radburn Incorporated, which by court appointment replaced the CHC as the community's development company in 1936, would retain at least three of the seats on the board of trustees. Its representation would then be "proportionately decreased," the committee proposed, "as the proportionate amount of their investment holdings in residential property decreases."[40] Thus the residents upheld the right of the development company to exert a strong influence over the political administration of the community—as long as it continued to own property there. Unlike their Sunnyside counterparts, Radburnites never challenged the sanctity of private property or the prerogative of a corporation to control its investments. To assure greater resident participation in the Radburn Association, the committee offered two plans. The first plan would have increased the size of the RA by establishing an executive committee from the resident-elected Citizen's Association: members of this committee would then become ex-officio representatives of the Radburn Association. The second plan would simply have created a process of direct election to the board, "open . . . to all homeowners, and their wives or husbands, and to all other adult residents who have resided here long enough to demonstrate a continuity of interest in the affairs of the community."[41] Although the committee discriminated against apartment dwellers, its suggestions yet provided for a broad base of democratic representation, especially compared to the well insulated organization established by the CHC in 1929.

The presiding members of the Radburn Association listened sympathetically to the residents' pleas for greater participation. Two years before the 1938 citizens' report was issued, one of the original trustees resigned, declaring that "more local representation [was] necessary" and he was "glad" to step down "to make room for part of it."[42] In the initial decade of Radburn's existence, the board often raised the sensitive issue of community control at its meetings. But the trustees, many of whom were employees of the CHC, could only agree upon this democratic principle in theory, and they politely ignored the residents' desires that they speed up the process of transition. They refused to implement either of the two plans presented by the Special Evaluation Committee of the Citizen's Association in 1938.

Instead of opening the meetings to all citizens, the board agreed to publish a summary of its discussions. It also permitted the "Manager and the President of the Citizen's Association . . . to receive direct complaints such as the trustees would receive at public meetings and to refer them to the trustees for action if they cannot be handled by the Manager of the Citizen's Association." And in place of direct elections, the trustees authorized the president to appoint a nominating committee which would select a slate of candidates for whom the residents would then vote. The individual with the "highest vote" would "be considered by the Board for membership."[43] This procedure has remained in effect to the present, although the Radburn Association—rather than the citizen's group—currently nominates candidates. More democratic than the original system, this is still not one of direct representation, although, since 1948, when the last nonresident of the board resigned, all members of the Radburn Association have lived in the community. The political structure in Radburn resembles that of a homeowner's association more than that of a conventional municipal government, and continuity is still emphasized more than democratic participation. But, in serving a homogenous population in a small geographic area, the RA has been remarkably responsive to the needs of its residents.

While Radburn residents quietly accepted foreclosures, and either continued to live in the repossessed houses as tenants or moved elsewhere, the legal battle between the CHC and the Sunnyside Home Owners Committee persisted. But the Queen's homeowners faced the same problem that a labor union does when it strikes against a bankrupt employer. Even if their suit had been recognized by the court, the CHC would not have had money to pay damages. Besides, the company's primary responsibility, according to the law, was to the investors, not the residents. Although the Sunnyside Home Owners Committee was allowed to participate in the bankruptcy hearings, its claims ranked below those of the lending institutions and the stock and bond holders. Nor could the residents' charge stand up in a court of law. The CHC limited its dividends, not its profits, and therefore could not be sued if it failed to sell houses at cost. The company never promised to hand over its profits to the residents; rather it intended to use the money for the capitalization of other projects. Experimentation in site planning did not mean the houses were of inferior quality. Finally, the company never misappropriated funds for its own benefit.

In response to the stultifying effects of the Depression, Sunnyside residents had struck out against the most visible and convenient "culprits"—Bing and the CHC. But both the company and the homeowners were victims of larger economic forces, forces beyond their control, forces Bing did not anticipate and the residents did not fully appreciate. When the bankruptcy proceedings ended, lending institutions—such as the Rockefeller family, Equitable Life Assurance, and the Irving Trust—received a good deal of protection from the courts for their investments in the "semi-philanthropic" company. But while the residents' grievances were heard, they were not redressed; and the CHC never recovered from the financial debacle and confrontations that took place during the 1930's. After the bankruptcy proceedings were completed, the company's assets were divided among its investors. Somewhere between Radburn and Sunnyside, the CHC's path to an American garden cities program had come to an abrupt end.

The Radburn Legacy

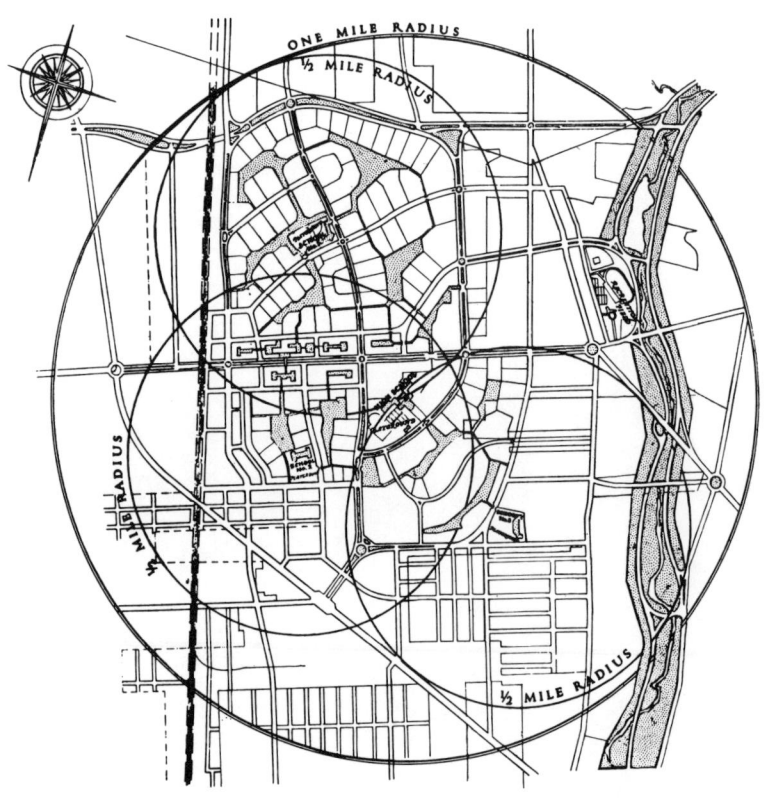

General Plan for Radburn (c. 1929): blueprint for a garden community of 25,000 people consisting of three neighborhood units clustered around a high school/civic building at the town's center. Radburn launched the garden city movement into the twentieth century by successfully confronting the problems created by the automobile. One-tenth of the community was finished, enough to illustrate the benefits of the superblock, but too small to demonstrate the full dimensions of the social plan. From Clarence S. Stein, *Toward New Towns for America* (Cambridge, Mass.: MIT Press, 1973). Copyright Clarence S. Stein, reprinted by permission of The MIT Press.

The Radburn Motif: the physical elements of the Radburn idea have been copied in America's planned communities for the past fifty years. Pieces of the Radburn idea can be found in numerous places, but the social and regional concepts behind the physical plan have been buried by speculative real estate practices.

Top: Pedestrian Underpass in Greenbelt, Maryland: a greenbelt town built by the New Deal's Resettlement Administration in the 1930's. Courtesy of the Library of Congress.

Bottom: Pedestrian Walkway and Neighborhood Shopping Center in Twin Rivers, New Jersey: one of a long list of planned unit developments built in the 1960's and 1970's as a response to unchecked suburban sprawl. From author's collection.

Aerial View of Radburn (c. 1940): a town built on the rolling farmland of Fair Lawn, New Jersey. Notice in the lower right hand corner that construction is underway for a conventional suburban subdivision, a precursor of the postwar suburban landscape. Courtesy of the Radburn Association Archives, Fair Lawn, N.J.

Aerial View of Radburn (c. 1975): a town now surrounded by the endless expanse of northern New Jersey's suburbs. The uniqueness of Radburn's clustered development and interior parkland stand in contrast to more conventional patterns of development, depicting both the uniqueness and limits of the Radburn idea. Courtesy of the Radburn Association, Fair Lawn, N.J.

Public Policy, Private Wealth   10

The Lost Vision of the Regional Planning Association of America

A social-economic system which in ordinary practice and on its own terms cannot provide a decent living environment is not a great civilization no matter what other things it can do.—Catherine Bauer[1]

The point is that the garden city is useful only as a concrete objective in a complete scheme of regional cities. . . . Saltaire, Pullman, Port Sunlight, Letchworth are drops in the bucket. . . . The aim of a garden city movement must be to change the shape of the bucket itself; that is to say, the frame of our civilization.—Lewis Mumford[2]

In order to take a fresh look at our barnacled, deteriorating twentieth century American scene, we must determinedly shake ourselves loose from the web of customary thinking and rash extrapolation. But in then setting out to improve our condition, we don't in any aspect, have to start from scratch. Radical humane thinking has gone before. Geddes, Howard, Mumford, MacKaye, Stein—a great inspiring body of thinking, exhortation and example that has been lying almost untouched as far as action in this country is concerned.—Albert Mayer[3]

DURING the 1920's, the Regional Planning Association of America's close relationship with the City Housing Corporation provided an opportunity for cooperation between progressive reformers and the business community. The association was a think tank with a sponsor, a group of intellectuals with access to capital that enabled them to translate at least a part of their vision into concrete, discernible forms. Despite close links to conservative political forces, RPAA members expressed reservations about the ability of private enterprise to finance a comprehensive program for community and regional development; the organization continually suggested that only an enlightened public policy could create garden cities for America. Bowing to the restraints of the American system of finance, however, the association called upon private institutions—such as large banks and insurance companies—to lead the way.

The RPAA thus encountered a dilemma common to many reform groups. It seriously doubted that private entrepreneurs possessed either the social consciousness or the financial resources to engage in comprehensive plans for regional growth. But the government—except for a brief period during World War I—had never assumed that housing and community development were public responsibilities. And in the "new era" of the Coolidge and Hoover administrations, there was no reason to believe that public institutions were about to alter their longstanding policy, especially since it conformed to the nation's abiding perception of the proper relationship between government and the economy.

Stein, Wright, Chase, Mumford, MacKaye, and other RPAA members never advocated ideological purity. For them, the problem was how to achieve gradual improvements that would head the nation down the path of garden city reform. This required a keen appreciation of what could be attained presently and what changes would have to await more fundamental alterations in American society. Two key factors, according to the members, would determine the organization's ultimate degree of success. First, the RPAA had to seize each opportunity that would advance its principles; and, second, it had to refine its techniques of land use and development in a series of experiments. These tactics superseded any hard and fast political principles in which the organization believed. Taking the initial step on the right path toward social reform was believed to be more significant than the ultimate destination. Thus the RPAA welcomed its affiliation with the CHC and cautiously encouraged large financial institutions to invest in its ideas.

But as might have been expected, differences existed between the two organizations' members, especially between Bing and Wright. With a deeply probing intellect and insatiable curiosity, Wright was never satisfied with a particular design. The unending changes he made in the blueprints exasperated Bing, who, as an astute businessman determined to protect both his own money and the money of his investors, stressed the need for rapid construction. Bing believed that Wright's ingenious experimentation, however fruitful in the long run, slowed the building process at hand and unnecessarily impeded the CHC's chances for financial success. Moreover, Bing was determined to meet the nation's undeviating demand for detached single-unit dwellings while Wright and Stein preferred to build row houses both to save space and money and to create the compact, communal environment they exalted as a physical expression of their social philosophy. Bing expressed doubts about the marketability of attached homes, especially in a community targeted, like Radburn, for middle and upper middle income families. Consequently, only about half the houses in Radburn were attached, and a majority of them were built after 1930 to save on construction costs and to reduce prices during the Depression. It was because such differences so often amounted to debates over what tactics to use to achieve similar goals that the CHC-RPAA partnership was both possible and productive. Both groups had a willingness to integrate theory and practice and an identification with Howard's ideals as the basis of a garden cities program for America.

THE stock market crash, as we have seen, ultimately destroyed the CHC and thus swept away the RPAA's only reliable source of capital. The Depression, however, might potentially have opened up as many opportunities for the RPAA as it closed. First an economic crisis of the magnitude of the Depression enabled critics and political leaders alike to challenge the fundamental economic principles behind land use in America. Unprecedented economic dislocation afforded an opportunity to introduce garden city principles on a larger scale. Second, while by 1933 the lid on private coffers had been nailed shut, the public purse was about to be unclasped for the first time in American history for housing construction and community development—not simply as an emergency war-related measure, as in 1918, but rather as part of a program for peacetime economic recovery and perhaps even for social reform. The sustained and unprecedented economic downturn had virtually halted private construction by the early 1930's, leading to deteriorated housing conditions and, more importantly, leaving hundreds of thousands of workers unemployed.[4]

To meet this crisis the Roosevelt administration had embarked on an array of federally funded home construction programs. Various individuals within the RPAA were employed to assist in the creation or implementation of these programs— although most were placed in subordinate, non-policy-making positions and the association was never contacted as a group. Stein and Wright were hired as consultants for the Resettlement Administration's greenbelt town program, and Wright served as one of the chief town planners for Greenbrook, New Jersey. (The plans for that greenbelt town, to be built just west of New Brunswick, were never carried out because of local opposition and unfavorable court decisions.) Stuart Chase was one of the chief advisors to Rexford Tugwell, a member of Roosevelt's "brain trust" and the architect of some of the New Deal's most liberal programs. Robert Kohn headed the Federal Housing Authority and later moved on to the New York Housing Authority. Benton MacKaye conducted the first surveys and drew the first maps for the Tennessee Valley Authority, and thus applied the broad brushstrokes for the nation's most ambitious attempt at comprehensive regional development.[5]

Thus the RPAA's self-proclaimed role as an educational forum had served its members well. Through its vigorous, informal dialogue they had gained valuable insights into the problems of housing and community development which they subsequently utilized to some degree in Roosevelt's government agencies. But as members of the RPAA became increasingly involved in their government work, they found increasingly less time for the association. And instead of serving to inject government policy with more progressive ideas, the RPAA's principles were often compromised by an uninspired federal bureaucracy and a vacillating leadership unable to sort out priorities and to fashion a consistent and coherent land use program for the nation.

Other problems plagued the organization and contributed to its eventual demise in 1933. In the early 1930's, Stein and Wright started to drift apart. Their partnership, finely knitting Stein's organizational talents with Wright's talent for ingenious site planning, had been frayed by Stein's growing health problems and a lack of commissions to sustain the pair's common efforts. As private funds evaporated, public money—despite Roosevelt's federal programs—did not directly assist the RPAA. Indeed, by establishing its own agencies and by drawing members away from the association, the government hastened the dissolution of the RPAA—and that without providing a more productive alternative. In 1930, Stein and Wright collaborated on the planning and construction of Chatham Village. Financed by the philanthropic Buhl Foundation founded on the same limited dividend principle practiced by the CHC, the community was built in Pittsburgh, Pennsylvania, as an experiment in moderately priced housing; and to this day, it remains one of the outstanding examples of urban design in America, its innovative responses to the problems of hillside housing still being studied. Its completion, however, marked the end of the partnership between Stein and Wright. Although their names have been inextricably linked by urban historians, architects, and planners, their considerable reputations as a team rest on their accomplishments in three small communities—Sunnyside Gardens, Radburn, and Chatham Village, all built by 1930.[6]

The RPAA had once hoped to recruit new, younger members and to establish a network of small forums or subgroups similar to their own throughout the nation. But as RPAA members left for various government posts or pursued their own personal interests with greater intensity, it became apparent that they had failed to accomplish this goal, thus placing the future of their organization in serious jeopardy. And with the demise of the RPAA, no agency existed outside of the government to push for a garden city program. The informal, personalized style of the RPAA had left garden city advocates without an effective lobby to support their cause. As historian Roy Lubove has pointed out, the self-consciously inner-directed policies of the organization, one characterized by friendship and oriented to personal growth, had "limitations in an organized world of competing power structures, particularly in the crucial transition from ideas to the realm of politics and administration." Although "anti-formalism" and collegiality may have "contributed to the vitality of the RPAA," Lubove has concluded, they were "undoubtedly at least partially responsible for its short life, and may have restricted its long-term influence."[7] These observations should not be discounted. But, the RPAA's limited impact on government policy may have had more to do with the overarching structure of the American political economy than it did with the internal structure of the RPAA.

In the years just before the association ceased formally to exist, it operated in much the same way it had in the past—despite the fact the meetings took place less frequently. Members of the RPAA would informally exchange ideas, discuss each others' work, and talk about the prospects for regional planning. The last official meeting was held at the University of

Virginia in 1931 and was attended by Franklin Roosevelt, then governor of New York. The topic was regionalism and the organization's approach came as no surprise to those who were familiar with its ideas. In an obvious reference to the Regional Plan of New York, Mumford spoke about the need to plan not just for the metropolis but for all environments—the cities, the villages, and the rural districts; he called for a renewed respect for balanced growth and "the settled mode of life." Espousing basic garden city principles of self-containment and limited growth, MacKaye argued that "the basic geographic unit of organic human society is the single town of definite physical limits and integrity"; he proposed that future growth be shaped by that enduring concept. Finally, Chase displayed the eclectic politics that characterized the RPAA throughout its history. Despite the collapse of the private sector, he proclaimed, "if industry itself chose to take charge of the planning machinery, and really marched on overproduction, business cycles, and low standards of living, I for one would raise no objection." Echoing a progressive theme dating back to the turn of the century, Chase concluded that "we do not care who controls the wild horses, so long as they are effectively controlled."[8]

Roosevelt listened intently to the ideas presented by the various members of the association. He had a keen appreciation for nature and a personal love for the landscape that enabled him to respect the RPAA's vision. Several of those who attended the meeting later claimed that in his off the record comments the future president then outlined a program remarkably similar to that eventually administered by the Tennessee Valley Authority, a New Deal agency which promoted something closely resembling the RPAA's brand of regionalism.[9] In office, however, Roosevelt followed a confusing, often contradictory, policy of housing reform and community development. In the dark days of 1933, 12.8 million people or nearly 25 percent of the nation's work force were unemployed, and 30 percent of the jobless were in the building trades.[10] Given the dimensions of the unemployment problem, it is not surprising that the first priority of the government's public works projects was to get people back to work. Yet virtually no attempt was made to tie that effort into a comprehensive plan for publicly financed community development. The Resettlement Administration's greenbelt town program, one of the few to see beyond the unemployment problem, planned initially to build fifty experimental communities: the total was pared to four when final blueprints were drawn for construction, and only three communities were ever completed—Greenbelt, Maryland, outside Washington, D.C., Greenhills, Ohio, just north of Cincinnati, and Greendale, Wisconsin, in Milwaukee County.

Whether the administration could have expanded the greenbelt town program is problematic, for, by the late 1930's, such projects for community and regional development were vehemently condemned as socialistic schemes by powerful Congressional voices—and "socialistic" was a label that few programs could overcome. Conservative opposition, together with the Roosevelt administration's hesitant financial commitment, rendered the impact of the greenbelt towns insignificant when compared to that of other New Deal housing legislation: the nearest thing America ever had to a government-sanctioned garden cities program barely had begun before it was abandoned.[11] Public housing for low income families, meanwhile, was defined as a form of welfare. Since each municipality could request public money on a discretionary basis, the more affluent suburban communities shunned the federal low income housing program and left the responsibility for housing the poor to urban municipalities where the poor already lived. Few attempts were made to integrate low cost housing into larger, more diverse, community settings. Moreover, exaggerated concerns for construction costs compromised the quality of what public housing was built, and often led to the creation of new urban slums for which the government must be held partially responsible. Thus when the opportunity for a radical reordering of the American landscape existed, conservative legislation quickly obscured it. Of the myriad New Deal community-oriented programs, only two—the National Resources Planning Board and the Resettlement Administration—were not made permanent. It should be no surprise that these two programs held great promise for significant social change and, except for the Tennessee Valley Authority, they were those most akin to the association's ideals.[12]

In the final analysis, the United States escaped from the Depression in much the same way it had fallen into that deep economic trough—by promoting and protecting capitalist investment. Nowhere was this promotion more evident than in the housing industry, where mortgages guaranteed by the Federal Housing and Veteran Administrations served as the powder for the postwar suburban explosion. Between 1946 and 1959, over 30 percent of all new housing units were purchased with FHA or VA mortgages. In the banner year of 1950, when there were 1.9 million housing starts, federally guaranteed loans accounted for 36 percent of the total; and in 1955, when 1.6 million units were constructed, 41 percent of the mortgages were issued with FHA or VA assistance.[13] By thus providing a substantial number of real estate entrepreneurs with risk-free investment opportunities, Washington underwrote suburban development—and thus sanctioned the American dream of a private homestead with substantial public commitment and money. Indeed, along with the goverment highway projects capped by the interstate highway system, begun in the 1950's, these guaranteed mortgages largely determined the contours of the postwar landscape.

The fundamental principles embodied in such housing and highway policies have consistently dominated American housing and community development programs since the New Deal. Urban renewal in the 1950's and community action grants in the late 1970's likewise socialized the cost of development, while allowing the increments in land values which resulted from public policies and public financial outlays to remain in private hands. Since the Depression, the federal government (at least until the Reagan administration) has come gradually to view the problems of urban America as national problems, and as symptoms of economic and political trends extending beyond city boundaries. (No agency has been more directly or more deeply involved in those problems than the Department of Housing and Urban Development, whose creation in 1965 was the culmination of a process dating back to the 1930's.) But even at their best, government programs for the past fifty years have lacked the

RPAA's social purpose and vision. Thus the formula for balanced growth proposed by the RPAA has rarely, if ever, been followed. Indeed national agencies have often promoted uneven development, accelerating the growth of the suburbs at the expense of the cities or the advance of one region to the detriment of another. Only sporadic attempts have been made to contain sprawl and the escalating land prices which come with it, along the metropolitan fringe, and those efforts have usually been initiated at the state, rather than federal, level. During both liberal and conservative administrations then, advocates of the garden city have been thwarted by political decisions which have received consistently strong support from powerful real estate interests, the building trades, utility companies, the automobile industry, unions, and even prospective homeowners who desire their own piece of the American dream. These factors have made the principles of the RPAA and the construction of Radburn a telling but, finally, much less than dominating influence in the history of American urban planning.

WITH the RPAA succumbing to internal and external pressures, Mumford and Wright, along with architects and planners Albert Mayer, Carol Aronovici, and Henry Churchill, formed the Housing Guild in 1934. The purpose of this group was to explore alternative methods for financing and constructing communities within a regional context, a problem magnified by the Depression. In words recalling the RPAA's the guild's planners argued that the key to the solution of the housing problem was to provide a substantial pool of low cost money for comprehensive community development. To achieve this goal, they called for legislation requiring banks and insurance companies to invest a certain portion of their enormous capital reserves in the construction of moderately priced housing. Lacking faith in the ability of private enterprise to provide adequate housing for all citizens, they argued also for extensive government loans for housing, loans in which the rate of interest charged to the borrowers would be fixed at the same level the government borrowed the money. This public capital would be given only to construction companies with centralized administrations capable of conducting large scale operations through rationalized schemes of production. A long period of amortization, fifty to sixty years, would reduce monthly payments and enable the builder to plan comprehensively without the fear of a cash flow crisis.[14] Thus the guild spoke about the need for public ownership and construction, but, following the lead of the RPAA, did not confine its arguments to government sponsored housing. Pointing to European precedents, it called for a multifaceted program that would utilize the resources of banks and other private institutions, as well as the government, to realize its goals; although it would prefer to rely on either a municipality, a cooperative, or a limited dividend company in place of the speculative developer. Mumford, Wright, and Mayer unabashedly proclaimed that the proposal was "the complete opposite of almost every plan in current reality, banking and building practice."[15] Nevertheless, the financial scheme still contained the ambiguities of the RPAA's proposals. Like the RPAA's, the guild's contentions were based on the premise that housing needs are as basic as education and that private industry had failed to meet certain health and social standards that every individual in a modern community has a right to enjoy. They estimated that at the height of the nation's greatest period of prosperity in the late 1920's, one-third of the population could not afford minimum standard housing, while by 1934, during the depths of the Depression, that fraction had climbed to over one-half. In the face of this failure, the reconstruction of both the urban and rural environments would depend on large scale projects for housing and community development, which would serve as part of a national economic policy for systematic growth. In line with the earliest proposals of the RPAA, members of the Housing Guild insisted that the government should initially concentrate its efforts on inexpensive undeveloped land outside the nation's densely populated cities. Once the crowded urban centers had been thinned out through a deliberate policy of decentralization, planners could then return to rebuild them in a low to moderate density pattern characteristic of Sunnyside and Radburn. For guild members, it made no sense to construct low cost housing on the most expensive and crowded land in the urban core, as dictated by the misdirected policies of the federal government. These policies, they argued, placed the nation's poorest people on the highest-priced land and diverted a great deal of capital needed for construction material and thoughtful design into mortgage payments.

The guild also rejected both the fantastic technical solutions offered by R. Buckminster Fuller and the more modest, almost mundane, experiments in prefabrication conducted by the government in an effort to produce affordable, commodious housing for the masses. Although those innovations might result in some cost reductions, they would not cure the housing ills facing America because they did not address the fundamental problem of the lack of availability of cheap capital for modestly priced homes. Moreover, the guild believed that the public did not identify with the modernistic residential living space created by architects who self-consciously built houses for "the machine age" and who took the principles of efficiency and geometric form to be the proper ideological and physical base for the new American community. For Mumford, Wright, and Mayer, twentieth-century technology should be put to more conventional uses: it could provide the instrument which would recreate the community environment of the traditional New England town.

In the final analysis, the Housing Guild—like the RPAA which preceded it—insisted that socially minded community development on a regional scale required comprehensive planning. Indeed, like Frederick Ackerman in 1919, they even hinted at the need for national planning, which would have meant the extensive involvement of the federal government almost by definition.[16] They called for the creation of a Housing Administration to train technicians, to engage in systematic research, and to establish a program for public education concentrating on housing issues. Although the administrative framework would be created by the government, the agency would take advantage of all existing institutions—the Federal Housing Authority, municipalities, limited dividend companies, and private, profit-making organizations. Thus the Housing Guild hoped that the ideas previously presented by the RPAA would be utilized to fight the ills of the Depression. Like the RPAA, the guild placed a heavy emphasis on education and personal interaction; it believed that many paths could lead to significant alterations in American patterns of land use; it advocated public sponsorship but did not object to participation by private enterprise; and it viewed reform as an evolutionary process where the ultimate destination was not as important as the direction in which one was heading. And like the RPAA, the guild's proposals were obscured by more conventional housing policies.

THE legacy of the RPAA resides in a comprehensive, nonspeculative approach to land use and development based on garden city principles. Never comfortable as political revolutionaries, nor at home among conventional capitalists, members of the RPAA occupied the highest ground of progressive, liberal reform. At times, theirs was an uncomfortable, almost hopeless, task—to plead for sizable public involvement in housing in an environment dedicated to private investment and control; to demand comprehensive planning in a society committed to piecemeal development; to believe in socially minded urban design in a nation still espousing the virtues of Adam Smith even as the government's role in the economy continued to expand. Members of the RPAA took Ebenezer Howard's peaceful path to reform and laid it out on the American political landscape. Experimentation, gradual improvements, and moral persuasion were the hallmarks of their journey. The limited progress they made signified both the success and failure of their tactical approach to reform.

Thus the Radburn idea was more a victim of policies pursued (or perhaps more precisely, not pursued) by the government in the 1930's, than it was of the stock market crash. The plans for balanced regional growth found in the Resettlement Administration, the Tennessee Valley Authority, and the National Resources Planning Board were overshadowed by the conservative programs of the Federal Housing Administration, which sought to use the federal government as an agency to protect and promote the private speculator by guaranteeing profitability to the housing industry. Instead of one element to be considered in a comprehensive plan, the city became an isolated concern—as much the victim of federal policy as the recipient of its reluctant "benevolence." The suburbs, allowed to grow in a haphazard fashion, emerged in their maturity with the problems mistakenly associated only with urban life. The American landscape therefore has been shaped by policies which actively promoted expansive, unplanned development, regardless of what such development has meant to the residential and commercial areas left behind; and the Radburn idea has become all too often but a textbook example of technical solutions to the problems created by the automobile. It is studied as a pleasing alternative to conventional suburban subdivisions, rather than as a tangible reminder of a reform movement spearheaded by an unique group of regional planners who called for a dramatic reordering of America's land use policies.

Today Radburn still speaks to many pertinent issues. It suggests approaches to the problems of energy and transportation; it presents an alternative to suburban sprawl and our increasingly extended metropolitan districts; it addresses questions concerning the preservation of farmland; and it offers sensitive solutions to the perplexing problems of community development. But what Radburn and the garden city movement that produced it can tell us about the nature of reform in the United States is perhaps most important. Certainly it is as much a part of any history of Radburn and the RPAA as the town's technical achievements and the organization's ultimate vision of balanced regional growth. "What we need in housing," wrote Mumford during the depths of the Depression, "is not a new deal with old marked cards—and with the old sharp players still sitting at the tables—what we need is a new set of cards and a complete new set of rules."[17] Although the RPAA never lost sight of its ultimate goals, it often had difficulty calling the rules it wanted to follow because it feared losing its place at the table where the political game was played. Without solving that dilemma, no player will ever come any closer to beating the dealers.

Notes

Introduction

1. Lewis Mumford, quoted in *How to Save Urban America: Regional Plan Association Choices for '76*, ed. William A. Caldwell (New York: New American Library, 1973), p. 4.

2. *New Jersey Business* 24 (April 1978): A-9. In 1978, the median income for all American families was $17,640. See U.S., Department of Commerce, Bureau of the Census, Current Population Reports, *Money Income of Families and Persons in the United States, 1978* (Washington, D.C.: U.S. Government Printing Office, 1980), p. 2. In 1979, 16.4 percent of the entire population had a college degree and 31 percent had some college training. See U.S., Department of Commerce, Bureau of Census, Current Population Reports, *Education Attainment in the United States, March 1978 and 1979* (Washington, D.C.: U.S. Government Printing Office, 1980), p. 1.

3. Carl Feiss, "New Towns for America," *Town and Country Planning* 28 (Jan. 1960): 235.

4. Clarence S. Stein, *Toward New Towns for America*, intro. by Lewis Mumford (1951; Cambridge, Mass.: M.I.T. Press, 1973), ch. 2; Carl Mecky and Daniel Schaffer, "Land Use in Radburn," unpub. ms., May 1978, Radburn Papers, Radburn Library, Fair Lawn, N.J.; "Report of the Special Evaluation Committee of the First Citizen's Association of Radburn, New Jersey," Nov. 1, 1938, p. 10, Radburn Papers.

5. Thomas Adams, Edward Bassett, and Robert Whitten, "Neighborhood and Community Planning: Problems of Unbuilt Areas," in *Regional Survey of New York and Its Environs*, ed. Thomas Adams, 8 vols. (New York: New York Committee on the Regional Plan of New York and Its Environs, 1929), vol. 7, *Neighborhood and Community Planning*,

p. 256; Lewis Mumford, *The City in History: Its Origins, Its Transformations, and Its Prospects* (New York: Harcourt, Brace and World, 1961), plate 51.

6. The N.J. Commission of State and National Historic Sites. The citation may be read in the Radburn Library.

7. Information obtained from a survey conducted among Radburn residents in September 1978, and from an interview with Ronald Gatti, manager of the Radburn Association, conducted by the author, March 1979, Fair Lawn, N.J. Radburn's ethnic diversity has evolved from the rich ethnic history of New York City, a diversity that has now spread throughout the entire metropolitan area. Although the suburban environment has become more varied throughout the entire nation, this trend has been most pronounced in the New York metropolitan region. Radburn's present-day mixed ethnic composition is, therefore, a result of this larger historical development, rather than its unique qualities as a planned community.

8. For examples of the extensive recreational and social programs now offered to Bergen County residents, see Ridgewood Parks and Recreation Department, "1981 Season," "1981 Summer Program and Calender of Events," and "New Player's Company 1981 Summer Season" (available from Ridgewood, N.J., Recreation Department). Also see "1981 Paramus Recreation Commission Programs" (available from Paramus, N.J., Recreation Department). Fair Lawn, of which Radburn is a part, also enjoys a full schedule of community activities. See "Borough of Fair Lawn Recreation and Parks Department 1979–1980 Recreation Guide" (available from Fair Lawn, N.J., Recreation and Parks Department).

9. John B. Lansing, Robert W. Marans, and Robert B. Zehner, *Planned Residential Environments* (Ann Arbor, Mich.: Braun-Brumfield, 1970), p. 144.

10. For a detailed description of the Radburn site plan, see Chapter 7 below; also see Stein, *Toward New Towns*, ch. 2.

11. Lansing et al., *Planned Residential Environments*, p. 185. The same study indicated that only about 10 percent of the population in the new towns of Reston, Virginia, and Columbia, Maryland, made extensive use of the walkway systems.

12. Thomas Ktsanes and Leonard Reissman, "Suburbia: New Homes for Old Values," *Social Values* 7 (Winter 1959–1960): 187–194. For a

discussion of the evolution of contemporary American suburbs, see Kenneth T. Jackson, "The Crabgrass Frontier: 150 Years of Suburban Growth in America," in *The Urban Experience: Themes in American History*, ed. Raymond A. Mohl and James F. Richardson (Belmont, Calif.: Wadsworth Publishing, 1973).

13. The term "lived in" is derived from Philippe Boudon's excellent sociological account of Le Corbusier's model community Pessac: see his *Lived-in Architecture: Le Corbusier's Pessac Revisited* (Cambridge, Mass.: M.I.T. Press, 1972).

Chapter 1

1. Ebenezer Howard, *Garden Cities of To-morrow* (1902; reprint ed., Cambridge, Mass.: M.I.T. Press, 1965), p. 59.

2. Frederic J. Osborn in the preface to Howard, *Garden Cities*, p. 10.

3. Lewis Mumford in *The Letters of Lewis Mumford and Frederic J. Osborn*, ed. Michael Hughes (New York: Praeger Publishers, 1971), p. 53.

4. Howard, *Garden Cities*. There is extensive literature on the English garden city movement, a good portion of which is written by advocates of Howard's ideas. For insightful essays by early proponents of the garden city, see Frederic J. Osborn's preface and Lewis Mumford's introduction to *Garden Cities*. For the best description of the problems and successes in building the first garden city at Letchworth, see. C. B. Purdom, *The Building of Satellite Towns* (London: J. M. Dent and Sons, 1925), with a follow-up on Letchworth's history through 1963 in C. B. Purdom, *The Letchworth Achievement* (London: J. M. Dent and Sons, 1963). For arguments supporting the need for an English garden cities program, see Frederic J. Osborn and C. B. Purdom, *New Towns After the War* (London: J. M. Dent and Sons, 1943), and Frederic J. Osborn, *Green-Belt Cities* (New York: Schocken Books, 1969). For analyses of the post–World War II English New Town Movement, see Frederic J. Osborn and Arnold Whittick, *The New Towns: The Answer to Megalopolis* (London: Leonard Hill, 1969), and Frank Schaffer, *The New Town Story* (London: Granada Publishing, 1970). For a laudatory description of Howard's life, see Dugald MacFadyen, *Sir Ebenezer Howard and the Town Planning Movement* (Manchester: University of Manchester Press, 1933). Although no scholarly biography of Howard has yet been written, interpretations of the roots and impact of his ideas may be

found in Walter Creese, *The Search for Environment* (New Haven: Yale University Press, 1966); Stanley Buder, "Ebenezer Howard: The Genesis of a Town Planning Movement," *Journal of the American Institute of Planners* 35 (Nov. 1969): 390–397; and William Petersen, "The Ideological Origins of Britain's New Towns," *Journal of the American Institute of Planners* 34 (May 1968): 160–170.

5. Mumford in the intro. to Howard, *Garden Cities*, p. 53. In formulating the concepts behind the garden city, Howard drew upon the rich diversity of European and American reformist thought. He readily acknowledged the influence of nineteenth-century reformers James Buckingham, Edward Gibbon Wakefield, Peter Kropotkin, and Henry George. In 1875, Howard journeyed to the United States and may have visited Riverside, Illinois, Frederick Law Olmsted's romantic suburb. More importantly, in 1888 he read Edward Bellamy's *Looking Backward*, a popular and influenial "utopian romance" which forecast a peaceful revolution through inevitable advances in the efficiency of industrial organization and production. The book sparked Howard's social activism and led to the publication of his *To-morrow: A Peaceful Path to Real Reform*. Thus the garden city represented an amalgamation of nineteenth-century intellectuals' thought applied to the problems found in England's industrial urban centers.

6. Howard, *Garden Cities*, pp. 51–53.

7. Ibid., p. 48.

8. Osborn, *Green-Belt Cities*, p. 59.

9. Robert Fishman, *Urban Utopias in the Twentieth Century: Ebenezer Howard, Frank Lloyd Wright and Le Corbusier* (New York: Basic Books, 1977), p. 75.

10. Howard, *Garden Cities*, p. 48.

11. Ibid., p. 159.

Chapter 2

1. Charles H. Whitaker, "What Is a House?" *Journal of the American Institute of Architects* 5 (Oct. 1917): 484.

2. Clarence S. Stein, "Housing and Reconstruction," *Journal of the American Institute of Architects* 6 (Oct. 1918): 472.

3. Frederick L. Ackerman, "The Real Meaning of the Housing Problem," *Journal of the American Institute of Architects* 6 (May 1918): 232.

4. Roy Lubove, *The Progressives and the Slums* (Pittsburgh: Pittsburgh University Press, 1962), p. 228.

5. Frederick C. Howe, "The Garden City Movement," *Scribner's Magazine* (July 1912): 1–19. For the importance Howe placed on decentralizing the population, see Frederick C. Howe, *The City: The Hope of Democracy* (New York: Scribner's Sons, 1905), especially p. 204.

6. A. L. Diggs, "Garden City Movement," *Arena* (Dec. 1902): 626–633; George Hooker, "Garden Cities," *Housing Problems in America: Proceedings of the Third National Conference on Housing* (New York: National Housing Association, 1913), pp. 13–28; Lawrence Veiller, *Housing Reform* (New York: Russell Sage Foundation, 1910), pp. 80–82; Lawrence Vieller, "Government Housing: The Example of England," *Housing Problems in America: Proceedings of the Eighth National Conference on Housing* (New York: National Housing Association, 1920), pp. 119–140; Lawrence Veiller, "Are Our Great Cities Menaced? The Garden City as a Way Out," *Architectural Record* 51 (Feb. 1922): 175–184; Gustav Stickley, "Rapid Growth of the Garden City Movement," *The Craftsman* (Dec. 1909): 296–310; Edward E. Pratt, "The Garden Cities in Europe," *American City* 7 (Dec. 7, 1912): 503–510; Thomas Adams, "Planning for Civic Betterment in Town and Country," *American City* 15 (July 15, 1916): 47–51.

7. Joseph L. Arnold, *The New Deal in the Suburbs: A History of the Greenbelt Town Program, 1935–1954* (Columbus: Ohio State University Press, 1971), ch. 1, especially pp. 6–7; Mel Scott, *American City Planning since 1890* (Berkeley: University of California Press, 1971), p. 90.

8. Ibid.

9. Scott, *American City Planning since 1890*, pp. 232–234.

10. Miles L. Colean, *Housing for Defense* (1940; reprint ed., New York: Arno Press, 1977), p. 3; Scott, *American City Planning*, p. 171. The campaign for publicly financed low and moderate income housing was spearheaded by future members of the RPAA, but in the months following the Armistice support came from throughout the planning profession. See Frederick L. Ackerman, "American Reconstruction Problems: Nation Planning," *Journal of the American Institute of Architects* 6 (Nov. 1918): 506–509; Frederick L. Ackerman, "Nation Planning," *National Municipal Review* 8 (Jan. 1919): 15–25; Charles H. Whitaker, "Post-War Committee: Preliminary Conclusions," *Journal of the American Institute of Architects* 7 (Sept. 1919): 390–395; Charles H. Whitak-

er, "The Senate and the United States Housing Corporation," *Journal of the American Institute of Architects* 8 (March 1920): 103–104; George Gove, "Community Values in Government Housing," *American City* 22 (Jan. 1920): 1–7; Richard S. Childs, "What Will Become of the Government Housing?" *National Municipal Review* 8 (Jan. 1919): 48–52; Ernest Cawfort, "The Present and Future Government of the War-Created Communities," *National Municipal Review* 8 (Jan. 1919): 52–60; John Ihlder, "Government Aid to Housing in War-Time—and After," *Journal of the American Institute of Architects* 5 (Oct. 1917): 489–490; Ewart G. Culpin, "The Remarkable Application of Town-Planning Principles to the War-Time Necessities of England," *Journal of the American Institute of Architects* 5 (April 1917): 157–159. For a volume of articles advocating postwar government-supported housing see Charles H. Whitaker, Frederick L. Ackerman, Richard S. Childs, and Edith Elmer Wood, *The Housing Problem in War and Peace* (Washington, D.C.: Octagon, 1918). For an excellent description of government wartime housing and its impact on the planning profession see Roy Lubove, "Homes and 'A Few Well Placed Fruit Trees': An Object Lesson in Federal Housing," *Social Research* 27 (Winter 1960): 469–486.

11. Park Dixon Goist, "The City as Organism: Two Recent American Theories of the City" (Ph. D. diss., University of Rochester, 1967), p. 324.

12. Secretary of Labor, William B. Wilson, U.S., Congress, Senate, Subcommittee of the Committee on Public Buildings and Grounds, Hearings: United States Housing Corporation, 66th Cong., 1st Sess., 1919, p. 486.

13. Frederick L. Ackerman, "The Significance of England's Program of Building Workmen's Houses," *Journal of the American Institute of Architects* 5 (Nov. 1917): 539.

14. Frederick L. Ackerman, "National Planning," *National Municipal Review* 8 (Jan. 1919): 15–25.

15. Lewis Mumford, "The Heritage of the Cities Movement in America: An Historical Survey," *Journal of American Institute of Architects* 7 (Aug. 1919): 349–354.

16. Patrick Geddes, "The Valley Plan of Civilization," *The Survey* 54 (July 1, 1925): 289; Patrick Geddes, *Cities in Evolution: An Introduction to the Town Planning Movement and to the Study of Civics* (1915; reprint ed., New York: Harper Torchbooks, 1968), p. 64; Goist, "The City as Organism," p. 279.

17. Geddes, *Cities in Evolution*, p. 74; Goist, "The City as Organism," p. 285; Geddes, *Cities in Evolution*, p. 116.

18. Geddes, *Cities in Evolution*, p. 73.

19. Henry M. Wright, Jr., "Radburn Revisited," *Ekistics* 33 (March 1972): 196; Goist, "The City as Organism," pp. 328–329; Henry Wright, Sr., "Allotment and Community Planning," *National Real Estate Journal* 21 (June 19, 1920): 15–20; Henry Wright, Sr., "Plotting City Areas for Small Homes," *Journal of the American Institute of Architects* 8 (Aug. 1920): 1–16; Henry Wright, Sr., "Shall We Community Plan?" *Journal of the American Institute of Architects* 9 (Oct. 1921): 320–324; Henry Wright, Sr., "Site Planning in Practice," *Journal of the American Institute of Architects* 11 (Oct. 1923): 405–407; Henry Wright, Sr., "The Six-Cylinder House with Stream-Line Body," *Journal of the American Institute of Architects* 14 (April 1926): 175–178; Lewis Mumford, intro. to Clarence S. Stein, *Toward New Towns for America* (Cambridge, Mass.: M.I.T. Press, 1973), pp. 11–17; Henry Wright, Sr., "War Housing in the U.S.," unpub. ms., Aug. 13, 1923, Henry Wright, Sr., Papers, Olin Library, Cornell University; Mumford, intro. to Stein, *Toward New Towns*, p. 12; Lubove, "Homes and 'A Few Well Placed Fruit Trees,'" pp. 469–486.

20. Henry M. Wright, Jr., "Radburn Revisited," p. 196; Clarence S. Stein, "Henry Wright, 1878–1936," *American Architect and Architecture* 149 (Aug. 1936): 23–24; Lewis Mumford, "Henry Wright," *The New Republic* 87 (July 22, 1936): 308–309, cont. in *The New Republic* 87 (July 29, 1936): 348–350; Henry Churchill, "Henry Wright: 1878–1936," *Journal of the American Institute of Planners* 26 (Nov. 1960): 295–296.

21. See Hugh B. Johnson, "In Memory of Benton MacKaye, 'Father of the Appalachian Trail,'" *Journal of the American Institute of Architects* 65 (Feb. 1976): 68D.

22. Goist, "The City as Organism," p. 361; Mumford, intro. to Benton MacKaye, *The New Exploration: A Philosophy of Regional Planning* (1928; reprint ed., Urbana: University of Illinois Press, 1962); Benton MacKaye, *Employment and Natural Resources: Possibilities of Making New Opportunities for Employment through the Settlement and Development of Agricultural and Forest Lands and Other Natural Resources* (Washington, D.C.: Government Printing Office, 1919), pp. 13–14; Benton MacKaye, *From Geography to Geotechnics*, ed. Paul T. Bryant (Chicago: University of Illinois Press, 1968), p. 49.

23. Lewis Mumford, "A Modest Man's Enduring Contributions to Urban and Regional Planning," *Journal of the American Institute of Architects* 65 (Dec. 1976): 20.

24. New York, Reconstruction Commission, Housing Committee, *Report on Housing Conditions*, March 26, 1920, pp. 36, 4.

25. *Ibid.*, pp. 54–55; Roy Lubove, *Community Planning in the 1920's: The Contribution of the Regional Planning Association of America* (Pittsburgh: University of Pittsburgh Press, 1962), pp. 72–73; Clarence S. Stein, "Amsterdam—Old and New," *Journal of the American Institute of Architects* 10 (Oct. 1922): 310–327.

26. Stein, unpub. ms., Aug. 17, 1947, Clarence S. Stein Papers, Olin Library, Cornell University.

27. New York, Commission on Housing and Regional Planning, Legislative Document 1924, *The Present Status of the Housing Emergency* (Albany, Dec. 22, 1923); Clarence S. Stein, "Housing the People," *The Nation* 122 (March 10, 1926): 246; Clarence S. Stein, "Housing New York's Two-Thirds," *The Survey* 51 (Feb. 15, 1924): 509–510; Clarence S. Stein, "The Housing Crisis in New York," *The Survey* 44 (Sept. 1, 1920): 652–662.

28. New York, Commission on Housing and Regional Planning, Legislative Document 1924, *Tax Exemption of New Housing* (Albany, March 14, 1924), pp. 16, 22, 15.

29. New York, Commission on Housing and Regional Planning, Legislative Document 1926, *Permanent Housing Relief* (Albany, Feb. 22, 1926), p. 33.

30. New York, Commission on Housing and Regional Planning, Legislative Document 1924, *Tax Exemption of New Housing* (Albany, March 14, 1924), p. 15.

31. Henry Wright, Sr., "Planning a Town for Wholesome Living," *Playground* 22 (March 1929): 683.

32. Clarence S. Stein, "New Communities," unpub. ms., undated, Stein Papers.

Chapter 3

1. Frederick L. Ackerman, "Our Stake in Congestion," *The Survey* 54 (May 1, 1925): 141–142.

2. Lewis Mumford, "The City of Tomorrow," *New Republic* 61 (Feb. 12, 1930): 332.

3. Clarence S. Stein, "Dinosaur Cities," *The Survey* 54 (May 1, 1925): 138.

4. Alexander Bing, Henry Wright, Sr., and Clarence S. Stein, "Preliminary Study of a Proposed Garden Community in the New York City Region," unpub. ms., 1923, Clarence S. Stein Papers, Olin Library, Cornell University.

5. Henry Wright, Sr., "Garden City Studies," unpub. ms., Aug. 28, 1923, Henry Wright, Sr., Papers, Olin Library, Cornell University.

6. Wright, "The Road to Good Homes," *The Survey* 54 (May 1, 1925): 165–166; also see Henry Wright, Sr., "Lo! The Poor One Family House," *Journal of the American Institute of Architects* 14 (March 1916): 118–121.

7. Bing, Wright, and Stein, "Preliminary Study," p. 30. For the most comprehensive analysis of Pullman, see Stanley Buder, *Pullman: An Experiment in Industrial Order and Community Planning, 1880–1930* (New York: Oxford University Press, 1970); also see Almont Linsey, *The Pullman Strike* (Chicago: University of Chicago Press, 1967). For contemporary indictments of the Pullman experiment, see Richard L. Ely, "Pullman: A Social Study," *Harpers Magazine* 70 (Feb. 1885): 452–466; Charles H. Eaton, "Pullman Paternalism," *American Journal of Politics* 5 (Dec. 1894): 571–579.

8. Bing, Wright, and Stein, "Preliminary Study," p. 18.

9. Stein, unpub. ms., Sept. 5, 1923, Stein Papers.

10. "Principles of the Garden City and Regional Planning Association of America," unpub. document, 1923, Stein Papers.

11. Lewis Mumford, intro. to Clarence S. Stein, *Toward New Towns for America* (1951; Cambridge, Mass.: M.I.T. Press, 1973), p. 15.

12. The International Garden Cities and Town Planning Federation served as a forum and promotional center for advocates of Howard's ideas from throughout the world. See Frederic J. Osborn, preface to Ebenezer Howard, *Garden Cities of To-morrow* (1902; reprint ed., Cambridge, Mass.: M.I.T. Press, 1965), p. 13.

13. John Moss-Eccardt, *Ebenezer Howard* (Aylesbury, United Kingdom: Shires Publications, 1973), p. 12; Robert Fishman, *Urban Utopias*

in the *Twentieth Century: Ebenezer Howard, Frank Lloyd Wright, and Le Corbusier* (New York: Basic Books, 1977), pp. 27–29.

14. Mel Scott, *American City Planning since 1890* (Berkeley: University of California Press, 1971), p. 223.

15. Lewis Mumford, "Regions to Live In," *The Survey* 54 (May 1, 1925): 152.

16. Clarence S. Stein, "Principles of the Garden City."

17. *Ibid.*

18. Lewis Mumford, "The Fate of Garden Cities," *Journal of the American Institute of Architects* 15 (Feb. 1927): 38.

19. Clarence S. Stein, "Address Before the City Housing Corporation," unpub. ms., Nov. 16, 1927, p. 3, Stein Papers.

20. Lewis Mumford, "Attacking the Housing Problem on Three Fronts," *The Nation* 110 (Sept. 6, 1919): 332.

21. Stein, "Dinosaur Cities," pp. 134–138; Lewis Mumford, "The Wilderness of Suburbia," *The New Republic* 28 (Sept. 7, 1921): 45.

22. Jane Jacobs, *The Death and Life of Great American Cities* (New York: Vintage Books, 1961), pp. 17, 20, 17.

23. Clarence S. Stein, "New York," unpub. ms., 1923–1924, Stein Papers; Lewis Mumford, *Green Memories: The Story of Geddes Mumford* (New York: Harcourt, Brace and Company 1947), p. 12.

24. Regional Planning Association of America (RPAA) Minutes, April 20, 1923, Stein Papers.

25. Patrick Geddes, *Cities in Evolution: An Introduction to the Town Planning Movement and to the Study of Civics* (1915; reprint ed., New York: Harper Torch Books, 1968), p. 60.

26. Lewis Mumford, "The Theory and Practice of Regionalism," *Sociological Review* 19 (Jan. 1928): 24, 19.

27. John Nolen, commenting on C. B. Purdom, "Financing Decentralization," Proceedings of the National Conference on City Planning: *Planning Problems of Town, City and Region: Papers and Discussions at the Ninth Congress of the International City and Regional Planning Conference of the International Federation for Housing and Town Planning* (Baltimore: Norman Remington, 1925), p. 199.

28. Stein, "New York," p. 12.

29. Lewis Mumford, "Realities versus Dreams," *JAIA* 13 (June 1925): 199.

30. Mumford, "Attacking the Housing Problem," p. 333.

31. Stein, "Address Before the City Housing Corporation," p. 2.

32. RPAA Minutes, June 7, 1923.

33. For the most comprehensive analysis of the development and impact of early zoning ordinances, see Edward Bassett, *Zoning: The Laws, Administration and Court Decisions During the First Twenty Years* (New York: Russell Sage Foundation, 1940). For a concise discussion of early zoning in America, see Scott, *American City Planning*, especially pp. 153–169. For a detailed, but convoluted, history of the 1916 New York zoning ordinance, see Seymour I. Toll, *Zoned America* (New York: Grossman Publishers, 1969).

34. Scott, *American City Planning*, pp. 154–155.

35. Ibid., p. 160.

36. Henry Wright, Sr., "The Architect, the Plan and the City," *Architectural Forum* 3 (Feb. 1931): 220. The RPAA was not alone in this argument. Planner George B. Ford, despite the fact that he served as a consultant in preparing New York City's zoning ordinance, voiced concern about introducing zoning without a more general and comprehensive plan for development.

37. Report of the Committee on Community Planning, *Proceedings of the Fifty-eighth Annual Convention of the American Institute of Architects* (1925), quoted in *The Urban Community: Housing and Planning in the Progressive Era*, ed. Roy Lubove (Englewood Cliffs, N.J.: Prentice-Hall, 1967), p. 117.

38. Theodora Kimball Hubbard and Henry Vincent Hubbard, *Our Cities To-day and To-morrow* (1929; reprint ed., New York: Arno Press, 1974), pp. 186–187; William H. Wilson, *Coming of Age: Urban America, 1915–1945* (New York: John Wiley and Son, 1974), p. 134.

39. Members of the RPAA also recognized and deplored the fact that zoning ordinances were used to create residential neighborhoods beyond the means of low income workers. The use of "exclusionary zoning," which dated back to the earliest days of "districting," soon emerged as a primary tool of suburban development. Today the debate on zoning focuses on unbuilt suburban environments targeted for residential development. However, until the late 1920's overzoned com-

mercial districts were the primary consequences of zoning, a reflection of the economic considerations which impelled the initial development of this planning tool. For a contemporary discussion of the problems related to zoning laws, see Richard F. Babcock, *The Zoning Game* (Madison: University of Wisconsin Press, 1966); Clifford Weaver and Richard F. Babcock, *City Zoning* (Chicago: American Planning Association, 1979); and Scott, *American City Planning*.

40. Edith Elmer Wood, *Recent Trends in American Housing* (New York: Macmillan, 1931), p. 84; Arthur Gleason, "The Lack of Houses: Remedies," *The Nation* 110 (April 24, 1920): 546–549.

41. Quoted in Wood, *The Housing of the Unskilled Wage Earner* (New York: Macmillan, 1919), p. 21.

42. Ibid., p. 65.

43. Henry Wright, Sr., "Housing Developments in the Past," unpub. ms., undated, Wright Papers; Frederick L. Ackerman, "American Reconstruction Problems—Nation Building," *Journal of the American Institute of Architects* 6 (Nov. 1918): 506; Stein, "New York," p. 4.

44. Clarence S. Stein and Henry Wright, Sr., "Community Planning and Housing," *Journal of the American Institute of Architects* 9 (Dec. 1923): 492–493.

45. Ibid.

46. Henry Wright, Sr., "The Sad Story of American Housing," *Architecture* 67 (March 1933): 128; Henry Wright, Sr., "Housing: How Much for How Much?" *The Survey* 55 (March 15, 1926): 674.

47. Roy Lubove, *Community Planning in the 1920's: The Contribution of the Regional Planning Association of America* (Pittsburgh: University of Pittsburgh Press, 1962), p. 1.

48. RPAA Minutes, Oct. 17–19, 1927; Stein, "Address Before the City Housing Corporation," p. 3.

49. Lewis Mumford, "The Culture-Cycle and City Planning," *Journal of the American Institute of Architects* 14 (June 1926): 291; Wright, "The Architect, the Plan and the City," p. 223.

50. Lewis Mumford, intro. to Benton MacKaye, *The New Exploration: A Philosophy of Regional Planning* (1928; reprint ed., Urbana: University of Illinois Press, 1962), p. 16.

51. *Planning the Fourth Migration: The Neglected Vision of the Regional Planning Association of America*, ed. Carl Sussman (Cambridge, Mass.: M.I.T. Press, 1976), pp. 50–51.

52. Paul Conkin, *Tomorrow a New World: The New Deal Community Program* (Ithaca, N.Y.: Cornell University Press, 1959), p. 23.

53. Alfred Bettman, "How to Lay Out Regions for Planning," *International City and Regional Planning Conference*, p. 289.

54. George B. Ford, "Regional and Metropolitan Planning: Principles, Methods, and Co-Operation," *Proceedings of the Fifteenth National Conference on City Planning* (Baltimore: Norman Remington, 1923), p. 3; G. Gordon Whitnall, "City and Regional Planning in Los Angeles," *Proceedings of the Sixteenth National Conference on City Planning* (Baltimore: Norman Remington, 1924), pp. 105–110; Hugh R. Pomeroy, "Regional Planning in Practice," *Proceedings of the Sixteenth National Conference on City Planning* (Baltimore: Norman Remington, 1924), p. 111.

55. The Regional Plan of New York consisted of eight volumes of research and analysis and two volumes of general descriptions and conclusions. See *Regional Survey of New York and Its Environs*, ed. Thomas Adams, 8 vols. (New York: New York Committee on the Regional Plan of New York and Its Environs, 1924–1931); *The Graphic Regional Plan: Atlas and Description*, ed. Thomas Adams (New York: New York Committee on the Regional Plan of New York and Its Environs, 1929); Thomas Adams, *The Building of the City* (New York: New York Committee on the Regional Plan of New York and Its Environs, 1931). For updates on the progress made in implementing the plan, see *From Plan to Reality I* (New York: Regional Plan Association, 1929). Two additional reports were published by the Regional Plan Association in 1938 and 1942. The Regional Plan Association, not to be confused with the RPAA, was established in 1929 as an outgrowth of the work of Adams and his staff. It still remains an important force in the planning of the New York metropolitan region.

56. Mumford, "Reality versus Dreams," p. 198.

57. Lewis Mumford, "The Plan of New York: I," *The New Republic* 71 (June 15, 1932): 121–126; also see his "The Plan of New York: II," *The New Republic* 71 (June 22, 1932): 146–153.

58. Lewis Mumford, "The Next Twenty Years in City Planning," *Plan-

ning *Problems of Town, City, and Region: Papers and Discussions at the Nineteenth National Conference on City Planning* (Philadelphia: William F. Fell, 1927), p. 46.

59. Thomas Adams, "A Communication," *The New Republic* 71 (July 6, 1932): 207.

60. Lubove, *Community Planning in the 1920's*, p. 121.

Chapter 4

1. Clarence S. Stein, quoted in *Planning the Fourth Migration: The Neglected Vision of the Regional Planning Association of America*, ed. Carl Sussman (Cambridge, Mass.: M.I.T. Press, 1976), p. 15.

2. Benton MacKaye, "An Appalachian Trail: A Project in Regional Planning," *Journal of the American Institute of Architects* 9 (Oct. 1921): 329.

3. Henry Wright, Sr., New York Commission on Housing and Regional Planning, Report (Albany, May 7, 1926), p. 2.

4. "Appalachian Trail Conference Member Handbook" (Harpers Ferry, W. Va.: Appalachian Trail Conference, 1978), p. 5.

5. Clarence S. Stein, "Community Planning and Housing," *Journal of the American Institute of Architects* 10 (April 1922): 126.

6. MacKaye, "Appalachian Trail," p. 326.

7. *Ibid.*, p. 327.

8. Regional Planning Association of America (RPAA) Minutes, June 23, 1923, Clarence S. Stein Papers, Olin Library, Cornell University; MacKaye, "Appalachian Trail," p. 327.

9. MacKaye, "Appalachian Trail," p. 329.

10. See Lewis Mumford, intro. to Benton MacKaye, *The New Exploration: A Philosophy of Regional Planning* (1928; reprint ed., Urbana: University of Illinois Press, 1962).

11. RPAA Minutes, April 20, 1923.

12. Benton MacKaye, *From Geography to Geotechnics*, ed. Paul T. Bryant (Chicago: University of Illinois Press, 1968), p. 24.

13. The Appalachian Trail Conference first met in March 1925. It was headed by Major William A. Welch, manager of Palisade Interstate Park.

14. Benton MacKaye, *Employment and Natural Resources: Possibilities of Making New Opportunities for Employment through the Settlement and Development of Agricultural and Forest Lands and Other Natural Resources* (Washington, D.C.: Government Printing Office, 1919).

15. *Ibid.*, p. 22.

16. *Ibid.*, p. 10.

17. *Ibid.*, p. 18.

18. Wright, Housing and Regional Planning Commission, *Report*.

19. *Ibid.*, p. 11.   20. *Ibid.*, p. 16.

21. *Ibid.*, p. 25.   22. *Ibid.*, p. 26.

23. *Ibid.*, p. 35.   24. *Ibid.*, p. 37.

25. *Ibid.*, p. 64.   26. *Ibid.*, p. 70.

27. Henry Wright, Sr., "Discussions on the Possibilities of Regional Planning," unpub. ms., Oct. 17–19, 1927, Stein Papers.

28. Benton MacKaye, "Memorandum on Regional Engineering Series," unpub. ms., July 21, 1930, Stein Papers.

29. Frederick L. Ackerman, "Our Stake in Congestion," *The Survey* 54 (May 1, 1925): 141.

30. Lewis Mumford, "The Fourth Migration," *The Survey* 54 (May 1, 1925), reprinted in Lewis Mumford, *The Urban Prospect* (New York: Harcourt, Brace and World, 1968), pp. 11–20.

31. Mumford, *The Urban Prospect*, p. 14.

32. Frederick L. Ackerman, "The Facts Behind Technology," (New York: New York Continental Committee on Technology, 1932); Frederick L. Ackerman, "The Technologist Looks at the Depression," unpub. ms., July 27, 1932, Stein Papers.

33. Stuart Chase, *Men and Machines* (New York: Macmillan, 1929), ch. 19; Stuart Chase, "The Concept of Planning," Address to the Round Table Conference on Regionalism, Institute of Public Affairs, University of Virginia, Aug. 8, 1931, Stein Papers.

34. MacKaye, *The New Exploration*, p. 33.

35. Mumford, "The Plan of New York: I," *The New Republic* 71 (June 15, 1932): 124.

36. *Planning the Fourth Migration: The Neglected Vision of the Regional Planning Association of America*, ed. Carl Sussman, (Cambridge, Mass.: M.I.T. Press, 1976).

Chapter 5

1. Alfred E. Smith, New York Commission of Housing and Regional Planning, Legislative Document 1926, *Permanent Housing Relief* (Albany, Feb. 22, 1926), p. 28. Quoted in Anthony Jackson, *A Place Called Home: A History of Low-Cost Housing in Manhattan* (Cambridge, Mass.: M.I.T. Press, 1976), p. 182.

2. Alexander Bing, "Sunnyside Gardens: A Successful Experiment in Good Housing at Moderate Prices," *National Municipal Review* 15 (June 1926): 335.

3. Lawson Purdy in "Expert Opinion," a City Housing Corporation promotional pamphlet, April 15, 1928, Stein Papers.

4. *First Annual Report to Stockholders of the City Housing Corporation* (New York: City Housing Corporation, 1925), Radburn Papers.

5. "Expert Opinion."

6. The term is derived from George Soule, *Prosperity Decade: From War to Depression, 1917–1929* (New York: Rinehart and Company, 1947).

7. Quoted in William E. Leuchtenburg, *The Perils of Prosperity, 1914–1932* (Chicago: University of Chicago Press, 1958), p. 202.

8. Charles and Mary Beard, *The Rise of American Civilization*, II (New York: Macmillan, 1927), p. 704.

9. "Your Share in Housing," City Housing Corporation promotional pamphlet, 1924, Radburn Papers. Among the wealthier CHC stockholders were Felix Warburg, Ann Morgan, and Ogden L. Mills. See "New York's First Satellite Town: An Interview with Mr. Alexander M. Bing," *National Municipal Review* 17 (March 1928): 142–146.

10. See the *First Annual Report to Stockholders of the City Housing Corporation* (New York: City Housing Corporation, 1925), Radburn Papers.

11. "Your Share in Housing." Also see Henry M. Propper, "Construction Work Now Under Way on the 'Town for Motor Age,'" *American City* 39 (Oct. 1928): 81–82.

12. *First Annual Report.*

13. For an excellent detailed discussion of housing reform during the late nineteenth and early twentieth centuries (with special attention to the problems of housing reform in New York City), see Roy Lubove, *The Progressives and the Slums* (Pittsburgh: University of Pittsburgh Press, 1962). Much of the background information in this chapter is derived from Lubove's earlier work.

14. *Ibid.*, p. 37.

15. *Ibid.*, p. 35.

16. *Ibid.*, p. 37.

17. Sam Bass Warner, Jr., *Streetcar Suburbs: The Process of Growth in Boston, 1870–1900* (New York: Atheneum, 1974).

18. Edith Elmer Wood, *The Housing of the Unskilled Wage Earner* (New York: Macmillan, 1919), p. 98; Lubove, *The Progressives and the Slums*, p. 39.

19. Elgin R. L. Gould, *Eighth Special Report to the Commissioner of Labor* (Washington, D.C.: Government Printing Office, 1895), p. 9.

20. Gould, *Eighth Special Report*, p. 419.

21. Lubove, *The Progressives and the Slums*, p. 101.

22. Wood, *The Housing of the Unskilled Wage Earner*, pp. 98–99.

23. Lawrence Veiller, *Housing Reform* (New York: Russell Sage Foundation, 1910), pp. 72–73; Edith Elmer Wood, *Recent Trends in American Housing* (New York: Macmillan, 1931), p. 284.

24. Wood, *Recent Trends*, p. 84.

25. *Ibid.*

26. Clarence S. Stein, "The Housing Crisis in New York," *The Survey* 44 (Sept. 1, 1920): 660. Also see New York, Housing Committee of the Reconstruction Commission, *Report on Housing Conditions* (Albany, March 26, 1920); New York, Commission on Housing and Regional Planning, Legislative Document 1924, *The Present Status of the Housing Emergency* (Albany Dec. 22, 1923); Stein, "The Housing Crisis in New York"; Wood, *Recent Trends*, p. 84; Miles L. Colean, *Housing for Defense* (1940; reprint ed., New York: Arno Press, 1977), p. 3. For a wide-ranging discussion of the post–World War I housing crisis, see the following articles: John I. Bright, "The Building Industry in the United

States," *Journal of the American Institute of Architects* 8 (Aug. 1920): 307–310; Luther H. Gulick, "Attacking the Housing Problem," *The Survey* 43 (March 20, 1920): 763–764; Arthur Gleason, "Houses: The Need," *The Nation* 110 (April 17, 1920): 511–513; Harry Brigham, "How to Meet the Housing Situation," *Atlantic Monthly* 127 (March 1921): 404–413; Alfred E. Smith, "A Housing Policy for New York," *The Survey* 45 (Oct. 2, 1920): 3–4; Clarence S. Stein, "The Housing Crisis in New York," *The Survey* 44 (Sept. 1, 1920): 652–662; "Housing and Reconstruction," *Journal of the American Institute of Architects* 6 (Oct. 1918): 469–472; Samuel Untermyer, "Who Is Responsible for the Housing Shortage?" *Housing Problems in America: Proceedings of the Ninth National Conference on Housing* (New York: National Housing Association, 1923), pp. 19–29; Edith Elmer Wood, "Using Postal Savings Funds," *Housing Problems in America: Proceedings of the Ninth National Conference on Housing* (New York: National Housing Association, 1923), pp. 125–132.

27. Report on Housing Conditions, p. 38.

28. See Charles H. Whitaker, Frederick L. Ackerman, Richard S. Childs, and Edith Elmer Wood, *The Housing Problem in War and in Peace* (Washington, D.C.: Octagon, 1918).

29. James Ford, ed., *Report of Housing Corporation: I, Organizations, Policies, Transactions* (Washington, D.C.: Department of Labor, 1920); Henry V. Hubbard, ed., *Report of Housing Corporation: II, Houses, Site-Planning, Utilities* (Washington: Department of Labor, 1919); *Second Annual Report of the United States Shipping Board* (Washington, D.C.: Government Printing Office, 1918), especially pp. 112–113, 143–147; *Housing the Shipbuilders* (Philadelphia: U.S. Shipping Board, Passenger Transportation and Housing Division, Emergency Fleet Corporation, 1920); Charles H. Whitaker, "Housing as a War Problem," *Housing Problems in America: Proceedings of the Sixth National Conference on Housing* (Chicago: National Housing Association, 1917), pp. 3–12; John Nolen, "What England Has Done in War Housing," *Housing Problems in America: Proceedings of the Sixth National Conference on Housing* (Chicago: National Housing Association, 1917), pp. 13–17; Joseph Leland, "What the Federal Government Has Done to House the Industrial Army," *Housing Problems in America: Proceedings of the Seventh National Conference on Housing* (New York: National Housing Association, 1918), pp. 50–69; Boyd Fisher, "Good Housing as a Reducer of Labor Turnover," *Housing Problems in America* (New York: National Housing Association, 1918), pp. 147–

174. Also see Roy Lubove, "Homes and 'A Few Well Placed Fruit Trees': An Object Lesson in Federal Housing," *Social Research* 77 (Winter 1960): 469–489.

30. U.S., Congress, Senate, Subcommittee of the Committee on Public Buildings and Grounds, Hearings: United States Housing Corporation, 66th Cong., 1st Sess., 1919, p. 486.

31. Quoted in Wood, *Recent Trends*, p. 78.

32. *Ibid.*

33. Lubove, "Homes and 'A Few Well Placed Fruit Trees,'" p. 485.

34. *First Annual Report.*

35. Harry E. Ward in "Expert Opinion."

36. *First Annual Report.*

37. Alexander Bing, "$2,000,000 City Housing Corporation: 15-Year 6% Mortgage Collateral Trust Sinking Fund Bonds," City Housing Corporation announcement, July 1, 1927, Radburn Papers.

38. *Ibid.*

39. *First Annual Report.*

40. Preston William Slosson, *The Great Crusade and After, 1914–1928* (Boston: Houghton, Mifflin, 1964), p. 66.

41. Arthur M. Schlesinger, Jr., *The Crisis of the Old Order, 1919–1933* (Boston: Houghton, Mifflin, 1964), p. 66.

Chapter 6

1. Henry Wright, Sr., "The Autobiography of Another Idea," *Western Architect* 39 (Sept. 1930): 139.

2. Richard T. Ely, "The City Housing Corporation and Sunnyside," *Journal of Land and Public Utility Economics* 2 (April 1926): 184.

3. Lewis Mumford, "Houses: Sunnyside Up," *The Nation* 120 (Feb. 4, 1925): 116.

4. Clarence S. Stein, *Toward New Towns for America* (Cambridge, Mass.: M.I.T. Press, 1973), pp. 21–22; Rosalind Tough, "Production Costs of Urban Land in Sunnyside, Long Island," *Journal of Land and Public Utility Economics* 8 (Feb. 1932): 49.

5. Clarence S. Stein, "Radburn and the Radburn Idea," unpub. ms., Aug. 19, 1948, Stein Papers, Olin Library, Cornell University.

6. Stein, *Toward New Towns*, chs. 1 and 5.

7. *Ibid*, p. 24.

8. "Sunnyside and the Housing Problem," City Housing Corporation promotional pamphlet, c. 1925, Stein Papers.

9. Stein, *Toward New Towns*, p. 22.

10. Henry Wright, Sr., *Rehousing America* (New York: Columbia University Press, 1935), p. 75; Lewis Mumford, "Houses—Sunnyside-Up," *The Nation* 120 (Feb. 4, 1925): 115–116; Clarence S. Stein, "A New Venture in Housing," *American City* 32 (March 1925): 277–281.

11. Stein, "A New Venture in Housing," p. 32.

12. Stein, *Toward New Towns*, p. 35.

13. Alexander Bing, "Sunnyside Gardens: A Successful Experiment in Good Housing at Moderate Prices," *National Municipal Review* 15 (June 1926): 335.

14. City Housing Corporation promotional pamphlets, Stein Papers: "Sunnyside and the Housing Problem"; "Your Share in Better Housing," April 1924; and "Brick Garden Homes at Madison Court," June 1927.

15. Stein, *Toward New Towns*, p. 34; Maurice Leven, Harold G. Moulton, and Clark Warburton, *America's Capacity to Consume* (Washington: Brookings Institute, 1934), p. 222. Deriving aggregate statistics for family incomes in America prior to the 1930's is a difficult task. The federal government did not conduct sample field surveys of family incomes for all income and occupation groups until the Depression. Researchers had to piece together their estimates from a variety of sources, including data from the Internal Revenue Service, local and state surveys, and figures collected for select occupations.

16. *Fourth Annual Report to Stockholders of the City Housing Corporation* (New York: City Housing Corporation, 1928), Radburn Papers; Stein, *Toward New Towns*, pp. 31–34; interview with Charles Ascher, conducted by the author, Dec. 1, 1977, New York City.

17. Lewis Mumford, letter to the author, Oct. 27, 1977.

18. This innovation served as a model for the Federal Housing Author-

ity established in the 1930's, whose policies subsequently provided the financial mechanism fueling post–World War II suburban sprawl.

19. Stein, unpub. ms., Sept. 4, 1947, Stein Papers.

20. Stein, unpub. ms., Sept. 10, 1947, Stein Papers; interview with Charles Ascher; "Brick Garden Homes at Madison Court."

21. Herbert Emmerich, "The Problem of Low-Priced Cooperative Apartments: An Experiment at Sunnyside Gardens," *Journal of Land and Public Utility Economics* 4 (Aug. 1928): 225–234.

22. Ibid., p. 233.

23. "Low Priced Garden Homes Next Door to Manhattan," City Housing Corporation promotional pamphlet, c. 1925, Radburn Papers.

24. Stein, *Toward New Towns*, p. 28.

25. Ibid.

26. Wright, *Rehousing America*, p. 41.

27. Stein, *Toward New Towns*, p. 28.

28. Loula Lasker, "Sunnyside Up and Down," *Survey Graphic* 25 (July 1936): 420; *Fourth Annual Report to Stockholders of the City Housing Corporation* (New York: City Housing Corporation, 1928), Radburn Papers.

29. "Expert Opinion," a City Housing Corporation promotional pamphlet, April 15, 1928, Stein Papers.

30. Ibid.

Chapter 7

1. Geddes Smith, "A Town for the Motor Age," *Survey* 59 (March 1, 1928): 695.

2. "Radburn, A Town Planned for Safety," *The American Architect* 137 (Jan. 1930): 42. Quoted in Eugenie Ladner Birch, "Radburn and the American Planning Movement," *Journal of the American Planning Association* 46 (Oct. 1980): 427.

3. Mumford, intro. to Clarence S. Stein, *Toward New Towns for America* (Cambridge, Mass.: M.I.T. Press, 1973), p. 17.

4. Interview with Charles Ascher conducted by the author, Dec. 1, 1977, New York City.

5. Quoted in the New York Times, Feb. 12, 1928.

6. Stein, Toward New Towns, p. 48; Material for Board of Directors Meeting, Nov. 6, 1929, Stein Papers. Also see "Radburn Revisited," A Report of a Snag Club Discussion, April 3, 1951, Radburn Papers, Radburn Library, Fair Lawn, N.J.

7. Regional Planning Association of America (RPAA) Minutes, Oct. 8–9, 1927, Stein Papers.

8. For the prices of houses in Radburn see Louis Brownlow, "New Town Planned for the Motor Age," International Housing and Town Planning Bulletin (Feb. 1930): 4–11.

9. For Radburn's demographic composition in its early stages of development, see Robert Bowman Hudson, Radburn: A Plan for Living (New York: American Association for Adult Education, 1934).

10. Ebenezer Howard, Garden Cities of To-morrow (1902; reprint ed., Cambridge, Mass.: M.I.T. Press, 1973), p. 59.

11. For a discussion of the Radburn Association see Charles Ascher, "How Can a Section of a Town Get What It Is Prepared to Pay For?" American City 40 (June 1929): 98–99; Charles Ascher, "The Extra-Municipal Administration of Radburn: An Experiment in Government by Contract," National Municipal Review 18 (July 1929): 442–446; Charles Ascher, "Community Life in Radburn," The Survey 66 (April 15, 1931): 99–100; Charles Ascher, "Private Covenants in Urban Redevelopment," in Urban Redevelopment: Problems and Practices, ed. Coleman Woodbury (Chicago: University of Chicago Press, 1953).

12. Interview with Charles Ascher.

13. RPAA Minutes, Oct. 8–9, 1927.

14. The planned community of Mariemont, Ohio (designed by John Nolen) was the first to be described as a "town for the motor age." See the New York Times, Aug. 24, 1924. However, the combined force of Radburn's revolutionary site plan, the extensive publicity the town received, and the widespread adaptation of the "Radburn idea" in twentieth-century New Towns have given Radburn exclusive title to the epithet.

15. Stein, Toward New Towns, p. 17.

16. Mark B. Lapping, "Radburn: Planning the American Community," *New Jersey History* 95 (Summer 1977): 92.

17. For an in-depth analysis of the superblock, see Stein, *Toward New Towns*, pp. 37–57.

18. Benton MacKaye, RPAA Minutes, Oct. 17–19, 1927.

19. Stein, "Annual Conference of the New Jersey Federation of Official Planning Boards," unpublished notes, Oct. 30, 1939, Stein Papers.

20. *New York Times*, Jan. 26, 1928.

21. Lewis Mumford, *The City in History: Its Origins, Its Transformations, and Its Prospects* (New York: Harcourt, Brace and World, 1961), plate 51.

22. Henry Wright, Sr., "Planning a Town for Wholesome Living," *Playground* (March 1929): 684.

23. Charles Ascher, letter to Ronald Gatti, Jan. 27, 1979, Radburn Papers.

24. Louis Brownlow, "Building for the Motor Age," *Housing Problems in America: Proceedings of the Tenth National Conference on Housing* (New York: National Housing Association, 1929), p. 149.

25. Clarence S. Stein, "Cities to Come," unpub. ms., c. 1955, Stein Papers.

26. Stein, *Toward New Towns*, p. 225.

27. See Clarence Perry, "The Neighborhood Unit, a Scheme of Arrangement for the Family-Life Community," *Neighborhood and Community Planning*. For the relationship between Radburn and Perry's concepts, see Lapping, "Radburn: Planning the American Community," pp. 93–94. Urban planners in Kohn and Hamburg, Germany, were designing neighborhoods similar to those proposed by Perry at the same time. Their plans were conceived and developed independently, and suggest that planners throughout the western world were responding to the automobile's impact in remarkably similar ways. See Lewis Mumford, "What Is a City?" *Architectural Record* (Nov. 1937): 59–62.

28. See the promotional literature distributed by the City Housing Corporation, Radburn Papers: for example, "Radburn Garden Homes," Sept. 1, 1930; and "Announcing Radburn, A New Town," c. 1930. Also see Henry M. Propper, "A New Town Planned for the Motor Age,"

American City 38 (Feb. 1928): 152–154; Henry M. Propper, "Radburn's Unique Plan Shows Results," *American City* 41 (Nov. 1929): 142–144; Geddes Smith, "The Radburn Way," *Outlook* 153 (Oct. 16, 1929): 257; Henry Wright, Sr., "Planning a Town for Wholesome Living," pp. 182–184.

29. Clarence S. Stein, "The Radburn Idea," unpub. ms., undated, Stein Papers.

30. Stein, *Toward New Towns*, p. 39.

31. "Radburn Garden Homes."

32. Clarence S. Stein and Catherine Bauer, "Store Buildings and Neighborhood Shopping Centers," *Architectural Record* 75 (Feb. 1934): 185, 178. The neighborhood or local shopping center would consist mainly of food stores with service stores such as laundries, drug stores, and shoe repair shops also available. The regional shopping center, serving customers throughout Bergen County, would contain department stores and specialty shops. Three local shopping centers were proposed for Radburn's first "neighborhood unit" of 10,000 people, but only one, designed by Frederick Ackerman, was constructed. Plans for the regional center never advanced beyond the discussion stage.

33. Stein, "The Radburn Idea"; Lapping, "Planning the American Community," p. 97.

34. Lewis Mumford, letter to the author, Nov. 16, 1977.

35. Stein, *Toward New Towns*, p. 17.

36. Stein, "Cities to Come."

37. For a discussion of the ideas and experiments which influenced the creation of the "Radburn Idea," see *ibid*. Also see Henry Wright, Sr., "The Autobiography of Another Idea," *Western Architect* 39 (Sept. 1930): 137–141, 153.

38. For a discussion of the "highwayless town" and "townless highway," see Benton MacKaye, "Roads vs. Shuttles," *American City* 44 (March 1931): 125–126; Benton MacKaye "Townless Highways to Relieve Through-Traffic Congestion and Restore a Rural Wayside Environment," *American City* 42 (May 1930): 94–96; and Benton MacKaye and Lewis Mumford, "Townless Highways for the Motorist," *Harpers* 163 (Aug. 1931): 347–356.

39. James Dahir, *Communities for Better Living: Citizen Achievement*

in Organization, Design and Development (New York: Harper and Brothers, 1950), pp. 189–190.

40. Thomas Adams, Edward Bassett, and Robert Whitten, "Neighborhood and Community Planning: Problems of Unbuilt Areas," in Regional Survey of New York and Its Environs, ed. Thomas Adams, 8 vols. (New York: New York Committee on the Regional Plan of New York and Its Environs, 1929), vol. 7, Neighborhood and Community Planning, p. 256.

41. Walter Creese, The Search for Environment: The Garden City, Before and After (New Haven: Yale University Press, 1966), p. 303.

42. Mumford, intro. to Toward New Towns, p. 17.

Chapter 8

1. Quoted in Lewis Mumford, "A Modest Man's Enduring Contributions to Urban and Regional Planning," Journal of the American Institute of Architects 65 (Dec. 1976): 22.

2. Robert Bowman Hudson, Radburn: A Plan for Living (New York: American Association for Adult Education, 1934), p. v.

3. Quoted in Anthony Baily, "Radburn Revisited," New York Herald Tribune (Sept. 27, 1964), p. 10.

4. Interview with William Elbow conducted by Nancy Moreland, June 14, 1978, Cape Cod, Mass., Radburn Papers, Radburn Library, Fair Lawn, N.J.

5. Interview with William Elbow.

6. Hudson, A Plan for Living, pp. 11–12.

7. See the promotional literature published by the City Housing Corporation, Radburn Papers: for example, "Radburn Garden Homes," Sept. 1, 1930; "Announcing Radburn, a New Town," c. 1930; "Radburn Model Homes," c. 1930; and "A New Lease on Living: Radburn, the Town for the Motor Age," c. 1931.

8. "Radburn Model Homes," p. 18.

9. John B. Rae, The Road and the Car in American Life (Cambridge, Mass.: M.I.T. Press, 1970), p. 50.

10. Michael Mikkelsen, "Riverdale Country Club: Riverdale-On-Hudson—New York City," Architectural Record 49 (Nov. 1920): 433.

11. A. Lawrence Kocher, "The Country House: An Analysis of the Architect's Method of Approach," *Architectural Record* 62 (Nov. 1927): 337.

12. Geddes Smith, "A Town for the Motor Age," *The Survey* 59 (March 1, 1928): 697.

13. Henry M. Propper, "Construction Work Now Under Way on the 'Town for the Motor Age,'" *American City* 39 (Oct. 1928): 82.

14. Maurice Leven, Harold G. Moulton, and Clark Warburton, *America's Capacity to Consume* (Washington, D.C.: Brookings Institution, 1934), p. 232.

15. Hudson, *A Plan for Living*, pp. 13–14.

16. Ibid., p. 15.

17. Ibid., p. 12.

18. Ibid., p. 12.

19. Robert A. Turner, "A Community-School Project," *Recreation* 29 (Sept. 1935): 194–196. For a favorable portrait of life in Radburn see Henry M. Propper, "Social Activities in the Town for the Motor Age," *National Municipal Review* 19 (Nov. 1930): 743–746.

20. "At Radburn: 1932 House Models," City Housing Corporation promotional pamphlet, 1932, Radburn Papers.

21. Hudson, *A Plan for Living*, pp. 16–63.

22. Ibid, p. 8.

23. Interview with John O. Walker conducted by Nancy Moreland, May 4, 1978, Alexandria, Va., Radburn Papers.

24. Interview with Charles Ascher conducted by the author, Dec. 1, 1977, New York City.

25. Interview with John O. Walker.

26. Evidence about Radburn's discriminatory policies are difficult to obtain. Written documents are not available, and residents are reluctant to discuss such a sensitive issue. In a recent interview, however, John O. Walker commented that each prospective homeowner had to fill out a questionnaire. This form was used to determine if the family would fit into Radburn's social environment. Other residents, most notably William Elbow, stated that would-be homeowners were screened to exclude Jews and Blacks. Black and Jewish families were, in fact, virtually

Garden Cities for America 258

excluded from Radburn throughout the 1930's. Interviews with John O. Walker and William Elbow.

27. Radburn Association Minutes, March 11, 1929, Radburn Papers.

28. Charles Ascher, "Radburn Protective Restrictions and Community Administration: Declaration of Restrictions, Certificate of Incorporation, and By-Laws of the Radburn Association" (Fair Lawn, N.J.: Radburn Association, 1929), pp. 1, 12, Radburn Papers.

29. Interview with Charles Ascher.

30. "Protective Restrictions," pp. 3, 29.

31. *Ibid.*, p. 2.

32. Radburn Association Minutes, March 11, 1929.

33. Charles Ascher, "How Can a Section of a Town Get What It Is Prepared to Pay For?" *American City* 40 (June 1929): 98.

34. "Radburn Garden Homes," p. 4.

35. Betty Fullerton, "The Test Is in the Living: A Critique of Radburn and Other Planned Communities," unpub. ms., c. 1948, Stein Papers.

36. "Protective Restrictions," p. 17.

37. Interview with William Elbow.

38. Charles Ascher, "Private Covenants in Urban Redevelopment," *Urban Redevelopment: Problems and Practices*, ed. Coleman Woodburn (Chicago: University of Chicago Press, 1953), p. 286.

39. The planners' concern about excessive community supervision was expressed in a conference held just prior to the construction of Radburn. See "Problems Connected with a Garden City," Regional Planning Association of America (RPAA) Minutes, Oct. 8–9, 1927, Stein Papers.

40. Radburn Association Minutes, Nov. 14, 1929; Nov. 3, 1930; Nov. 2, 1931.

41. *Ibid.*, Oct. 6, 1930.

42. *Ibid.*, Nov. 3, 1930.

43. *Ibid.*, Dec. 2, 1929.

44. Mark B. Lapping, "Radburn: Planning the American Community," *New Jersey History* 95 (Summer 1977): 85–100.

Chapter 9

1. Alexander Bing, "To the Home Owners—Sunnyside Gardens," letter, February 27, 1935. United States District Court for the Southern District of New York, Proceedings for the Reorganization of the City Housing Corporation (No. 60286), Federal Archives, Bayonne, N.J.

2. Benjamin Ginzburg, "Sunnyside Back and Forth," *Survey Graphic* (Aug. 1936): 496.

3. Loula D. Lasker, "Sunnyside Up and Down," *Survey Graphic* 25 (July 1936): 441.

4. *Fourth Annual Report to Stockholders of the City Housing Corporation* (New York: City Housing Corporation, 1927), Radburn Papers, Radburn Library, Fair Lawn, N.J. Also interview with Charles Ascher conducted by the author, Dec. 1, 1977, New York City.

5. *Sixth Annual Report to Stockholders of the City Housing Corporation* (New York: City Housing Corporation, 1929), Radburn Papers; Roy Lubove, *Community Planning in the 1920's: The Contribution of the Regional Planning Association of America* (Pittsburgh: University of Pittsburgh Press, 1963), p. 62.

6. *New York Times*, April 27, 1930, Section 12 ("Real Estate"), p. 12; *New York Times*, May 26, 1930, p. 20.

7. *Fifth Annual Report to Stockholders of the City Housing Corporation* (New York: City Housing Corporation, 1928), Radburn Papers.

8. *Business Week Magazine*, July 9, 1930, p. 19.

9. *Eighth Annual Report to Stockholders of the City Housing Corporation* (New York: City Housing Corporation, 1931), Radburn Papers; *Ninth Annual Report to Stockholders of the City Housing Corporation* (New York: City Housing Corporation, 1932), Radburn Papers; *Tenth Annual Report to Stockholders of the City Housing Corporation* (New York: City Housing Corporation, 1933), Radburn Papers.

10. Quoted in Clarence S. Stein, unpub. notes, Sept. 4, 1947, Stein Papers.

11. See Radburn Association Minutes, May 16, 1929; Dec. 2, 1929; Dec. 7, 1931; Dec. 17, 1930; Dec. 20, 1933; Dec. 20, 1932, Radburn Papers.

12. Anton H. Frederich, "Case History of a Community of Mortgaged Home-Owners," *Survey Graphic* 22 (June 1933): 311–312.

13. Anton H. Frederich, quoted in Lasker, "Sunnyside Up and Down," p. 423.

14. Ginzburg, "Sunnyside Back and Forth," p. 496.

15. Stein, unpub. notes, Oct. 8, 1943, Stein Papers.

16. Lasker, "Sunnyside Up and Down," p. 420.

17. Betty Fullerton, "The Test Is in the Living: A Critique of Radburn and Other Planned Communities," unpub. ms., c. 1948, Stein papers, p. 6; Lasker, "Sunnyside Up and Down," p. 422.

18. *New York Times*, Aug. 2, 1934, p. 27.

19. Lasker, "Sunnyside Up and Down," p. 425.

20. For a sampling of the CHC's self-proclaimed mission, see the company's promotional literature in the Radburn Library: for example, "Sunnyside Gardens," c. 1928; "Radburn Garden Homes," Sept. 1, 1930; and "Announcing Radburn," c. 1930.

21. Lasker, "Sunnyside Up and Down," p. 440; *New York Times*, March 25, 1935.

22. 340 of the 600 homeowners in Sunnyside participated in the strike. *New York Times*, April 11, 1935.

23. Ibid.

24. Ibid., April 16, 1935; ibid., Nov. 15, 1935.

25. Ginzburg, "Sunnyside Back and Forth," p. 496.

26. *New York Times*, Jan. 15, 1936.

27. Lasker, "Sunnyside Up and Down," p. 423.

28. *New York Times*, June 23, 1936.

29. Clarence S. Stein, "Sunnyside: The Organization of the Community," unpub. ms., Aug. 26, 1947, Stein Papers.

30. Alexander Bing, "Sunnyside Back and Forth," *Survey Graphic* 25 (Aug. 1936): 496.

31. *New York Times*, April 10, 1933.

32. See Hudson, *A Plan for Living*, ch. 1. Also an interview with John O. Walker conducted by Nancy Moreland, May 4, 1978, Alexandria, Va., Radburn Papers.

33. Interview with William Elbow conducted by Nancy Moreland, June 14, 1978, Cape Cod, Mass., Radburn Papers.

34. Ibid., "Report of the Special Evaluation Committee of the First Citizen's Association of Radburn, New Jersey," Nov. 1, 1938, p. 5, Radburn Papers.

35. Radburn Association Minutes, Nov. 18, 1935; Dec. 30, 1935, Radburn Papers.

36. Charles Ascher, "How Can a Section of a Town Get What It Is Prepared to Pay For?" *American City* 40 (June 1929): 99.

37. "Report of the Special Evaluation Committee," p. 8.

38. Ibid., p. 20.   39. Ibid., p. 21.

40. Ibid.   41. Ibid.

42. Robert Carlisle in the Radburn Association Minutes, Nov. 14, 1936.

43. Radburn Association Minutes, Feb. 20, 1939.

Chapter 10

1. Catherine Bauer, *Modern Housing* (1934; reprint ed., New York: Arno Press, 1974), p. 114.

2. Lewis Mumford, "The Fate of Garden Cities," *Journal of the American Institute of Architects* 15 (Feb. 1927): 38.

3. Albert Mayer, *The Urgent Future* (New York: McGraw-Hill, 1967), p. 7.

4. The dwindling number of housing starts was startling. In 1932, there were only 134,000 housing starts in the United States as compared to 937,000 in 1925 at the peak of the housing boom between the wars. In 1933, housing starts sunk to a dismal 93,000 units. This dramatic downward spiral had a dire impact on both housing stock and employment. See "New Housing Units Started, by Ownership, Type of Structure, Location and Construction Cost: 1889–1970," *Historical Statistics of the United States, Colonial Times to 1970* (Washington, D.C.: U.S. Bureau of the Census, 1975), p. 640.

5. Clarence S. Stein, *Toward New Towns for America* (Cambridge, Mass.: M.I.T. Press, 1973), pp. 182–183; Joseph L. Arnold, *The New Deal in the Suburbs* (Columbus: Ohio State University Press, 1971), pp. 38–39, 61–77, 88–90, 93–103.

6. *Planning the Fourth Migration*, ed. Carl Sussman (Cambridge, Mass.: M.I.T. Press, 1976), p. 40. Also Roy Lubove, *Twentieth Century Pittsburgh: Government, Business and Environmental Change* (Pittsburgh: University of Pittsburgh Press, 1969), pp. 71–82.

7. Roy Lubove, *Community Planning in the 1920's: The Contribution of the Regional Planning Association of America* (Pittsburgh: Pittsburgh University Press, 1963), p. 127.

8. Lewis Mumford, "Regional Planning"; Benton MacKaye, "Cultural Aspects of Regionalism"; Stuart Chase, "The Concept of Planning," Address to the Round Table Conference on Regionalism, Institute of Public Affairs, University of Virginia, Aug. 3, 1931, Stein Papers.

9. Interview with Charles Ascher conducted by the author, Dec. 1, 1977, New York City.

10. "Unemployment: 1890 to 1970," *Historical Statistics of the United States, Colonial Times to 1970* (Washington, D.C.: Bureau of the Census, 1975), p. 135; Mark I. Gelfand, *A Nation of Cities: The Federal Government and Urban America, 1933–1965* (New York: Oxford University Press, 1975), p. 59.

11. Arnold, *The New Deal in the Suburbs*; Paul Conkin, *Tomorrow a New World: The New Deal Community Program* (Ithaca, N.Y.: Cornell University Press, 1959).

12. John L. Hancock, "Planners in the Changing American City, 1900–1940," in *American Urban History*, ed. Alexander B. Callow, Jr. (New York: Oxford University Press, 1973), p. 609.

13. U.S., Housing and Home Finance Agency, "Housing Statistics: Historical Supplement" (Washington, D.C.: The Agency, Oct. 1961), p. 8.

14. Lewis Mumford, Henry Wright, Sr., and Albert Mayer, "New Homes for New Deal: A Concrete Program," *The New Republic* 78 (March 7, 1934): 91–94.

15. Mumford, Wright, and Mayer, "New Homes," p. 92.

16. Frederick L. Ackerman, "National Planning," *National Municipal Review* 8 (Jan. 1919): 15–25.

17. Mumford, Wright, and Mayer, "New Homes," p. 94.

Index

A

Ackerman, Frederick L., 35, 39, 41, 56, 57–58, 72, 93, 117, 123, 256; on growth, 49; on regional planning, 29, 35; on speculation, 58, 72, 91. See also Sunnyside Gardens

Adams, Thomas, 74–76, 116; on Radburn, 4, 164

Adler, Felix, 32, 106, 110

Agar, John G., 106

AICP. See New York Association for the Improvement of the Condition of the Poor

Amalgamated Clothing Workers' Union, 129

American Architect, on Radburn, 145

American City, on garden cities, 31

American Institute of Architects (AIA), 46, 71. See also Journal of the American Institute of Architects

American Irving Trust Company, 193, 208

American Radiator Company, 159

Appalachian project, 81–87

Appalachian Trail. See Appalachian project

"Appalachian Trail: A Project in Regional Planning" (MacKaye), 81

Appalachian Trail Conference, 84–85, 247

Architectural Record, on country clubs, 171

Aronovici, Carol, 227

Ascher, Charles, 56, 127, 149, 179; on Radburn, 152, 155, 177, 180, 183–184

Astral Apartments (Brooklyn, N.Y.), 109

Attached houses, 156, 220–221

Atterbury, Grosvenor, 33

Auger, Tracy, 56

Australia, land use in, 86

Automobiles, 61, 90, 163, 170–172; in Radburn, 7–8, 152–155, 156, 160–161, 163

B

Bauer, Catherine, 56; on socialeconomic systems, 217

Beard, Charles and Mary, on social reform, 104–105

Bellamy, Edward, 236

265

Belmont, August, 32
Bergen County (N.J.), 147–148; demography, 3. *See also* Fair Lawn; Radburn
Bettman, Alfred, on regional planning, 73
Bing, Alexander, 41, 51–54, 56, 105, 179, 220; and CHC, 51, 103, 105–106, 117, 147, 194, 197–198, 200; on the Depression, 189; on speculation, 101; on Sunnyside, 115, 202. *See also* City Housing Corporation
Bing, Leo S., 105, 106
Bird, Charles S., Jr., 106
Bittenheim, Harold, 56
Black, Russel Van Nest, 56
Bliss, William D. P., 32
Block associations, in Sunnyside, 130–131, 184
Bourneville (Eng.), 19
Bridgeport (Conn.), 113
"Broadside flats" (Wright), 39
Brownlow, Louis, 179
Bruère, Robert, 56, 72
Buckingham, James, 236
Buhl Foundation, 222
Burbank (Calif.), 65–66
Business, and social reform, 51, 104–105, 118, 219; Chase on, 224. *See also* Limited dividends, history of
Business Week, on Radburn, 192

C

Cadbury, George, 19
Capital. *See* Financing
Carlisle, John, 177
Central Park (New York City), 163
Chase, Stuart, 11, 56, 221–222, 224; on engineering, 93; on industry, 224
Chatham Village (Pittsburgh, Pa.), 222–223
CHC. *See* City Housing Corporation
Chicago World's Fair (1893–1894), 31
Children, planning for, 157–158; in Radburn, 6–8, 175, 204
Childs, Louis, 32
Churchill, Henry, 227
Citizen's Association (Radburn), 176, 177, 184–185; Special Evaluation Committee, 205–207
City and Suburban Homes Company, 109–110
City Beautiful movement, 31
City Housing Corporation (CHC), 11, 12, 51, 103–107, 111, 113, 115–118, 219–221; advisory board, 116–117; bankruptcy, 193–194, 208–209; board of directors, 106; and Radburn, 147–149, 159, 170, 177, 179–182, 184, 186–187, 192–195, 202–209; and Sunnyside, 121–122, 127–133, 195–202
Cluster housing, 71; in Radburn, 154–155, 156; in Sunnyside, 124
Coal, 37, 61, 89
Coffin, William Sloane, 106
Columbia (Md.), 8, 234
Commerce, planning for, 65–66, 157; in Radburn, 160–161, 256
Committee on Community Planning (AIA), 46, 71

Garden Cities for America 266

Community planning, 10, 65, 70; MacKaye on, 224; in Radburn, 160, 172. See also Regional planning
Company towns, 54
Congestion, of population, 32, 58, 62–63, 64. See also Population growth
Construction costs, 45, 53–54, 68–69, 112, 113, 225; and CHC, 116; in Sunnyside, 122
Construction schedules, 54, 116; in Sunnyside, 123
Continental Committee on Technocracy, 93
"Conurbations" (Geddes), 37, 61
Co-operative apartments, 129–130
Copeland, Royal, 199
Cost of housing. See Construction, cost of; Financing; Housing costs, for consumers; Land, cost of
Country Club District (Kansas City, Mo.), 160
Country clubs, 170–172
Craftsman, on garden cities, 31
Creese, Walter, on open space, 164
Cul-de-sacs, in Radburn, 8, 154–155, 156

D
Davis, William Morris, 39–40
Death and Life of Great American Cities (Jacobs), 59
Decentralization, of population, 59, 90–91. See also Population movement
De Forest, Robert W., 34; on restrictive legislation, 67

Department of Housing and Urban Development, 226
Depression, 224–226, 262; Bing on, 189; and Radburn, 12, 160, 187, 191–192, 194–195, 202–209; and Sunnyside, 125, 127, 128–129, 194–202, 208
Desmond, Thomas C., 106
Detached houses, 52–53, 220
Districting. See Zoning
Duluth (Minn.), 66
Dunbar (Paul Lawrence) Apartments (Harlem, N.Y.), 129–130

E
Economy, and housing, 111–112, 117, 221; Bauer on, 217. See also Depression
Eidlitz, Otto M., 116
Eighth Special Report to the Commissioner of Labor (Gould), 109
Elbow, William, on Radburn, 169, 259
Electricity, 37, 61, 90
Elliman, Douglas L., 106
Elliot, John, 200
Ely, Richard, 106, 117; on Sunnyside, 119, 122
Emergency Fleet Corporation, 114–115, 116
Emmerich, Herbert, 148, 179
Employment and Natural Resources . . . (MacKaye), 40, 85
Energy, 37, 61, 89, 90
Engineers, 65, 93
England, urban planning in, 17–22, 35, 113
Englewood (N.J.), 149

Index 267

"Epoch I" (Wright), 88–89
"Epoch II" (Wright), 89–90
"Epoch III" (Wright), 90–91
Equitable Life Assurance Company, 193, 199, 201, 208
Erie Railroad, 149, 159, 192

F
Fair Lawn (N.J.), 147–148, 203–204
Families, planning for, 157–158; in Radburn, 6–7. See also Children, planning for
Family Day, in Radburn, 6–7
Federal Housing Authority, 22, 230, 253
Financing, 34, 42–43, 45–46, 52, 54, 55, 69, 226; by CHC, 127–128, 193–194, 196–198, 202; of CHC, 103–107, 193–195; and Housing Guild, 227–229; Howard and, 19, 20–21; of Radburn, 11, 132, 155. See also Limited dividends; Speculation
Ford, George B., 243; on regional planning, 73
Ford, James, 34
Forest Hills (N.Y.), 33, 151, 178
Fort Lee (N.J.), 3
"Fourth Migration" (Mumford), 92
Frazer, Spaulding, 177
Fuller, R. Buckminster, 229

G
Garden Cities Association of America, 32–33
Garden Cities of To-morrow (Howard). See *To-morrow: A Peaceful Path to Real Reform*
Garden City Association (Eng.), 19, 20, 74
Garden city movement, 10, 12, 59–60, 230–231; in England, 17–22, 163; Jacobs on, 59; literature on, 235–236; Lubove on, 31; Mumford on, 15, 17–18, 49, 57, 217; and population growth, 18, 55, 152; and Radburn, 10, 149–152, 162–163; and social reform, 17–18, 21–22, 33, 93–94, 219–221, 231; in U.S., 31–34, 35, 46–47, 55–57, 223, 225, 230–231. See also names of individual persons and organizations
Garden suburb, 52
Geddes, Patrick, 36–37, 71, 84
George, Henry, 236
George Washington Bridge, 148, 159, 192
"Geotechnics" (Geddes), 40, 84
Germany, urban planning in, 31, 64, 255–256
Gilbert, Charles K., on CHC, 104
Ginzburg, Benjamin, on philanthropists, 189
Glen Rock (N.J.), 149
Gould, Elgin R. L., 109. See also City and Suburban Homes Company
Government, and urban planning, 73, 86–87, 118, 224–231; housing construction, 34, 35, 42–43, 57, 113–116, 118, 221–222, 225, 226, 227–229, 230–231. See also names of individual agencies and commissions
Greenbelt (Md.), 225

Greenbelt town program, 221, 225
Greenbrook (N.J.), 221
Greendale (Wisc.), 225
Greenhills (Ohio), 225
Greenpoint (Brooklyn, N.Y.), 109

H
Harkness tract (Brooklyn, N.Y.), 51, 54, 121
Hawes, Mrs. Henrietta, 179
"Heritage of the Cities Movement in America: An Historical Survey" (Mumford), 35–36
Hofheimer Foundation, 198
Holland, housing legislation in, 43, 113
Homestead Act (1862), 86
Houses, design of, 39, 52–53, 229; in Radburn, 155–156, 162, 170; in Sunnyside, 124–125. See also names of housing types
Housing, low cost, 34, 44, 51–52, 67–68, 227–229; government construction of, 113–115, 225; history of, 107–111; in Radburn, 150–151, 172–173; in Sunnyside, 127–132. See also Poor, housing for
Housing Act of 1919 (Eng.), 21
Housing costs, for consumers, 108, 112; in Radburn, 5, 150–151, 172–173, 193–194, 202; in Sunnyside, 125–126, 127–129, 193–194, 195–198
Housing Guild, 227–230
Housing shortage, 34, 42, 66–67, 111–112, 262

Howard, Ebenezer, 15, 17–22, 31–32, 55, 71, 236
Howe, Frederick C., 31
Hudson, Robert, on Radburn, 167, 169, 174
Hudson Guild Farm, 84, 149
Hudson Valley, 89, 91

I
Improved Dwellings Association (Boston, Mass.), 109
Independent, on CHC, 104
Industrial towns. See Company towns
Industry, planning for, 18, 40, 61, 65–66, 82, 85–86; in Radburn, 150, 159–160. See also Technology, effect of, on environment
Interest rates, 45, 69, 108. See also Financing; Limited dividends
International Garden Cities and Town Planning Federation, 55, 241
International Town, City and Planning Conference (1925), 71–72
Investment capital. See Financing
Irving Trust Company, 193, 208

J
Jacobs, Jane, on garden cities, 59
JAIA. See Journal of the American Institute of Architects
James, Darwin R., on CHC, 104
Journal of the American Institute of Architects (JAIA), 34, 35, 36, 39, 46, 81

K

Kellogg, Paul, 72
Kessler, George, 38
Kocher, A. Lawrence, on country houses, 172
Kohn, Robert D., 38, 41, 56, 117, 222
Kropotkin, Peter, 236
Ktsanes, Thomas, on suburbs, 10

L

Land, cost of, 51–52, 53; and CHC, 116; in Radburn, 121, 148–149; in Sunnyside, 121, 132
Land use, 32, 42, 55, 62–63, 86; and CHC, 116; linear, 10, 61; polynucleated, 10, 35, 60–61, 88, 152; in Radburn, 161–162, 163–165. See also Site planning
Lasker, Loula, on limited dividend housing, 189
Lehman, Arthur, 200
Lehman, Herbert H., 199
Le Play, Frédéric, 36
Letchworth (Eng.), 20–21, 22, 71, 74, 162
Lever, W. H., 19
Limited dividends, 11, 20, 45, 52, 54, 103, 106; Bing on, 101; and CHC, 106–107, 113, 192, 193, 200–201, 208; history of, 107–111; Lasker on, 189; in Sunnyside, 125, 131; Wood on, 109, 110
Llewellyn Park (N.J.), 151
Looking Backward (Bellamy), 236
Lord, Frank, 106

Los Angeles (Calif.), 66, 73–74
Low cost housing. See Housing, low cost
Lubove, Roy: on garden cities, 31; on housing reform, 107; on RPAA, 69, 223

M

MacKaye, Benton, 11, 39–40, 56, 72; Appalachian project, 79, 81–87; on community planning, 224; on "folk flows," 93; on industry, 40; on regional planning, 39–40, 91, 163
Macy, V. Everit, 106
Manager of Radburn, 9, 178, 182–183, 207
Mariemont (Ohio), 33, 254
Martin, John, 106
Mass transit, 63. See also Railroads
Mayer, Albert, 227; on planning, 217
Mikkelsen, Michael, on Riverdale Country Club, 171
Mills, Ogden L., 248
Morgan, Ann, 248
Mortgages. See Financing
Multi-unit houses, 39, 128–129, 156
Mumford, Lewis, 11, 35–37, 56, 60, 72, 75–76, 127; on Appalachian project, 84; on garden cities, 15, 17–18, 49, 57, 217; on growth, 58, 76; on "migrations," 92–93; on Radburn, 4, 49, 145, 154, 164; on regional planning, 36–37, 56, 75–76, 224; on RPAA, 55, 70, 162; on social planning, 3, 36, 62,

Garden Cities for America   270

94, 231; on Sunnyside, 119, 127
Municipal services, 68, 71, 73; in New York City, 60; in Radburn, 159, 170, 185–187; in Sunnyside, 123

N

National Housing Association, 115
National Resource Planning Board, 225, 230
National Women's Trade Union League, 115
"Neighborhood unit" concept, 33, 157–158; in Radburn, 158–159, 160
Neighborliness, promotion of. See Social planning
"Neotechnic order" (Geddes), 37–38, 60–61
Netcong (N.J.), 71, 149
Neville, Ralph, 19
New Exploration: Regional Planning (MacKaye), 84, 93
New Jersey Bell Telephone Company, 159
New Republic, on CHC, 104
New York Association for the Improvement of the Condition of the Poor (AICP), 107, 109–110
New York City, 60, 64, 66; demography, 89, 90; housing shortage, 111–112. *See also* names of individual places and organizations
New York Commission on Congestion of Population, 64
New York Commission on Housing and Regional Planning, 43–46, 71; Wright report, 75, 87–92
New York Housing Authority, 222
New York Housing Committee (Reconstruction Commission), 41–43; on housing conditions, 112–113
New York Metropolitan Life Insurance Company, 124
New York Reconstruction Commission, 41. *See also* New York Housing Committee
New York state, 87–92. *See also* names of individual places and organizations
New York Tenement House Building Company, 109
New York Times, on Radburn, 154, 191
Nolen, John, 34, 254
"Nothing Gained by Overcrowding" (Unwin), 71

O

Old Mill (Radburn), 149
Olmsted, Frederick Law, Jr., 33
Olmsted, Frederick Law, Sr., 163, 236
Open space, 18, 83, 157; Appalachian project, 81–87; Creese on, 164; in Radburn, 125, 149–150, 151, 153, 155, 157, 162, 163, 164, 170, 172; in Sunnyside, 123–124, 125, 130–131
Osborn, Frederic J.: on Howard, 15; on Letchworth, 20
Ownership, of land, 32, 55, 86, 118, 226, 228; and CHC, 116,

Index   271

Ownership, of land (cont.) 127–129, 147–149, 151. See also Financing; Speculation

P

"Paleotechnic era" (Geddes), 37, 60–61
Palos Verdes Estates (Calif.), 33, 178
Paramus (N.J.), 7
Parker, Barry, 20, 71
Parkland. See Open space
Pasadena (Calif.), 66
Paul Lawrence Dunbar Apartments (Harlem, N.Y.), 129–130
Pedestrians, in Radburn, 7–8, 152, 153, 160
Pennsylvania and Long Island Rail Road Company, 121
Perry, Clarence, 33, 157–158
Peters, Ralph, 32
Phipps Apartments (Sunnyside, N.Y.), 122
Physical planning, 7–8. See also Site planning
Politics, 93–94; in Radburn, 177–187, 205–208. See also Government, and urban planning; Social reform; names of individual persons and organizations
Poor, housing for, 43–44, 66–67, 107, 111, 225; in England, 17, 19, 20, 21. See also Housing, low cost
Population growth, 32, 58–59, 62–64, 65–66; and garden cities, 18, 55, 152; in New York state, 87–91
Population movement, 58–59, 61, 70, 72–73, 82, 92–93; in New York state, 87–91
Port Authority (New York City), 73
Port Sunlight (Eng.), 19
Potter, Henry C., 32
Pratt Institute, 109
Pray, Sturgis, 84
"Preliminary Study of a Proposed Garden Community" (Bing, Stein, and Wright), 51–54
Progressives and the Slums (Lubove), 107
Proskauer, Mrs. Joseph M., 106
Public housing corporations, 113–115. See also names of individual agencies
Pullman (Ill.), 54
Purdy, Lawson, 117; on profit, 101

Q

Queens (N.Y.), 122. See also Sunnyside Gardens
Quincy (Mass.), 113

R

RA. See Radburn Association
Radburn (Fair Lawn, N.J.), 4–13, 191–192; Adams on, 4, 164; *American Architect* on, 145; Ascher on, 152, 155, 177, 180, 183–184; automobiles, 7–8, 152–155, 160–161, 163; Brownlow on, 156; *Business Week* on, 192; cluster housing, 154–155, 156; commerce, 160–161, 256; cul-de-sacs, 8, 154–155, 156; demography, 5–6, 7, 173–175, 177, 234, 258–259; Depression, 12, 160,

187, 191–192, 194–195, 202–209; as "experience," 5, 9–10, 12, 169–170, 175, 176, 187–188; financing, 11, 132, 155; and garden city movement, 10, 149–152, 162–163; government, 177–187, 205–208; house design, 155–156, 162, 170; housing costs, 5, 150–151, 172–173; as "idea," 5, 8, 12–13, 152, 162–165, 230–231; industry, 150, 159–160; land costs, 121, 148–149; Mumford on, 4, 49, 145, 154, 164; *New York Times* on, 154, 191; open space, 125, 149–150, 151, 153, 155, 157, 162, 163, 164, 170, 172; pedestrians, 7–8, 152, 153, 160; recreation, 6–7, 170, 175–177; regional planning and, 164, 230–231; site planning, 7–8, 147, 152–162, 164–165; social planning, 8–10, 157–159, 161–162, 176–177, 180–182; social values, 169–170, 175, 176, 177, 187–188; Stein on, 152, 154, 158, 159, 161, 162; "superblocks," 153–155, 156, 158, 160–161, 162; taxes, 9, 159, 178, 185–186; Wright on, 70, 155, 167
Radburn Association (RA), 6, 151, 177–187, 204–208
Radburn Incorporated, 206
Railroads, 37, 61, 88–89; and Radburn, 159, 192
Recreation, 157; Appalachian project, 81–87; in Radburn, 6–7, 170, 175–177; in Sunnyside, 131

"Regional ecology" (MacKaye), 39
Regional Plan Association, 245
Regional planning, 10, 36–37, 39–40, 56, 58–61, 65, 72, 73–74, 87, 222, 225, 227–230; Ackerman on, 29; Bettman on, 73; Ford on, 73; MacKaye on, 91, 163, 224; and Radburn, 164, 230, 231; Stein on, 55; Wright on, 91
Regional Planning Association of America (RPAA), 10–11, 34, 46–47, 55–77, 164, 219–227; financing, 103–118, 219–221; membership, 34–47, 56, 71, 221–223; political position, 93–94, 219–221. See also City Housing Corporation; Radburn; Sunnyside Gardens
Regional Plan of New York (Sage Foundation), 74–75, 157, 224
Reissman, Leonard, on suburbs, 10
Resettlement Administration, 225, 230
Reston (Va.), 8, 234
Restrictive legislation, 66–67
Return on investment. See Limited dividends; Speculation
Revolving capital fund, 52, 54, 195; and Radburn, 149; and Sunnyside, 125, 132, 200–201, 208
Ridgewood (N.J.), 7
Riis, Jacob, 110
Rise of American Civilization (Beard and Beard), 104–105
Riverdale Country Club, 171

Index 273

Riverside Buildings (New York City), 108
Roads, 63, 163; in Radburn, 8, 153–154. See also Automobiles; Cul-de-sacs; Transportation
Rockefeller, John D., 191, 193
Rockefeller family, 208
Roland Park (Md.), 151, 178
Roosevelt, Eleanor, 106, 199, 201
Roosevelt, Franklin D., 221, 224
Route 4 (N.J.), 148, 159
RPAA. See Regional Planning Association of America
Russell Sage Foundation, 74, 198

S
Saddle River (N.J.), 7, 149
Safety, planning for, 157; in Radburn, 7–8, 153–154
Sage (Russell) Foundation, 74, 198
St. Louis City Planning Commission, 39
Saunders, Bertram, 179
Schlesinger, Arthur, Jr., on 1920's, 117
Schools, 157–158; in Radburn, 158, 203–204
Scott, Mel: on regional planning, 33; on RPAA, 56; on zoning, 64–65
Senate Committee on Public Buildings and Grounds, 114
Shaler, Nathan Southgate, 40
Shopping facilities. See Commerce, planning for
Simkhovitch, Mrs. V. G., 117
Simon, Robert E., 106

Site planning, 52–54, 65; in Radburn, 7–8, 152–162, 164–165; in Sunnyside, 122, 123–125, 130, 131
Slum clearance, 51
Smith, Alfred E., 41, 43, 71; on CHC, 103–104; on speculation, 101
Smith, Charles S., 110
Smith, Geddes, on Radburn, 145, 172
Social planning, 8–9; Mumford on, 3, 36, 62, 94, 231; in Radburn, 8–10, 157–159, 161–162, 176–177, 180–182; in Sunnyside, 130–132. See also Social reform
Social reform, 41–43, 57, 104–105, 219; Beard and Beard on, 217; and garden city movement, 17–18, 21–22, 33, 93–94, 219–221, 231. See also Social planning
Social values, 9; in Radburn, 169–170, 175, 176, 177, 187–188; suburban, 9–10. See also Social planning
Soule, George, 87
Speculation, 42, 45, 57–58, 62–63, 67–68, 69, 91–92, 108; Ackerman on, 91; and CHC, 108, 132, 194; in Sunnyside, 132. See also Financing; Limited dividends
Sporn, George, on Radburn, 167
Steam, 89
Steffens, Lincoln, on social reform, 104
Stein, Clarence S., 11, 38, 40–43, 46, 51–54, 56, 60, 71, 72, 81–82, 123, 200, 221, 222–

223; on Appalachian project, 79, 82; and Commission on Housing and Regional Planning, 43–46, 71, 87; on congestion, 58, 70; and Housing Committee, 41–43; on neighborhoods, 157, 158; on New York City, 49; on planning, 55, 62, 63; on Radburn, 152, 154, 158, 159, 161, 162; on speculation, 29, 67; on Sunnyside, 130, 196, 202. See also Sunnyside Gardens

Stickley, Gustav, 31

Strong, Josiah, 32

Subdivision, 53

Suburban development, 3–5, 12–13, 58–59, 226–227, 231. See also Garden city movement; names of individual communities

Sunnyside Gardens (Queens, N.Y.), 11, 121–133; Bing on, 115, 202; block associations, 130–131, 184; cluster housing, 124; construction costs, 122; demography, 126–127, 130; Depression, 125, 127, 128–129, 194–202, 208; Ely on, 119, 122; house design, 124–125; housing costs, 125–126, 127–129; land costs, 121, 132; Mumford on, 119, 127; open space, 123–124, 125, 130–131; recreation, 131; site planning, 122, 123–125, 130, 131; social planning, 130–132; Stein on, 196, 202; Wright on, 119, 130

Sunnyside Gardens Community Association, 131

Sunnyside Home Owners Committee, 196–202, 208

"Superblocks," 153; in Radburn, 153–155, 156, 158, 160–161, 162

Survey Graphic, 72

T

Taxes, 34, 44, 63; in Radburn, 9, 159, 178, 185–186

Technology, effect of, on environment, 37–38, 58, 61–62, 88–89, 90, 93, 117, 229

Tenement House Law (New York City), 108, 112, 124

Tennessee Valley Authority, 222, 224, 226, 230

To-morrow: A Peaceful Path to Real Reform (Howard), 17, 236

Toward New Towns for America (Stein), 157

Town meetings, in Radburn, 9

Transportation, 37, 61, 63, 70, 88–89, 90, 163, 170–172; in New York state, 88–89, 90, 91; in Radburn, 7–8, 148, 152–155, 159, 160–161, 163, 192. See also Automobiles; Railroads

Triborough Bridge Authority (New York City), 73

Tugwell, Rexford, 222

Two-family houses, 128–129

U

United States Housing Corporation, 114–115

United States Shipping Board, 38–39

Unwin, Raymond, 20, 71, 148

Index 275

Utilities. *See* Municipal services

V

"Valley section" (Geddes), 36–37
Vanderbilt, Cornelius, 110
Veblen, Thorstein, 35
Veiller, Lawrence, 32, 34, 64, 66, 115
Village, 33

W

Wagner, Robert F., 199
Wakefield, Edward Gibbon, 236
Wald, Lillian, 117
Walker, John O., 179, 182–183, 185; on Radburn, 176, 177, 259
Walkways. *See* Pedestrians
Warburg, Felix, 248
Ward, Harry E., on low cost housing, 116
Warner, Sam Bass, on real estate investors, 108
Welwyn (Eng.), 21–22, 162
Westchester County (N.Y.), 163, 171
Whitaker, Charles H., 34–36, 46, 56; on houses, 29. *See also Journal of the American Institute of Architects*
White, Alfred T., 107–109, 110
Whitnall, G. Gordon, 73–74
Wilson, William, on government housing, 114
Wood, Edith Elmer: on government housing, 114; on housing shortages, 66; on limited dividend companies, 109, 110; on restrictive legislation, 67
Wright, Henry, Sr., 11, 38–39, 46, 51–54, 56, 71, 72, 116, 123, 200, 220, 221, 222–223; Commission on Housing and Regional Planning report, 75, 87–92; on group housing, 39, 71, 220; on planning, 79; on Radburn, 70, 155, 167; on regional planning, 91; on road frontage, 124; on speculation, 68; on Sunnyside, 119, 130; on zoning, 65. *See also* Sunnyside Gardens

Y

Young, George W., 110

Z

Zoning, 63–66, 243–244; in Radburn, 147, 155; in Sunnyside, 122, 130; Wright on, 65